Self-Care in Later Life

Marcia G. Ory, PhD, MPH, is chief, Social Science Research on Aging, Behavioral and Social Research Program, National Institute on Aging, National Institutes of Health, Bethesda, Maryland, where she has been employed since 1981. She holds a doctorate from Purdue University and a Master's of Public Health from The Johns Hopkins University. As director of Psychosocial Geriatrics Research, she oversees a large research portfolio on aging, health and behavior. She has published widely in her main areas of interest which include aging and health care, health and behavior research, and gender differences in health and longevity. She is especially interested in self-care in later life and has provided national leadership for research development in this area.

Gordon H. DeFriese, PhD, is professor of Social Medicine in the School of Medicine, professor of Epidemiology and Health Policy and Administration in the School of Public Health, and director of the Cecil G. Sheps Center for Health Services Research at the University of North Carolina at Chapel Hill, where he has been since 1971. Dr. DeFriese has focused his research in the field of aging around practices related to self-care that may offset specific forms of physical limitations and, therefore, increase the prospects of older adults' living independently. His other research interests are broad, addressing the fields of preventive health services, the epidemiology of medical care, rural health care, and health program evaluation.

Self-Care in Later Life

Research, Program, and Policy Issues

Marcia G. Ory, MPH, PhD
Gordon H. DeFriese, PhD
Editors

Foreword by
Richard S. Schweiker

Springer Publishing Company

Springer Publishing Company, Inc.
536 Broadway
New York, NY 10012-3955

Cover design by: Margaret Dunin
Acquisitions Editor: Helvi Gold
Production Editor: T. Orrantia

98 99 00 01 02/5 4 3 2 1

Library of Congress Cataloging-in-Publication Data

Self-care in later life : research program, and policy issues /
    [edited by] Marcia G. Ory, Gordon H. DeFriese.
        p.   cm.
    Includes bibliographical references and index.
    ISBN 0-8261-1186-6
    1. Aged—Medical care—Social aspects—United States. 2. Aged—
Care—Government policy—United States. 3. Aged—Health and
hygiene—United States. 4. Self-care, Health—United States.
    I. Ory, Marcia G.   II. DeFriese, Gordon H.
RA564.8.S4625   1998
362.1′9897′00973—dc21   97-43506
                                                                                                        CIP

Printed in the United States of America

To our parents for their love, wisdom, and inspiration

Contents

Contents

Contributors

Lucille Davis, RN, PhD, Chicago State University, Chicago, IL

Kathryn Dean, PhD, Population Health Studies, Copenhagen, Denmark

Gordon H. DeFriese, PhD, University of North Carolina, Chapel Hill, NC

Alfred P. Duncker, PhD, Administration on Aging, Washington, DC

Laura N. Gitlin, PhD, Thomas Jefferson University, Philadelphia, PA

Thomas R. Konrad, PhD, University of North Carolina, Chapel Hill, NC

Elaine A. Leventhal, MD, PhD, University of Medicine and Dentistry of New Jersey, New Brunswick, NJ

Howard Leventhal, PhD, Rutgers University, New Brunswick, NJ

Marcia G. Ory, PhD, MPH, National Institute on Aging, Bethesda, MD

Thomas Prohaska, PhD, University of Illinois at Chicago, IL

William Rakowski, PhD, Brown University, Providence, RI

Chantal Robitaille, MA, Rutgers University, New Brunswick, NJ

Eleanor Palo Stoller, PhD, Case Western Reserve University, Cleveland, OH

Donald M. Vickery, MD, Health Decisions, Inc., Golden, CO

Alison Woomert, PhD, Battelle Research Institute, Research Triangle, NC

May L. Wykle, RN, PhD, Case Western Reserve University, Cleveland, OH

Foreword

Americans are constantly reminded of the many threats to their health and longevity. At the same time, current systems of health care actively discourage our use of unnecessary services and encourage our self-reliance in time of minor acute health events as well as over the longer term as we develop chronic, though manageable, health conditions. As we grow older, some aspects of advancing age may bring noticeable decrements in either physical or cognitive function. The issue of greatest worry for most older adults is the prospect of having to live the latter years of life in a nursing home or other facility not of their choosing as their health and social circumstances pose limitations to their ability to live independently.

Over the next several decades, the number of older adults living to advanced ages will increase significantly. Though most older adults will enter these advanced ages in relatively good health and able to live in the community without the need of institutional care, some will find the challenges of independent living impossible. There is a need to know more about the threshold that will confront our older adult population as they enter the latter years of life. The challenge to our scientific community and to those who work with and serve our older adult population through health and social programs is to find ways of strengthening the capacity of older adults to adapt, to deal with the threats to their independence in ways that will assure their safety and way of life, and to lessen their dependence on institutions which offer care arrangements of last resort.

Over the past several decades, a group of American and European social scientists and health professionals have been quietly but actively accumulating a body of scientific understanding of the factors which enable older adults to manage the threats to their independence, particularly as they experience serious limitations of cognitive and physical function. Under the rubrics of "self-care" and "self-help," these scientists have shown that not only are these skills and capacities of older adults ones that can be specifically defined, but they can be taught to laypersons through a series of curricula. Those taught will be able to practice these skills reliably and with safety and efficacy when they are necessary to everyday management of the routines of living.

Much of this research has shown that the ability of older adults to practice these skills varies considerably within the elderly population of our nation, and that there are significant personal variabilities in both the capacity to learn and the inclination to seek such learning opportunities among older adults. Moreover, research has shown that many older adults have devised very innovative ways of coping with limitations in their functional capacities, and that these innovative strategies can become the curricula of interventions to instruct others of a similar age and capacity in how to deal with comparable problems or limitations.

Self-care practice and self-care education have therefore become important strategies for the prevention of serious secondary consequences of functional limitations among our older adult population. As chairman of Partnership for Prevention, a nonprofit public policy research and educational organization founded in Washington, DC, I am particularly pleased that we have been able to co-sponsor with two important federal agencies, the National Institute on Aging (of the National Institutes of Health) and the Administration on Aging (of the U.S. Department of Health and Human Services), a national invitational conference on research issues related to self-care and aging in 1994. The papers which appear in this book are based on the seminal papers from that conference and, collectively, make a significant contribution to the expanding literature on the role and potential for self-care as a strategy for improving the health and independence of older adults in America.

I commend these papers to interested readers with the hope that they will stimulate further research and action in this field in the interest of a healthier and more empowered older adult population capable of meeting the challenges of their increasing numbers in the decades ahead.

RICHARD S. SCHWEIKER
Chairman, Partnership for Prevention
Former Secretary, US Department of
Health and Human Services
Former US Senator from Pennsylvania

Acknowledgments

It is a pleasure to recognize the contributions of individuals and organizations that helped to make this volume possible. First, we owe a tremendous debt to our colleague, Alfred P. Duncker of the Administration on Aging who worked closely with the editors to organize the Self-Care and Aging Conference out of which this volume emerged. At every stage of conference planning, he was supportive of our efforts and involved in critical decisionmaking.

This collection of papers and the conference from which they grew could not have been possible without the financial support and encouragement of several agencies of the federal government. The largest share of the cost of the conference was supported by the Administration on Aging. Financial support was also provided by the National Institute on Aging, the Office of Research on Women's Health, and the Office of Alternative Medicine, all of the National Institutes of Health. We wish to recognize the staff of Partnership for Prevention, Inc. which sponsored and organized the two-day conference held in Washington, D.C. in the spring of 1994. The American Council of Life Insurance, and its President, the Honorable Richard S. Schweiker, who served as Chairman of Partnership for Prevention, provided the facility and food for the event.

The Cecil G. Sheps Center for Health Services Research of the University of North Carolina at Chapel Hill provided key staff for leading the conference. Among these were Leslie Towns Navarra, Associate Director for Planning and Public Information, who served as general conference director; and Faculty Research Fellows Shulamit Bernard, Jean Kincaid, Alison Woomert, and Donna Rabiner. Martha Greenwald took responsibility for amassing the manuscripts from the conference and for preparing computer-readable versions of each. Our appreciation also goes to Darby Lipman, who worked with us at the National Institute on Aging to facilitate the publication effort.

The conference could not have taken place without the financial support and encouragement of Donald M. Vickery, President of Health Decisions, Inc., and the Board of Directors of The Self-Care Institute, who thought that such a project would meet a need for conceptual and practical clarification of many of the basic issues surrounding the practice of self-care among older adults.

We are also grateful to Ursula Springer and Helvi Gold of the Springer Publishing Company, who worked closely with us throughout the publication process and who took great interest in the dissemination of these contributions to the aging field.

For all of these contributions, as well as to the authors of these excellent chapters, we are most grateful. We hope that this volume will help to illuminate many of the exciting research and policy issues surrounding the field of self-care and aging.

MARCIA G. ORY
GORDON H. DEFRIESE

Introduction: The Nature, Extent, and Modifiability of Self-Care Behaviors in Later Life

Marcia G. Ory,
Gordon H. DeFriese, and
Alfred P. Duncker

A decade or so ago, *self-care* was a term used more often than not in a polemical way. Self-care was often advocated as a means to offset the perceived "medicalization" by professionals of common health and illness events (DeFriese, Woomert, Guild, Steckler, & Konrad, 1989). Since that time, the term has evolved in usage to identify a participative role for laypersons in shaping both the processes and outcomes of the care they receive from professionals, a role extending to the self-management of chronic conditions. In recent years, American social scientists have turned their attention from self-care as a self-defensive reaction to a concern with understanding the nature, causes and consequences of a whole array of health behaviors—leading to a resurgence of interest in self-care as a researchable area.

At the same time, health professionals and patient education activists, particularly those concerned with the management of specific chronic diseases, have incorporated self-care concepts and educational methods into their practices to better assist their patients (and their families). Self-care, in the space of a decade, has quietly been incorporated into the vocabulary and interventional approach of a variety of clinical disciplines with focal interests in assisting persons with specific forms of health and functional limitations. As managed care has come to play such an important role in the restructuring of American health care, so has self-care been given greater emphasis in the form of "demand management" strategies for increasing consumer self-reliance and decreasing the dependence on professionals for common health problems and concerns.

Much of the interest in self-care has focused on the maintenance of functional health and independence among persons with various forms of physical or cognitive limitations. Hence, the question of the potential value of self-care as a means of enhancing the long-term social and health independence of older adults is one of considerable national policy significance. Among the more prominent issues related to self-care are: (1) the patterns, dynamics and processes of self-care behaviors practiced by older adults in Western industrialized societies; (2) the design, implementation, and evaluation of self-care programs; (3) the theoretical underpinnings explaining self-care processes and intervention approaches; (4) the role of technology in promoting self-care and successful aging; and (5) the socio-cultural context of self-care practices, programs and policies.

This volume represents an important step in the process of assessing the potential contribution which self-care may make to the field of aging and health. It brings together some of the nation's leading authorities on various aspects of self-care and the measurement of health status among older adults. The chapters of this volume are based, in part, on materials presented at the 1994 National Invitational Conference on Research Issues Related to Self-Care and Aging. Updated to reflect new information on self-care and aging, the chapters presented here summarize the current state of knowledge regarding self-care among older adult populations; identify research, practice and policy gaps; and make recommendations regarding short- and long-term actions which may promote self-care practices among older adults. We see this volume as a valuable resource for researchers, practitioners, and policy makers interested in learning what older people can do for themselves to enhance their health and functioning.

DEFINING SELF-CARE

This volume defines self-care to include a broad range of behaviors undertaken by individuals, often with the assistance and support of others, that have the intent and effect of maintaining or promoting health and functional independence. Also included are those actions persons take to detect and diagnose, prevent or treat common illnesses and conditions, either acute or chronic. The definition of self-care promulgated by a special work group convened by the World Health Organization (WHO, 1983) is particularly relevant to the purposes and orientation of the volume:

> Self-care in health refers to the activities individuals, families and communities undertake with the intention of enhancing health, preventing disease, limiting illness, and restoring health. These activities are derived from knowledge and skills from the pool of both professional and lay experience. They are undertaken by lay people on their own behalf, either separately or in participative collaboration with professionals.

Following from this definition, we have emphasized several key components of self-care behaviors, including the intent and purpose of a wide range of self-care practices, the knowledge base underlying health behavior and behavior change skills, and the relationship of self-care to other informal and formal types of care used by older people.

ORGANIZATION OF THIS VOLUME

The focus of chapter 1 is on epidemiological studies of health and illness among older adults, with special attention to the role of self-care in the maintenance of independent functioning among elderly populations. Thomas Konrad summarizes available information indicating the extent to which self-care practices occur among different subgroups of older persons and are associated with various forms and degrees of morbidity, the risk of institutionalization, and/or mortality. New data from the National Survey of Self-Care and Aging are presented to document the patterns of self-care behaviors by age and gender.

In chapter 2, Eleanor Palo Stoller shifts the focus to the current knowledge available regarding factors that tend to either encourage or discourage the practice of self-care skills by older adults. This chapter gives attention to the contexts of self-care practice and discusses the role of social support networks in facilitating and encouraging lay initiative in personal health as well as the situational/environmental factors which make self-care practice more or less likely. Stoller deals with the notion of symptom-response and examines differences in the extent to which persons define a given symptom or health deficit as requiring either self-care or other response.

Self-care associated with the identification and diagnosis of acute health and illnesses conditions, and care of chronic conditions, have stressed symptom recognition skills, the ability to monitor changes in health status, and the development of self-management skills. In chapter 3, Thomas Prohaska discusses the research bases underlying programs designed to foster self-care activities and recommends priorities for self-care interventional/educational programs for older adults. Topics include issues such as participant recruitment, retention, public health versus clinical approaches to self-care, and the importance of stages of care in self-care activities. Examples of self-care programs designed to target specific self-care activities are examined in the context of research issues on self-care. Prerequisites for successful development and maintenance of appropriate self-care practices are examined (e.g., family involvement prior to and during the medical encounter and communication skills within health care settings).

Psychosocial interventions for promoting health-enhancing behaviors and discouraging health-impairing ones represent one of the best opportunities for reducing preventable illness, injury, and disability in old age. In chapter 4, William Rakowski provides a comprehensive review of self-care intervention research conducted to date, with special attention to the self-care behaviors that have been targeted for change, characteristics of the populations that have been studied, the types of interventions proposed, the effectiveness of different intervention strategies, and the gaps in existing research efforts. Rakowski illustrates the various ways the measurement of self-care behavior itself may "fit" with the attempt to understand the larger spectrum of health consequences and outcomes. This synthesis of existing literature is critical for identifying the most promising strategies for promoting self-care behaviors. Specific recommendations about the feasibility of designing and testing psychosocial interventions to promote self-care behaviors in late life are highlighted.

In order to move beyond descriptive self-care research, it is critical to attend to the underlying social, behavioral and biological processes motivating health beliefs and behaviors in later life. In chapter 5, Leventhal,

Leventhal, and Robitaille discuss the advantages of theory-based research over descriptive research. Comparing and contrasting several different theoretical approaches, this chapter delineates the attributes of the self-care process and illustrates how different theories address key parameters. The authors propose a dynamic self-regulation model which not only views the individual as an active problem solver, but also recognizes the influence of the sociocultural context in determining older people's views of health and their health care actions. The linkage between theory and clinical application is addressed with attention to how practitioners can use knowledge about determinants of health beliefs and behaviors to shape older people's health promotion and treatment behaviors.

Assistive technologies have become an important dimension of any assessment of the role of self-care in the total spectrum of health care services needed and used by persons with chronic and debilitating conditions. In chapter 6, Laura Gitlin reviews the extant literature on the use of assistive technology in self-care practice, providing a new perspective on the role of social science in the cumulative understanding of the role technology plays in extending the adaptability of human beings to the demands of their environments. Gitlin also addresses the current theoretical models for understanding the role of technology in self-care, discusses the problems of measurement associated with the study of technology adaptation and use, and emphasizes the implications of this body of literature for health and social policy.

Although most self-care research published in the United States has focused on middle-class, White Americans, it is important to understand similarities and differences in factors that predict self-care behaviors and their consequences across diverse populations both in the U.S. and in other Western industrialized societies. Toward this goal, we have included two cross-cutting chapters on the sociocultural context of self-care practices, programs, and policies. In chapter 7, Davis and Wykle examine cultural origins and beliefs about self-care in minority and ethnic populations with specific reference to the experience of older African Americans. Recognizing the dramatic diversity within the Black population, these authors lament the lack of studies that have examined minority differences while also taking socioeconomic and regional differences into account. Focusing on low-income Black elders, this chapter provides a cultural context for understanding the importance of self-care in promoting health among groups traditionally cut off from majority social institutions. Much more research is needed to understand how self-care practices differ between and among different ethnic/cultural groups.

Chapter 8 provides an international perspective to enhance our understanding of factors influencing self-care practice and research in the United States. Kathryn Dean reveals how social systems interact with academic disciplines to influence the kind of attention given to different health care approaches and to set research priorities. As in chapter 1, the evolution of the self-care concept and related disciplinary perspectives are addressed. However, in Europe and elsewhere, there appears to be a stronger connection between social policies and self-care practice than in the U.S. Underscoring the advantages of a cross-cultural sharing of self-care concepts, methodologies, and solutions, Dean calls for a new research paradigm to address the place of self-care in health care in different countries. A more integrative perspective of self-care practice and policy that combines both individual and social approaches promises to bring greater health benefits for all.

This volume's afterword provides an integrative summary of research priorities and policy/practice implications of prominent issues related to self-care in later life. As editors of this volume, we are joined by our colleague, Donald M. Vickery, in offering a synthesis of the volume's content. We conclude with recommendations for addressing the dearth of systematic studies on the nature, extent, and modifiability of self-care behaviors across the life course. Research on self-care has passed the nascent stage and the opportunity now exists to move the field forward by adhering to some of the principles for future investment in self-care research and aging identified in this afterword.

EMERGENT SELF-CARE THEMES

The Nature, Extent and Process of Self-Care Practices

As indicated in the chapters to follow, one of the major advances in self-care research over the past few years has been the specification of different types of self-care behaviors. Inconsistent research findings can be attributed, in part, to a failure to specify the antecedents and consequences of specific self-care behaviors. Three general categories of self-care practices are of importance in understanding the relationships among self-care practices and health outcomes: (a) steps taken by lay persons to compensate or adjust for functional limitations affecting routine activities of daily living, (b) actions taken to either prevent disease or promote general health status through health promotion or other lifestyle modification efforts, and (c) medical self-care for the diagnosis or treatment of minor symptoms of ill health or the self-management of chronic health conditions.

It is now clear that older adults who have experienced one or more significant declinations in functional capacity may offset these limitations through the use of assistive devices, modification of the living environment, or through one of several types of activity modifications. The point of these self-care practices is to restructure the physical or social environment of the individual so as to retard the progression of a "functional limitation" which, if unattended, may become a "disability." Findings reported from the first wave of the NIA-supported National Survey of Self-Care and Aging indicate that there is no direct relationship of age to the extent of self-care practice. Rather, the tendency to engage in these practices is mediated by the presence of physical impairments, the social circumstances in which one lives, and the availability of social support.

With regard to general health-promoting behaviors among older adults, it appears that there are significant secular changes taking place within the older age groups, some with negative, and others with positive implications. As an example, on the one hand, there are indications of increased interest among hypertensive men in monitoring blood pressure and adhering to a medication regimen. On the other hand, there are disturbing signs of an increase in the number of older women smokers and reduced rates of smoking cessation among this group. These trends are some of the many aspects of lifestyle change and health-promoting self-care practices which may have to be taken into account in the design and implementation of programs in the years ahead.

There is considerable evidence that many older adults tend to "normalize" illness symptoms and health complaints and to attribute them to the fact of aging itself. Many of the reactions of older adults to the symptoms of ill health are grounded in cultural and ethnic traditions. However, few studies have examined cultural differences in medical self-care behaviors systematically, taking into account the interacting influences of socioeconomic status differentials or within-group cultural differences. There is even less appreciation of international differences as the context for self-care practices.

Self-care, informal care, and formal care are often traditionally viewed as three distinct types of self-care, with substitution among care providers as a major policy issue for those concerned about escalating health care costs. Recent studies suggest, however, that these are arbitrary demarcations and that there is an interplay of different types of care over the illness episode among various subpopulations.

Among the factors accounting for the variability among individual older adults in reaction to illness symptoms are characteristics of the symptoms themselves, such as severity, pain, acuity, and pattern of experience (i.e., intermittent, nonspecific, mild/slow onset). Situational factors, such as the social roles played by the individual and the settings within which the individual lives and experiences these symptoms are also relevant. We know that older women tend to react differently to illness symptoms than do men. Among both men and women, patterns of lay consultation with peers, as well as significant persons in one's primary group (such as adult children), can have significant influence on the way in which a symptom is perceived and the likelihood of an active response.

Much of the most illuminating recent research has contributed to an emerging general model of health behavior that acknowledges the dynamic nature and situation-specific qualities of meanings associated with illness, its symptoms and various types of functional limitations. Our understandings of the behavior of older adults (and those in their primary relationships) in the face of illness symptoms or functional decrements seem to require an increased emphasis on both the epidemiology of these conditions among these older adult populations, as well as a deeper and more intensive understanding of the process through which individuals attempt to regulate the quality of their environments and make behavioral and environmental adjustments to the shifting health conditions they face day-by-day. Among the most important considerations of theoretical and practical importance to research in these areas are such factors as self-assessed health status (which seems to be a powerful predictor of the seriousness with which symptoms are treated via self-care), the body awareness of the individual (which is a psychological phenomenon more prominent among older males than among older women, although women tend to use more formal health care services than men), and the extent of confidence older persons have in the efficacy of formal medical care and physicians in particular.

Though we have known for several decades about the variability among social groups in patterns of response to illness symptoms, we are now much more aware of the intra-individual variability in response to symptoms (both over time and across different life situations) associated with these important factors. Still, we cannot ignore social structural influences on self-care practices, and are now being urged to turn our attention to family and community-level influences, as well as "upstream" approaches and supports for self-care behaviors.

There seems to be an increasing societal level of skepticism about the capabilities and effectiveness of medical therapies by physicians, which has permeated even the older adult population. When combined with worries about the cost and experiences of lower quality and otherwise unacceptable processes of formal care, these factors have tended to make self-care for common acute illnesses and the day-to-day self-management of chronic conditions a much more prevalent response in the last decade or so.

The Design and Evaluation of Interventions to Encourage Self-Care Practice Among Older Adults

There is now a growing research basis for the design and evaluation of self-care programs. As indicated in the chapters that follow, there emerges a body of carefully designed studies testing the effectiveness of diverse interventions based on theoretical models of health behavior and behavioral change (i.e., cognitive rational decision-based models). There is now an awareness of the importance of considering the stages of behavioral change and the need to tailor interventions according to specific stages (e.g., whether individuals are in the precontemplation, contemplation, preparation, action, or maintenance stage). Several common components of self-care programs can be identified, including:

1. the provision of information to impart knowledge relevant to the practice of self-care skills
2. methods to motivate the older individual to adopt relevant and appropriate self-care behaviors
3. meaningful and timely feedback on the consequences of self-care practices
4. attention to environmental factors that continue to support the desired patterns of self-care practices and behaviors

An extensive variety of formal courses and curricula have offered opportunities for older adults to acquire specific types of self-care skills. Many of these interventions have been studied rigorously and reported in the formal literature, and a substantial number of programs have involved randomized assignment to intervention or control groups. The lessons from this body of experience and literature can inform future efforts to design and evaluate interventions for each of the three broad categories of self-care.

One of the issues apparent from a review of extant literature on the subject concerns which self-care practices (or sets of practices) can serve as primary dependent measures of intervention effect. Though the question of the most appropriate fit of self-care in this chain of effect may pose difficult theoretical and design questions, there are clearly situations where self-care can and does adequately serve as the appropriate outcome. In smoking cessation self-care education interventions, for example, the self-care practice has been previously established to be related to longer-term health consequences and no longer requires the additional effort to establish the epidemiological relationship with other health outcomes. In such a situation, it is sufficient to demonstrate the intervention's impact in terms of the targeted health behavior (e.g., smoking cessation) as an outcome.

Though self-care educational interventions for older adults, like most health promotion programs for other adult age groups, have encountered problems in both the recruitment and retention of participants, evidence from carefully evaluated interventions to address lifestyle and health promotion goals indicates that these programs have demonstrable positive effects among those who participate most actively, as measured by changes in key outcome variables. Nevertheless, results are mixed, and reasons for differences have been difficult to isolate because of the diversity of interventions and studies in this body of literature. This suggests that the *dose-response* relationship between self-care interventions and their presumed and targeted outcomes deserves further investigation. Further research can elucidate the extent to which recruitment and retention of older adult participants can be enhanced by including in these courses family and friends who are likely to offer social support for the learning and practice of self-care skills.

There is a growing recognition of the importance of translating the benefits of self-care education and practice into a form which can be more widely disseminated through population-based and public health–oriented programs designed to improve the health of large groups of older adults. Some means of varying the messages and the mode of transmission to accommodate the highly variable target audiences seems needed. There is considerable concern over the absence in this body of literature and experience of a genuine public health application of self-care concepts and approaches meeting the health needs of older adults from diverse backgrounds.

A great deal of the intervention literature seems to focus on the technological aspects of self-care instruction and eventual practice. Many of the most widely cited self-care studies are multicomponent intervention approaches, which lack the capacity to disentagle the separate effects of individual program components on knowledge gained, skills demonstrated, survival, functional health status, health care utilization or cost. We recommend that there be some future effort to conceptualize studies of self-care educational approaches to broad public health aspects of aging, with the emphasis on scope and reach, as well as on health outcomes or the use of assistive technologies. Moreover, there is room in such studies for participation of researchers from different disciplines who may have quite different interests in self-care; some may focus on the setting within which self-care skills are learned or practiced; others may focus on the intervention methods themselves; and a third group may focus on the response of specific target groups to these interventions.

CONCLUSION

Over the past 25 years, self-care behaviors have been associated with a multitude of health outcomes. Recent research studies have expanded the knowledge base by specifying different types of self-care behaviors, identifying factors influencing the development and maintenance of different types of self-care behaviors in different populations, and evaluating the effectiveness of social and behavioral interventions for modifying self-care practices throughout the life course. This complexity of research presents a formidable challenge, but, unlike in the early years of self-care research, there is now a concerted multidisciplinary research effort, combining the best conceptualizations and methodologies from both the social and clinical sciences.

REFERENCES

DeFriese, G. H., Woomert, A., Guild, P. A., Steckler, A. B., & Konrad, T. R. (1989). From activated patient to pacified activist: A study of the self-care movement in the United States. *Social Science and Medicine, 29,* 195–204.

World Health Organization (WHO). (1983, November 21–25). *Health education in self-care: Possibilities and limitations.* Report of a scientific consultation, Geneva, Switzerland.

CHAPTER 1

The Patterns of Self-Care Among Older Adults in Western Industrialized Societies

Thomas R. Konrad

One of the most striking features of the demographic transition of the last several decades is an increase in the number and proportion of the population over age 65, especially that portion of the population that is over age 85 (Hobbs & Damon, 1996; Taeuber, 1983). Yet how this increase in longevity is related to population morbidity and disability in the later years is less clear and more controversial. Longer life may be not only a consequence of improved health status of the individuals who are experiencing it, but may also be a factor in increasing the disability of the population of this age group, which continues to experience nonfatal disabling conditions. The assessment of the joint impact of postponement of death of the frail elderly and better management of chronic nonfatal diseases of the nonfrail elderly on different segments of the population over age 65 is challenging, although recent studies suggest declines in chronic disability rates over the past decade (Manton, Corder, & Stallard, 1997).

The heterogeneous nature of the older population, along with the increasing cost of medical care, the widespread recognition of the limits of effectiveness of medical technology, and the distinct possibility that dramatic breakthroughs could affect mortality or morbidity rates for certain diseases all suggest a complex range of scenarios. Strategies employed by people themselves to prevent or delay the onset of disease, or to minimize the impact of impairments on their functioning assume an important role in the array of resources available to older persons as they face the challenges of aging in the 21st century.

In this chapter, we place various epidemiological approaches that have been used to link health behaviors and health outcomes among older adults into historical context. First, we will examine the framing of questions relating to self-care and aging over the last several decades, especially from the perspectives of epidemiology and gerontology. Second, we profile selected epidemiological studies of health and illness among older adults by focusing on the role of self-initiated behaviors in the maintenance of health and independent functioning among older populations. Third, we present selected data from a longitudinal national study of prevalence of self-care practices among older adults as a way of illustrating how focused analysis of a national sample of older adults can use the techniques and data of behavioral epidemiology to inform health policy and program design efforts. Finally, we outline how a research agenda on self-care and older populations can be more effectively guided toward examining those self-care practices and health outcomes which might be most effective in enhancing the quality of life of our older population.

HISTORICAL BACKGROUND AND CONCEPTUAL FRAMEWORKS

Over the last several decades, the basic paradigms of social gerontology, social epidemiology, and the study of self-care have evolved in a parallel fashion. This is not surprising, given the tendency for intellectual currents to flow in the same direction and for underlying paradigms to influence developments in a variety of disciplines. In retrospect, three distinct phases, displayed schematically in Table 1.1, can be seen in that evolution.

As pointed out by Holstein (1986) and articulated most prominently by Cummings and Henry (1961), during the first phase (1960s), the notion of *disengagement* emerged in the field of social gerontology. This viewpoint was consistent with a belief that inevitable, irreversible, and parallel declines occur as a normal and expected part of the aging process. Individuals were thought to experience parallel declines in a variety of spheres— biological, psychological, and social—with their advancing age.

Social epidemiology in this era was concerned with identifying population subgroups displaying certain morbidity and mortality profiles.

TABLE 1.1   Phases in the Study of Social Gerontology, Social Epidemiology, and Self-Care

Phase of Theoretical Development	Social Gerontology	Social Epidemiology	Studies of Self-Care
First phase (1960s)	*Disengagement perspective:* Gradual withdrawal from a variety of roles seen as normal and appropriate for older persons	*Risk factor epidemiology:* Emphasis on membership in various social categories (e.g., age, race, sex, occupation, etc.)	*"Lay care" vs. medical care:* Self-care as mainly a behavioral response to illness or other physical conditions, not a proactive health maintenance strategy
Second phase (1970s, 1980s)	*Activity perspective:* New skills and activities can be learned and initiated	*Behavioral epidemiology:* Emphasis on modifiable lifestyle elements	*Self-care as empowerment:* Reflects individual overcoming dominance of the medical model of care
Third phase (1990s)	*Continuity and contingency perspectives:* Interaction of environment and coping with aging; importance of temporal perspective	*Multivariate-multilevel epidemiological models:* Modifiable risks within high-risk groups; global community-wide assessments	*Conditional and situational approaches:* Dynamic interaction between capacities of person and demands of environment

Exploration of the reasons these underlying sociodemographic regularities occurred was secondary to the mechanics of establishing reliable information about the membership in different social categories and their corresponding mortality rates. Nonetheless, such an approach could easily yield the impression that humankind inevitably breaks down by age and sex, reinforcing the fatalistic undercurrent latent in the gerontology literature of the period.

During this same era, self-care (or "lay care") was examined primarily as a deficit to explain the failure of persons to make use of the health care system. It is not surprising that such an approach was developed initially during the pre–Medicare era, when there were more barriers to access to medical care, especially for older persons. The health behavior context in which such phenomena were investigated had to do with the correction of lay-inspired "misinformation."

In the second era (1970s, 1980s), when "labeling" became a watchword of much sociological theory, one observer noted potential widespread and destructive effects on older people:

> The consequences of stereotyping are considerable, not only in the every-day world but also in the way policy is conceived and research is formulated and executed. Thus, there is the danger that current preoccupations will create a socially manufactured and distorted view of old age which will be mistakenly seen as a permanent feature of life in so-called developed societies. (Ford, 1986)

Of particular importance was the assertion that the equation of old age with disability was fundamentally flawed. Research began to demonstrate that "old age disabilities are *not*: (1) universal; (2) necessarily irreversible; or (3) determined solely by biological processes, apart from social and psychological processes" (Riley & Bond, 1983; p. 243). This reappraisal of aging as a socially constructed phenomenon also involved a more critical evaluation of the methodological approaches in social gerontology. It was argued that cohort studies should be employed to help account for observed correlations between age and various negative health and functional status indicators. Numerous observers suggested that cohort approaches could illuminate the fact that what might appear in cross-sectional studies as declining health or functional status could merely be a spurious but an historically obsolescing relationship. Such a pattern could change as more recently born, more independent, better educated, and healthier cohorts begin to come of age.

During this same time period, the behavioral approach in epidemiology began to bear fruit (Berkman & Breslow, 1983). As the adults in Alameda County aged, it was becoming clear that "healthy habits" could affect the mortality of populations. Risk factors were seen as not only modifiable but as discretionary and affecting mortality in both the middle and older years.

Also during the 70s and 80s, considerable focus on self-care began to occur both as a social phenomenon—some would say a social movement—and also as a policy domain. As aging was seen in a positive light—as a phase of the changing life span—so self-care was also seen as a positive development. Sometimes the self-care notion involved enlisting individual participation of lay persons in a collaborative effort with the physician to deal with problems of health. At other times, however, self-care was thought to supplant medical care, and in doing so, was thought of as a positive and liberating experience for the individual and for the community. Although initially this self-care emphasis was understood to be in part a reaction to the dominance of the medical model in the delivery of health care, it was also understood to be a naturally occurring phenomenon which had existed prior to and apart from the formal health care system, but which had not until then attracted much scholarly attention (Dean, 1989; Dean, Hickey, & Holstein, 1986; Levin & Idler, 1981).

The third and current stage (1990s) in the evolution of social gerontology steers a mid-course between the undue pessimism of the postwar years and the excessive optimism characteristic of the oversocialized conception of aging. The contemporary notion of aging and health is one in which the later years of life are significantly determined by patterns of living established in middle age. Although these later years may not allow endless possibilities, they can provide some vital and unexpected second chances; therefore, we have characterized them as having the attributes of continuity and contingency. By *continuity,* we mean that the health and social situation of elders is a product of a lifetime of positive and negative factors which are the results both of situations in which people have found themselves and situations they have chosen. While many of these factors are not reversible for a current generation of elders, some are. *Contingency* means that many of the apparent relationships seen in cross-sectional observations of the current generation of elders are by no means certain to replicate themselves as the coming cohorts age. On the contrary, as better health information about the risks and benefits of various health behaviors and lifestyles diffuses through the population, we would expect that there would be more deliberate attention to health, both societally and individually.

Contemporary social epidemiology has also shifted its focus. The development of multivariate and multilevel statistical models and techniques, the availability of large national longitudinal databases, and the refinement of elaborate survey designs and extensive measurements have made the enterprise of social epidemiology more complex and challenging. Now the emphasis has moved beyond examining simple measures of mortality and morbidity to using a number of time-related concepts such as active life expectancy, disability-free years, and the compression of morbidity (Manton et al., 1997; Strawbridge, Cohen, Shema, & Kaplan, 1996; Wolfson, 1996). Not surprisingly, this change in research emphasis leads epidemiologists to explore hypotheses involving relatively complex chains of causality over lengthy durations, and requires the examination of extensive longitudinal panel study data.

In a similar fashion, the study of the self-care phenomenon has become more complex and is now characterized by both conditional and situational approaches. A *conditional* perspective helps explain how self-care becomes activated and why some segments of the population are more likely to engage in self-care activities. A *situational* model emphasizes the notion of self-care as purposive action taken to reduce a gap between the capacities of the individual person and the demands of that person's task environment. Theory and research in the present era has before it the job of selectively identifying the conditions under which self-care is activated naturally, and understanding when it is "appropriate" (i.e., when it has therapeutic/palliative kinds of effects).

The self-care movement, if it ever really existed as a single phenomenon, has crystallized into a variety of diverse programs. Many of these are adjuncts of the health care system rather than functioning independently of it (DeFriese, Woomert, Guilder, Steckler, & Konrad, 1989, see also chapter 8 in this volume for discussion of the development of the self-care movement in the international arena). If self-care is to be incorporated programmatically into a national health policy strategy, programs must be well designed and rigorously and comparatively evaluated. Ultimately, the relationship between self-care and health outcomes will need to be carefully examined. Expected health and functional status outcomes require specification, and hypothesized causal relationships between self-care activities and outcomes will need to be tested. In this respect, the epidemiology of self-care in the general population becomes an important background against which to compare the experiences of health-oriented self-care programs. As more detailed programmatic efforts to develop self-care and health promotion activities for seniors are initiated, we will need to know if particular elements in a regimen of self-care are effective, and which might have untoward, unexpected, or harmful effects. This means that more complex measures and analytical methods must be employed. Finally, realistic time horizons that describe the trajectories over which various outcomes might be expected to emerge will need to be explicated and this temporal dimension will need to be incorporated into the study of self-care.

EPIDEMIOLOGICAL EVIDENCE ABOUT AGE, PSYCHOSOCIAL RISK FACTORS, AND HEALTH-RELATED OUTCOMES

The results of many investigations have led to a distinct new way of viewing age as a sociological or epidemiological variable. Most studies relating age and health are beginning to

> suggest that independent effects of age are small. Rather, age is statistically related to social and psychosocial variables that directly influence behavior and health and thus should perhaps be considered in more technical terms as a summary collector of causal influences. The task then is to disentangle the summary effects and identify the combinations of factors that lead to the preservation or breakdown of health. (Dean, 1992, p. 50)

Kaplan and Strawbridge (1994) review recent evidence that supports the importance of behavioral and social factors in predicting healthy aging, or "optimal" levels of health and functioning. The fact that heterogeneous levels of functioning occur suggests that behavioral and social interventions might modify risk factors and reduce or possibly reverse progression of disease and dysfunction. The authors recognize the importance of prevention in all stages of the health-disease continuum, and they have laid out summary evidence from the Alameda County study, Longitudinal Survey on Aging (LSOA), the second National Health and Nutrition Examination Survey (NHANES II), the Established Populations for Epidemiologic Studies of the Elderly (EPESE), and other longitudinal studies that support the critical role of behavioral and social predictors of healthy aging, defined as longevity and enhanced physical function.

The strongest evidence in the abundant literature linking behaviors to mortality or longevity emerges in two behavior areas: smoking and physical activity. Both smoking and low levels of physical activity are strongly associated with increased risk of death among older adults, and both are modifiable behaviors. For example, not only was smoking strongly associated with risk of death among older adults in the Alameda study, but smoking cessation by older adults effectively reduced the risk of death in subsequent years. When compared with the continuing nonsmokers, the risk of death was greatest (76%) for the continuing smokers, but was only 33% higher for the smokers who quit during the first study period.

In a similar fashion, the life-extending benefits of exercise are manifest. Subjects 70 years or older who reported no leisure physical activity had a 37% higher mortality risk than those reporting some activity. Furthermore, when compared with older subjects who maintained the same levels of leisure activity over time, increasing leisure activity levels decreased mortality risks in subsequent years, while decreasing activity levels increased subsequent mortality risk. Results from other studies show similar beneficial effects.

Additional evidence suggests that increased mortality risks occur among older adults having low levels of social network participation, low levels of social activities participation, and low socioeconomic and educational levels. Although this association is not consistently found, the powerful role of social activities in enhancing health and functioning represents modifiable factors rather than structurally determined facts. The review of evidence regarding the relationship of behavioral and social factors with functional health concentrates on physical function. However, cognitive, psychological, and social domains of functional health ultimately must also be considered. Of particular importance is understanding the role of psychological variables and symptoms, especially depressive symptoms, in inhibiting social participation and physical activity.

Evidence shows that preventing and delaying chronic illness (e.g., arthritis, diabetes, hypertension, cardiovascular disease, myocardial infarction, stroke) and acute incidents such as falls (e.g., hip fracture) offers great potential for preventing declines in physical function. Nevertheless, the mechanisms linking chronic and acute conditions to functioning need much further study. Preliminary evidence suggests that smoking, alcohol consumption, lack of physical activity, and lack of maintenance of appropriate weight may predict subsequent difficulties with physical functioning, especially mobility (Guralnick, Land, Blazer, Fillenbaum, & Branch, 1993; Guralnik, LeCroix, et al., 1993). A small amount of literature suggests that socioeconomic status, marital status, social network participation, and social support may also predict physical functioning (Kaplan, 1996). Several studies show the potential importance of behavioral and social factors in modifying physical functioning among older adults (LaCroix, Guralnick, Berkman, Wallace, & Satterfield, 1993).

Finally, prediction of healthy aging depends on health care, as well as social and physical environments. Despite meager evidence about effects of the health care delivery environment on functional status, studies show potential benefits of rehabilitative services and predict that interventions to increase exercise capacity may postpone frailty (Hadley, Ory, Suzman, Weindruch, & Fried, 1993; Ory & Williams, 1989). Existing evidence does suggest that modifying the social environment through interventions affecting social support and autonomy may have beneficial impacts on physical functioning. Modification of the physical environment and removal of physical barriers to activity clearly deserves more study (see Gitlin in this volume), and the human factors movement seems especially well equipped to take up this challenge (Barr, 1994).

NEW EVIDENCE ABOUT SELF-CARE AND AGING

The Definition of Self-Care

One of the major difficulties in examining and reviewing work in the area of behavior, psychosocial risk factors, and health outcomes has to do with identifying and bounding what is actually meant by *self-care*. The definition promulgated by a work group convened over a decade ago by the World Health Organization (WHO) has proven a useful starting point for a discussion of the term. As first introduced in the volume overview, WHO's definition states:

> Self-care in health refers to the activities individuals, families and communities undertake with the intention of enhancing health, preventing disease, limiting illness, and restoring health. These activities are derived from knowledge and skills from the pool of both professional and lay experience. They are undertaken by lay people on their own behalf, either separately or in participative collaboration with professionals. (World Health Organization, 1983)

Self-care behavior takes place in the context of attempts to maintain control of life and to do so with competence, autonomy, and self-reliance. It includes the deliberate effort of lay persons to balance a variety of personal risks and resources in the achievement of specific goals and objectives in everyday experience. Obviously, this domain could include a wider spectrum of behaviors than those merely aimed at "filling a gap" in one's ecology of social life. Various observers and advocates have drawn the definition either more or less broadly, and much of what is described as "coping" with life's challenges using social, physical, and psychosocial resources could be considered under the rubric of "self-care." The study of self-care behavior, and the capacities this behavior both requires and represents, however, involves examining activities through which individuals mobilize personal and social resources proactively to sustain and enhance the quality and length of their own and each others' lives.

Domains of Self-Care

This chapter attempts to expand the understanding of health behavior by presenting selected findings from a national probability survey of the non-institutionalized older adult population being conducted at the University of North Carolina at Chapel Hill. The findings reported here focus on the current self-care practices of older adults. In the first phase of this study, an in-person interview survey instrument entitled "The National Survey of Self-Care and Aging" was employed to elicit descriptions of self-care practices from community-dwelling adults aged 65 and older. The interview was designed to provide national estimates of the prevalence of self-care activities on several broad dimensions by measuring the extent and type of subjects' self-care activities. Interviews for this national survey were completed during the fall and winter of 1990–1991 with 3,485 noninstitutionalized adults age 65 and older, whose names were selected from Medicare beneficiary files. This stratified random sample includes approximately equal numbers of adults of each gender in each of the three age categories, 65 to 74, 75 to 84 and 85 and older. Oversampling the oldest age groups assures representation of those likely to be frail and the most difficult to reach in community surveys. Furthermore, the geographically clustered sample was selected in proportion to the size of both nonmetropolitan and metropolitan populations and clustered within 50 primary sampling units across the United States. The design applies weights to achieve a nationally representative sample of both well and frail elderly persons of all three age groups.

Subjects were asked about three different types of self-care behavior:

1. What steps had they taken in adjusting to decrements in physical functioning?

2. What kinds of preventive and health promotive behavior were they engaging in that was consistent with a "healthy lifestyle"?
3. How did they engage in medical self-care behavior (i.e., diagnosing and self-treating minor symptoms and/or monitoring chronic medical conditions)?

Self-Care: Adaptation to Functional Limitations

The first analysis of these data focused on a specific range of purposeful activities in which older persons engage and through which they compensate for declining physical, cognitive or mental functioning which can detract from one's quality of life. Inquiries were made of subjects about the extent of their difficulties in performing basic activities of daily living (ADL), such as eating and getting dressed; and instrumental activities of daily living (IADL), such as managing money and using the telephone. Questions about these aspects of functioning were drawn from other national surveys of older adults (Weiner, Hanley, Clark, & Van Nostrand, 1990). New items were developed to assess the kinds of self-care/self-help activities in which persons may be engaged in meeting ADL and IADL requirements. The three broad categories of self-care activities are:

1. Self-care/self-help behaviors that may involve the use of *assistive devices* (Centers for Disease Control, 1992; DeWitt, 1991; see also Gitlin chapter in this volume). This category may encompass a broad range of devices, from simple homemade tools to sophisticated and expensive equipment such as motorized wheelchairs.
2. Self-care/self-help behaviors that involve some systematic *modification of a person's living environment.* Modifications could include structural alterations of a person's home to facilitate access or mobility (e.g., by installing grab bars or a ramp), or could involve physically relocating to a more accommodating residence (e.g., one without stairs or with a door wide enough to allow passage of a wheelchair).
3. Intra-individual factors that could be a source of assistance through activity accommodations (e.g., doing things more slowly or less often), psychosocial coping (e.g., cognitive adaptation to the situation, prayer, distraction), or some other lifestyle or behavior change.

If we follow the logic of Verbrugge and Jette's (1994) characterization of the process of disablement, we can describe *disability* as a gap between personal capability and environmental demand. It then becomes clear that the progression from functional limitation to disability may be slowed by restructuring the physical, social, and even cultural environment. Given this perspective, adaptive changes that people make in their customary way of doing things, their acquisition and application of technology to affect and overcome functional limitations (e.g., on mobility, transfer, hearing), and even the reconstruction of the built environment as self-care responses to functional limitations are all strategic devices employed by individuals to prevent or delay their own functional limitations from being transformed into disabilities.

It is on this basis that we have examined the epidemiology of the use of equipment, environmental modification and behavioral adaptations as different types of self-care adjustments to decrements in functional status. The distribution of adaptive strategies by age and gender subgroups is exemplified in Table 1.2. Despite the strong age gradient reflected in the zero-order relationships, our multivariate analysis suggests more complex relationship between age per se and self-care adaptation. The relationship between age and adaptation is strongly mediated by the presence of physical impairments, functional limitations, and social support. Notable effects of age on the acquisition of equipment and environmental modifications remain when statistical controls are applied, especially in terms of adaptations which are aimed at promoting physical mobility (Norburn et al., 1995). However, in general, age effects are not linear; individuals between age 75 and 84 are more likely to make changes in their environments or use equipment than are individuals in the younger or older age groups. One interpretation of this phenomenon might be that "the years between 75 and 84 may be a time of transition, with a greater proportion of individuals in this age group engaging in activities which would promote a balance between their capacities and their experienced environmental demands" (Norburn et al., 1995; p. S107). Another possible interpretation is that there is an emergent cohort effect. In other words, more recent generations may be less likely to be characterized by a passive acceptance of limitations on mobility, and more likely to make use of equipment and to reinvent their environments in order to improve mobility.

Self-Care: Healthy Lifestyle Practice

The second major focus of the National Survey of Self-Care and Aging is on the kinds of preventive and health-promoting behavior practiced by sur-

**TABLE 1.2   National Prevalence of Selected Self-Care Adaptations
to Functional Limitations by Age and Gender**

Type of practice	Male 65–74	Male 75–84	Male 85+	Female 65–74	Female 75–84	Female 85+
Avoid lifting heavy objects	35	45	55	49	53	63
Do things less often or more slowly	31	52	57	49	57	67
Avoid walking	11	17	25	18	21	34
Avoid bending or stooping	11	15	27	20	22	36
Avoid stairs	8	12	20	19	21	32
Avoid reaching overhead	4	11	17	17	24	34
Avoid gripping and opening things	5	11	16	20	20	30

Note. From *National Survey of Self-Care and Aging,* Cecil G. Sheps Center for Health Services Research, University of North Carolina at Chapel Hill, 1996.

vey respondents. The overall national prevalence of several of the healthy habits used in the Alameda County studies was estimated from survey responses and is displayed in Table 1.3. Generally, persons in this age group are quite likely to abstain from alcohol or to drink in moderation (one or two drinks in a sitting), and to eat breakfast regularly. About half the population generally avoid eating between meals, while two thirds report themselves as being physically active (often hunt, fish, exercise, garden, or at least sometimes engage in physical sports, swimming, or long walks). Slightly more than half of this age group report getting seven or eight hours of sleep daily. Furthermore, about the same proportion report height and weight consistent with appropriate ratios as defined for their age and sex.

TABLE 1.3   National Prevalence of Selected Healthy Lifestyle Practices

Type of practice	Male 65–74	Male 75–84	Male 85+	Female 65–74	Female 75–84	Female 85+
No eating between meals	48	46	52	40	42	47
Adequate sleep	62	56	57	56	48	42
Never smoked	35	38	47	60	73	72
Moderate drinking	78	82	86	92	95	94
Eats breakfast	84	92	97	82	84	92

Note. From *National Survey of Self-Care and Aging,* Cecil G. Sheps Center for Health Services Research, University of North Carolina at Chapel Hill, 1996.

These observations support the notion that the relationship between a "healthy" lifestyle and aging will not be easily understood without more sophisticated analyses. In this case, the choice of a measure of "healthy habits" is important in determining whether or not we observe a bivariate relationship with age. Thus, while there is little evidence of a strong age or gender difference for an overall summary score of the seven healthy habits, it is evident that significant gender and age variation exists when many of these lifestyle elements are examined individually. Further, some habits appear to decline with age (notably, getting an adequate number of hours of sleep), others appear to increase with age (e.g., drinking in moderation). Thus, attempts to summarize the relationship between age and various healthy lifestyle behavior patterns may oversimplify a complex constellation of behaviors. This should not be surprising, given the fact that the internal consistency of the index of seven healthy habits is relatively low; that is, a person who avoids one type of unhealthy behavior is not necessarily the same one who avoids another. Thus, not only are more sophisticated multivariate modeling and sensitivity to cohort effects necessary, but also summary measures of complex concepts such as healthy lifestyle require robust measurement techniques.

Age and gender differences are particularly striking for individuals who report that they have smoked at any time during their lives. Curiously enough, when only those who have ever smoked are considered as a denominator, the proportion of individuals still smoking is higher for women than for men, especially in the older age categories. Thus only 8% of males age 85 and over who ever smoked are still smoking while the comparable figure for women that age is 28% (Woomert et al., 1994). This suggests that even though older women are less likely to have ever smoked than older men, they may have more difficulty quitting smoking. Although complete multivariate analyses of these data have yet to be done, we expect that the effects of education will be reflected in health habits and health behavior, and that because more recent cohorts of older persons tend to have higher levels of education, reliance on age alone will mask more subtle effects of other socioeconomic variables.

Self-Care: Medical Diagnostic and Therapeutic Tools and Techniques

One unique feature of our national study is the inclusion of items describing patterns of medical self-care. An indication of the distribution of these activities in the older population can be deduced by examining the prevalence of common household items that constitute the *sine qua non* of a bathroom medicine chest in most American homes—a thermometer, a bathroom scale, a hot water bottle or a heating pad, and a first aid kit (see Table 1.4). The national survey data reveal that on average at least 8 out of every 10 older Americans are likely to have all or most of these in their bathroom. However, there are disparities by age and gender in the reported availability of these items; persons in the oldest-old category generally are less likely to have them, and women (especially those in the youngest age group) are slightly less likely to have them than are men. None of these items seems especially costly, complex, or novel, nor does it seem apparent that the usefulness of these items declines with age. Yet a downward sloping age gradient, especially for men, is evident for all of them. This pattern suggests that a cohort effect may be involved, i.e., that more recently-born cohorts of persons are more likely to have these medical self-care items. A somewhat disturbing trend is found with the presence of smoke alarms, which if anything, might be more essential for the oldest-old. Here again, however, younger males are the most likely to have these

TABLE 1.4 National Prevalence of Health Self-Care Items in Homes of Elders

Type of health self-care item	Male 65–74	Male 75–84	Male 85+	Female 65–74	Female 75–84	Female 85+
Thermometer	86	82	78	79	79	78
Bathroom Scale	90	87	84	83	84	79
Hot Water Bottle	89	88	85	88	88	82
First Aid Kit	92	90	86	90	88	87

Note. From National Survey of Self-Care and Aging, Cecil G. Sheps Center for Health Services Research, University of North Carolina at Chapel Hill, 1996.

devices. The age gradient is much less marked for women, but the rates are also lower with greater age.

A similar pattern was suggested when respondents were asked about the availability of medical books (i.e., "doctor" or "self-care" books) in their homes. The percentages of males in the three age groups having these books ranged from 60% in the youngest (65–74) age group to 47% in the oldest (85+) group, while for women the comparable percentages were 53% in the youngest group and 40% in the oldest group. Here again, a cohort effect seems a plausible interpretation and the more recent cohort of older persons is more likely to have some health information available in their homes. The reasons why men seem to be more likely than women to have medical or health self-care books are unclear. Each of these downward sloping trends with age probably reflects a cohort effect; we suspect that this cohort effect may be a result of the fact that more recent cohorts of elderly persons are better educated.

When we look at the relationship between age and gender and the availability of two common diagnostic medical tools—a blood pressure cuff and a stethoscope—we see the same age gradient for men in particular (see Table 1.5). Almost one third of the men in the 65 to 74 age group report having a blood pressure cuff and about one in six have a stethoscope. For women, the situation is somewhat more complex, showing a decreasing prevalence of these medical items in the two younger groups, but an

TABLE 1.5   National Prevalence of Medical Self-Care Equipment in Homes of Elders

Type of health self-care item	Male 65–74	Male 75–84	Male 85+	Female 65–74	Female 75–84	Female 85+
Stethoscope	16	13	11	10	8	14
Blood pressure cuff	32	24	18	21	17	19

Note. From *National Survey of Self-Care and Aging,* Cecil G. Sheps Center for Health Services Research, University of North Carolina at Chapel Hill, 1996.

increase again in the oldest group. Clearly, the utility of these items does not decline with age, and again, a cohort effect seems likely.

This notion is strengthened by the fact that the age and gender gradient characteristic of the use of medical self-care equipment is replicated in the exercise of medical self-care practices. For example, among the 65 to 74 age group, 24% of males and 14% of females reported taking their own blood pressure during the past 12 months. This figure declines to 9% of males and 8% of the females in the 85 and above age group. Similarly, among the 65 to 74 age group, 19% of males and 14% of females reported taking their own pulse during the past 12 months, while only 12% of males and 10% of the females in the oldest group did so. Testing urine with a dipstick was being done by about 10% of elders in the youngest age group and only 4% in the oldest age group. Breast self-examination also displays a steep age gradient, with 44% of the 65 to 74 year old women reporting having done a breast self-exam regularly during the previous 12 months, while only 20% of the women 85 and above did so.

The hopeful interpretation from this snapshot of medical self-care resources and activities is that many older Americans are taking a more proactive role in their health and are acquiring at least some of the tools and skills that in past decades were chiefly under the control of physicians and other health care professionals. Some of the societal emphasis on taking charge of one's own health that has emerged out of a confluence of various social and cultural forces over the last few decades is apparently coming of age. If higher levels of education prove to be associated with the acceptance of healthy lifestyles and the effective use of medical self-care skills and devices, then a hopeful trend may be expected as current middle-aged persons reach older ages, because the trend in average level of education is going up. However, we do not know how effectively or appropriately these tools and skills are being applied and cannot assume that such efforts will continue to be employed as these younger seniors age further.

Even if the emphasis on the acquisition of self-care tools and skills is a new historical phenomenon in this most recent generation of seniors, it remains to be seen whether or not they will continue to engage in such activity as they age. An alternative interpretation of these cross-sectional data could be that these skills decay with increasing age, that equipment is lost or broken and not repaired or replaced, or that motivation to engage in self-care declines with greater social disengagement or lack of focused social support. Further analyses of these data will yield more clues as to which interpretation is correct, or if some combination of age and cohort effects is involved. Fuller explanations for the age gradient can only be clearly ascertained by well-conducted longitudinal or follow-up studies in which such information is obtained.

RESEARCH AND POLICY AGENDA

Several different themes emerge from our examination of theoretical approaches, current research directions, and contemporary data on self-care behaviors of the U.S. population over age 65.

First, there seems to be evidence of changes in health lifestyle and self-care practices that are reflected in the experiences of different age groups as they reach retirement years. Effective design of self-care programs and lifestyle and behavior modification campaigns requires targeting with these positive and negative trends in mind. Not only do we need to understand better what problems to anticipate but also we need to know what trends to take advantage of as new cohorts move into their late years. Careful monitoring of the health knowledge, attitudes, and practices of individuals in the late middle-age years seems warranted so that more and better life course–oriented health promotion campaigns can be designed and implemented.

A second major theme that emerges is the fact that there is a great deal of variability in the older population in the practice of self-care and healthful habits. While some of this variability is due to predictable sociodemographic variables such as gender, educational level, and marital status, there may be much more subtle cultural and psychosocial variables that affect how people view self-care and whether they are disposed to engage in it. Much more research about the epidemiology of readiness for and acceptance of self-care in the older population needs to be done so that well-designed and appropriately targeted campaigns can actually be implemented.

A third major area where there are many unanswered questions is in the patterning of self-care and health behavior. More studies are needed examining any clustering of various self-care and lifestyle practices, and documenting the relationships between beliefs and behavior change (Ferrini, Edelstein, & Barrett-Connor, 1994; Frenn, 1996). We do not know, for example, if the kinds of individuals who take an active, assertive posture with respect to self-treatment for minor conditions are the same persons who develop active coping strategies for dealing with functional limitations, who use positive strategies for coping with depression, or who carefully watch their diet and exercise. Longitudinal data could also add depth to such knowledge by identification of the extent to which some health-related activities of late life serve as precursors to other ones later on. Knowledge about the covariation in the population could help program design in at least three ways: First, it could lead to improved targeting of health-focused programs by identifying seniors who might be more or less receptive to various types of programs. Second, such knowledge could lead to better program design. Health educators need to know whether to focus efforts on a single type of health promotion activity or on several types of activities that cluster together. Finally, an increased understanding of the longitudinal relationship between these various health-related behaviors could help health program planners know how such elements ought to be sequenced within a larger health behavior modification strategy. Effective program design requires identification of those segments of the older population who should be the focus of health promotion efforts. Once these target populations are identified, then those activities that should be encouraged or discouraged should be specified. Finally, those who design health promotion programs should be clear about whether health behaviors will be dealt with one at a time or simultaneously.

A final theme that seems evident is *priorities and payoffs*. Clearly, smoking cessation and physical exercise modification have demonstrated their potentials to enhance and lengthen life. Further epidemiological studies and programmatic evaluations are needed to examine the effectiveness and implementability of health promotion and self-care programs in other areas as well. Ultimately, however, there is little doubt that well-designed self-care programs and the societal encouragement of the widespread adoption of sound self-care practices will play a critical role in enhancing the quality of life of seniors.

CONCLUSION

The population over age 65 (Hobbs & Damon, 1996) has increased dramatically both in absolute numbers as well as proportionally over the last two decades. This phenomenal growth, which served to galvanize the health policy and research communities, has recently become the subject of widespread journalistic and political expressions of concern about the future stability of long-standing supportive structures for older Americans. Yet the current debate about the stability of the Medicare program, Social Security, and private pension plans, the role of the government versus individuals and families in long-term care, and the role of individual choice in financing these changes reflects an underlying concern about dependency in the last years of life. Whatever the outcome of the debate about financing and organization of health care for older Americans, this tension will not cease. Increasingly, however, the salience of self-care to this debate is coming to be recognized (Uhlenberg, 1996). As we come to have a more sophisticated appreciation of how self-initiated actions can affect the patterns of frailty and dependency, we can design better programs and policies to deal creatively and effectively with the tension between the realities of frailty and dependency and our common aspirations for dignity and autonomy in the later stages of life.

REFERENCES

Barr R. A. (1994). The promise of human factors research. In R. P. Abeles, RP, H. C. Gift, & M. G. Ory (Eds.), *Aging and quality of life: Charting new territories in behavioral sciences research.* New York: Springer Publishing.

Berkman L., & Breslow, L. (1983). *Health and ways of living: The Alameda County study.* New York: Oxford University Press.

Centers for Disease Control. (1992). *Advance data: Assistive technology devices and home accessibility features: Prevalence, payment, need and trends* (U.S. Public Health Service, no. 217). National Center for Health Statistics.

Cummings, E., & Henry, W. E. (1961). *Growing old.* New York: Basic Books.

Dean, K., Hickey T., & Holstein B. E. (1986). *Self-care and health in old age: Health behaviour implications for policy and practice.* London: Croom Helm.

Dean, K. (1989). Conceptual, theoretical and methodological issues in self-care research. *Social Science and Medicine, 29*(2), 117–123.

Dean, K. (1992). Health-related behavior: Concepts and methods. In *Aging, health and behavior.* Ory, M. G., Abeles, R. P., Lipman, P. D. (Eds.). Newbury Park, CA: Sage.

DeFriese, G. H., Woomert, A., Guild, P. A., Steckler, A. B., Konrad, T. R. (1989). From activated patient to pacified activist: A study of the self-care movement in the United States. *Social Science and Medicine, 29*, 195–204.

DeWitt, J. C. (1991). The role of technology in removing barriers. *Milbank Quarterly, 69* (Suppl. 1–2), 332.

Ferrini, R., Edelstein, S., & Barrett-Connor, E. (1994). The association between health beliefs and health behavior change in older adults. *Preventive Medicine, 23*(1),1–5.

Ford, G. (1986). Age as a labeling phenomenon. In K. Dean, T. Hickey, & B. E. Holstein (Eds.), Self-care and health in old age (p. 35). London: Croom Helm.

Frenn, M. (1996) Older adults' experience of health promotion: A theory for nursing practice. *Public Health Nursing, 13*(1), 65–71.

Guralnik, J. M., LaCroix, A. Z., Abbott, R. D., Berkman, L. F., Satterfield, S., Evans, D. A., & Wallace, R. B. (1993). Maintaining mobility in late life: I. Demographic characteristics and chronic conditions. *American Journal of Epidemiology, 137,* 845–868.

Guralnik, J. M., Land, K. C., Blazer, D., Fillenbaum, G. G., & Branch, L. G. (1993). Education status and active life expectancy among older blacks and whites. *The New England Journal of Medicine, 329*(2), 110–116.

Hadley, E. C., Ory, M. G., Suzman, R., Weindruch, R., & Fried, L. (Eds.) (1993, September). Physical frailty: A treatable cause of dependence in old age. *The Journals of Gerontology, 48* (Special Issue), 1–88.

Hobbs, F. B., & Damon, B. L. (1996). *65+ in the United States* (U.S. Bureau of the Census, Current Population Reports, Special Studies, P23-190). Washington, DC: U.S. Government Printing Office.

Holstein, B. E. (1986). Health related behavior and aging: Conceptual issues. In K. Dean, T. Hickey, & B. E. Holstein (Eds.), *Self-care and health in old age.* London: Croom Helm.

Kaplan, G. A. (1996). People and places: Contrasting perspectives on the association between social class and health. *International Journal of Health Services, 26*(3), 507–519.

Kaplan, G. A., & Strawbridge, W. J. (1994). Behavioral and social factors in healthy aging in R. P. Abeles, H. C. Gift, M. G. Ory (Eds.), *Aging and quality of life: Charting new territories in behavioral sciences research* (pp. 57–78). New York: Springer Publishing.

LaCroix, A. Z., Guralnik, J. M., Berkman, L. F., Wallace, R. B., & Satterfield, S. (1993). Maintaining mobility in late life. II: Smoking, alcohol consumption, physical activity, and body mass index. *American Journal of Epidemiology, 137*(8), 858–869.

Levin, L. S., & Idler, E. L. (1981). *The hidden health care system: Mediating structures and medicine.* Cambridge, MA: Ballinger.

Manton, K. G., Corder, L., & Stallard, E. (1997) Chronic disability trends in elderly United States populations: 1982–1994. *Proceedings of the National Academy of Sciences, USA,* 94, 2593–2598.

Norburn, J. E. K., Bernard, S. L., Konrad, T. R., Woomert, A., DeFriese, G. H., Kalsbeek, W. D., Koch, G. G., & Ory, M. G. (1995). Self-care and assistance from others in coping with functional status limitations among a national sample of older adults. *Journal of Gerontology: Social Sciences, 50*(2), S101–S109.

Ory, M. G., & Williams, T. F. (1989). Rehabilitation: Small goals, sustained interventions. *The Annals of the American Academy of Political and Social Science, 503,* 61–76.

Riley, M. W., & Bond, K. (1983). Beyond ageism: Postponing the onset of disability. In M. W. Riley, B. B. Hess, & K. Bond (Eds.), *Aging in society: Selected reviews of recent research.* Hillsdale, NJ: Erlbaum.

Strawbridge, W. J., Cohen, R. D., Shema, S. L., & Kaplan, G. A. (1996). Successful aging: Predictors and associated activities. *American Journal of Epidemiology, 144,* 135–141.

Taeuber, C. M. (1983). America in transition: An aging society. *Current population reports* (Series P-23, No. 128). Washington, DC: U.S. Bureau of the Census.

Uhlenberg, P. (1996). The burden of aging: A theoretical framework for understanding the shifting balance of caregiving and care receiving as cohorts age. *The Gerontologist, 30,* 761–767.

Verbrugge, L. M., & Jette, A. M. (1994). The disablement process. *Social Science and Medicine, 38*(1), 1–14.

Weiner, J. M., Hanley, R. J., Clark, R., & Van Nostrand, J. F. (1990). Measuring the activities of daily living: Comparisons across national surveys. *Journal of Gerontology: Social Sciences, 45,* S229–S237.

Wolfson, M. (1996). Health-adjusted life expectancy. *Health Reports, Statistics Canada, 8*(1), 41–46.

Woomert, A., Konrad, T. R., Ory, M. G., DeFriese, G.H., Norburn, J. E. K., & Bernard, S. (1996, May). *Health promotion and disease prevention in late life: Findings from the National Health Study of Older Adults.* Working paper; supported by the National Institute of Aging Self-Care Assessment of Community-Based Elderly project. Chapel Hill: Cecil G. Sheps Center for Health Services Research, University of North Carolina at Chapel Hill, 1996.

World Health Organization. (1983). *Health education in self-care: Possibilities and limitations* (Report of a scientific consultation). Geneva: World Health Organization.

CHAPTER 2

Dynamics and Processes of Self-Care in Old Age

Eleanor Palo Stoller

S elf-care is the predominant form of primary care in illness (Dean, 1989b; Rakowski, Julius, Hickey, Verbrugge, & Halter, 1988; Stoller, Forster, & Pollow, 1994). Although much of the behavior of sick people is a direct product of the symptoms they experience, existing literature reports significant variability in responses by different people to similar symptoms. These differences emerge from personal experience, cultural definitions, and the social interactions that develop around illness (Dill, Brown, Ciambrone, & Rakowski, 1995). A fundamental assumption in the literature on illness behavior is that the experience of illness "is shaped by sociocultural and other social psychological factors, irrespective of their genetic, physiological, and other biological bases" (Mechanic, 1986, p. 1). Response to illness is frequently conceptualized as individual behavior, yet self-care is embedded in family, community, and institutional frameworks (Backett & Davison, 1995; Norburn et al., 1995; Royer, 1995).

This chapter explores the social context of self-care practices in old age, including the role of informal support networks, environmental factors, and situational contexts in facilitating or impeding the likelihood of particular practices. Self-care has been defined broadly as activities undertaken by individuals to promote health, prevent disease, limit illness, and restore health (DeFriese, Konrad, Woomert, Norburn, & Bernard, 1994; Levin & Idler, 1983). The critical component of this definition is that self-care practices are lay initiated and reflect a self-determined decision-making process (Royer, 1995; Segall & Goldstein, 1989). In this chapter, attention is limited to self-care in response to illness. The focus is on interpretation and management of symptoms, either as indicators of new conditions or as exacerbations of ongoing chronic conditions.

The first section begins with a review of the literature on illness behavior, covering symptom interpretation, lay consultation, and self-treatment. It draws on research from multiple disciplines, and includes sociological, anthropological, and psychological perspectives. This review also incorporates more subjective aspects of illness experience, including strategies people develop for managing symptoms, repertoires of lay knowledge, and the impact of illness on identity (Conrad, 1994). The second section identifies a range of conceptual and methodological issues which emerged from this review. Finally, the third section discusses implications for practitioners, policy analysts, and researchers.

COMPONENTS OF ILLNESS BEHAVIOR

Symptom Interpretation

People experience a number of bodily sensations which must be interpreted (Alonzo, 1979); recognition and evaluation of symptoms is a fundamental aspect of self-care (Dean, 1986). Both perception and interpretation of bodily sensations are grounded in cultural context and in social learning (Angel & Thoits, 1987; Dean, 1992). The first step in interpreting perceived symptoms is "classifying the noticed discomforts roughly in terms of popular cultural perspectives and developing hypotheses about likely cause(s)" (Chrisman & Kleinman, 1983, p. 576). This view of symptom definition is analogous to Mechanic's (1978) concept of *illness attribution*—the ways in which pain and symptoms are defined, accorded significance and socially labeled. Interpretations are multidimensional, including attributions of cause and assessments of pain and discomfort, disruption of desired activities, and perceived seriousness.

Causal Attributions

In his analysis of illness narratives, Kleinman (1988) stresses the importance of the explanatory models of illness that patients and their families develop. The initial response to a new symptom is often to normalize the symptom, by attributing it to some cause other than disease. In most instances, the cause is located retrospectively by examining occurrences in previous days (Chrisman & Kleinman, 1983). Commonsense models of illness, which incorporate multiple dimensions such as identity (symptoms and label), consequences (perceived impact), time-lines (onset, duration, and periodicity), assumed causes, and controllability will be explored in depth in chapter 5 of this volume.

Older people frequently attribute symptoms to the aging process (Kart, 1981; Leventhal, Leventhal, & Schaefer, 1992; Leventhal & Prohaska, 1986; Prohaska, Keller, Leventhal, & Leventhal, 1987). Stoller found evidence of normalizing symptoms among the elderly respondents in her recent health diary study (1993a). Over half (54%) of her respondents attributed at least one of their symptoms to normal aging ("something that happens to most people as they get older"), and 5% attributed all of their symptoms to normal aging. Normalizing symptoms by attributing them to aging does not always exclude disease-related explanations. Older people can attribute symptoms to an underlying disease but conclude, accurately or erroneously, that the prevalence of particular diseases increases with age or that progression of certain pathological conditions occurs as people age. Thus, people do not necessarily treat aging and illness as two mutually exclusive causes (Prohaska et al., 1987).

The overwhelming majority (89%) of Stoller's (1993a) respondents reported a cause outside of a disease framework for at least one of their symptoms, and 16% attributed all of their symptoms to exclusively nonmedical causes. The most common nonmedical interpretation was weather or season of the year, cited by 60% as a cause for at least one symptom. A smaller minority attributed symptoms to stress or to behavior or life style.

Daily symptoms are most often attributed to diseases, particularly chronic conditions. Three-quarters of Stoller's (1993a) respondents incorporated a disease-related interpretation in explaining their symptoms, although only 6% interpreted all of their symptoms within a medical framework. The most common disease attribution, reported by 62%, was a flare-up of a chronic condition. This medical interpretation was often used in conjunction with a nonmedical interpretation. Qualitative analysis of the health diaries suggested that respondents with these mixed interpretations believed that certain diseases or medical conditions are associated with old age. Others explained a symptom as a flare-up of a chronic condition but attributed the flare-up to a specific behavior, a stressful situation, or season of the year. Even nonmedical explanations were often based on quasi-biological models of human functioning, reflecting the trickling down of clinical knowledge into the popular health culture (Chrisman & Kleinman, 1983).

Attributions couched in medical terms do not always reflect tenets of scientific medicine. This discrepancy is most clearly evident when lay theories of disease are grounded in ethnic or rural subcultures (Hansen & Resick, 1990). For example, rural Blacks and poor Whites in Appalachia complain of "high blood," "sugar," "fallin' out," and "nerves" (Kleinman, 1988). Less obvious are the ways in which older people reinterpret clinical explanations. People have come to understand their illnesses "through a process of reappraisal that produced modifiable explanations, logical to them in terms of their everyday thinking and, most importantly, useful in terms of their everyday needs" (Hunt, Jordan, & Irwin, 1989, p. 954). As a result, explanations given by patients and physicians can reflect different understandings, even though expressed in similar terminology.

The distinction between medical and nonmedical interpretations is only one aspect of causal attributions. Another important dimension involves imputation of responsibility (Davison, Frankel, & Smith, 1992). Davison and colleagues conceptualize personal responsibility as a continuum, anchored by conditions such as diabetes, brain hemorrhage, and many common infectious diseases on the "least fault" end and sexually transmitted disease, cirrhosis of the liver, and lung cancer on the other. Blaxter's qualitative study (1983) of women in Scotland yielded a number of possible causes, including infection, heredity or family tendency, environmental agents (e.g., climate, dampness, working conditions, "poisons"), neglect, inherent susceptibility, behavior, aging, and randomness or chance (i.e., speaking of disease as "just happening"). She reported a preference for external causes, which "assigned blame but located the cause outside of oneself" (1983, p. 66). In contrast, explanations invoking randomness or inevitability were more threatening and less popular. Attributions suggesting that sufferers brought disease on themselves appear least common. Neither of these studies, however, focused on elderly respondents, so their generalizability to older people remains an empirical question.

Seriousness, or perceived threat, is another component of symptom interpretation. Few of the respondents in Stoller's (1993a) health diary study believed that their symptoms were "definitely serious." Heart palpitations and vision problems were the only symptoms rated as "definitely serious" by more than 20% of the people experiencing them. A considerably larger proportion expressed some uncertainty regarding the clinical import of their symptoms. Over half of people experiencing weakness, dizziness, urination difficulties, joint or muscle pain, shortness of breath, heart palpitations, or swelling indicated that their symptom was "possibly" or "probably" serious (Stoller, 1993a).

Research on self-care has focused more attention on the interpretation of symptoms than on lay theories of disease—the beliefs and perceptions that underlie self-care practices. Investigators have explored general models of disease causation, including exposure to disease agents and environmental pathogens; psychological distress; unhealthful behaviors or lifestyles (e.g., dietary patterns, lack of exercise, smoking), access to and quality of medical care, punishment for violating norms or religious taboos, fate or God's will, other supernatural forces (e.g., voodoo, rootwork, "evil eye"), chance or luck, and genetics or heredity (Blaxter, 1983; Furnham, 1994; Kleinman, 1988; Klonoff & Landrine, 1994; Schiaffino & Cea, 1995). Other researchers have studied lay understandings of particular diseases, including diabetes (Hampson, Glasgow, & Toobert, 1990), arthritis (Hampson, Glasgow, & Zeiss, 1994), cancer (Matthews, Lannin, & Mitchell, 1994) and hypertension (Heurtin-Roberts, 1993). Only a minority of studies utilize samples of elderly people (Strain, 1996), although differences in knowledge, attitudes, and beliefs about disease reflect the lifetime experiences of individuals in a given age cohort (Haug, Wykle, & Namazi, 1989). As a result, we know very little about how elderly people's lay theories of illness and disease-specific understandings influence self-care practices and implementation of professional recommendations for managing chronic conditions.

Factors Influencing Interpretation

A number of factors influence older people's interpretations of the symptoms they experience. One is the nature of the symptoms themselves. Symptoms that are severe and rapid in onset are likely to be interpreted as signs of illness (Leventhal et al., 1992; Prohaska et al., 1987). In contrast, symptoms that are intermittent, nonspecific, relatively mild and of slow onset are more likely to be normalized outside a disease framework (Alonzo, 1986; Leventhal et al., 1992; Levkoff, Cleary, & Wetle, 1987; Prohaska et al., 1987). Symptoms that are particularly painful, that persist beyond an expected period of time, that defy explanations, and disrupt normal routines are more likely than other symptoms to raise considerations of possible seriousness (Dean, 1986).

Multiple chronic conditions can also sensitize people to the potential import of new symptoms. Older people do not confront symptoms in isolation.

Rather, symptoms are interpreted within a context of health and illness experienced over a lifetime. People experiencing multiple health problems are likely to interpret each new symptom as an assault on their already precarious condition, whereas elderly people who believe their health is good have more confidence in their own resilience and are less likely to interpret any particular symptoms as potentially threatening (Haug et al., 1989). Stoller (1993a) also found that when symptoms occur within a context of poor health, older people begin to question their potential seriousness and to consider disease-related explanations. Among her respondents, people who reported a larger number of other symptoms and who rated their health as poor reported more negative interpretations of specific symptoms than people reporting fewer symptoms and better health. They were less likely to dismiss symptoms as not at all serious and more likely to interpret their symptoms within a medical framework. Familiar symptoms which older people had experienced more frequently in the past were also less likely to be dismissed as not serious and to be attributed to exclusively nonmedical causes. In a study of elderly adults with arthritis and heart/circulatory problems, Strain (1996) found that poorer self-rated health was associated with anticipation of further deterioration. These results indicate that older people experiencing health-related problems are likely to interpret additional symptoms as further evidence of their declining health. A complementary explanation suggests that people who experience few symptoms and who assess their health positively are more likely to normalize and minimize the potential import of new and unfamiliar symptoms. (Stoller, 1993a). These results are consistent with Ford's conclusion that chronic ill health sensitizes people to the need to attend to symptoms (1986).

Other factors influencing symptom interpretation relate to characteristics of individuals. For example, perceptions of serious rather than benign symptoms are associated with living alone, having low income, being widowed or divorced, experiencing stressful problems, low satisfaction with social support, low internal locus of control, inability to find ways to relax, and belief in the efficacy of medical care (Dean, 1986).

Finally, evaluation of symptoms is also a function of situational factors. Alonzo (1984, 1989) argues that different roles and different social settings vary in the degree to which they will accommodate manifestations of illness. From the standpoint of the older respondent, the primary concern is containing signs and symptoms of disease in such a way that role compromise is minimized. Alonzo stresses the fact that individuals must not only cope with multiple health-related problems but must manage them across multiple situations. Interpretation of any particular problem, therefore, varies with the demands and tolerance of the situation. Consistent with this perspective is Stoller's (1993a) finding that the number of important roles and activities reported by her respondents was positively related to assessments of pain and interference for several symptoms. These positive coefficients suggest that people with more activities they deem important are more likely to be frustrated by the presence of symptoms that limit their ability to pursue these activities. They are also more likely to encounter situations that are less able to accommodate side involvement with illness.

> The extent to which illness can be contained is a function of both the severity and nature of the symptoms and the tightness and particular requirements of the situation. The point is that individuals move backward and forward between situations with different demands all the time and have a multitude of options for living with a degree of illness short of entry into the sick role. (Ford, 1986, p. 153)

Lay Consultation Patterns

Many people experiencing illness episodes discuss their condition with a lay consultant—instead of, prior to, or after consulting a professional provider (Brody, Kleban, & Oriol, 1985; DeFriese & Woomert, 1983; Fleming, Giachello, Andersen, & Andrade, 1984; Verbrugge, 1987). Symptom-related discussions are part of the information gathering that often accompanies "vigilant coping" (Leventhal et al., 1992). Family members are consulted most frequently, and family members are often "the first and only person with whom older individuals will discuss their symptom experience" (Glasser, Prohaska, & Roska, 1992, p. 59). Spouses are the primary lay consultants among old people who are married, especially married men (Stoller, 1993b). Married men are more likely than married women to rely exclusively on their spouses for advice about symptoms. Married women often draw on advice from other women, including both other relatives and friends (Chappell, 1989; Stoller, 1993b). However, Chappell (1989) reports that this gender difference disappears in the case of serious conditions. Spouses reportedly talk over most health problems, and these discussions more often focus on the husband's health than on the wife's (Dean, 1986). Women are also more likely than men to assume responsibility for the health of their spouse and other family members (Depner & Ingersoll-Dayton, 1985; Umberson, 1992). When married people consult someone other than their spouse, they are more likely to consult women than men (Stoller, 1993b).

Widowed respondents, especially widowed men, are less likely than married people to discuss their symptoms with lay consultants. Stoller (1993b) found that when widowed elders discussed a symptom with someone else, the consultant was most often an adult child. Slightly over one third of widowed parents consulted someone other than an adult child, and these lay consultations also demonstrated a strong preference for women, most of whom were friends or neighbors. Lay referral networks among widowed elderly confirmed the salience of women as lay consultants. At the same time, men also exhibited some preference for same-gender consultants. While widowed men and women were equally likely to select women consultants, widowers were significantly more likely to speak to a man than were widows. Less is known about the consultation patterns of divorced or never-married elders, and the small numbers of respondents in most studies undermine confidence in the stability of available estimates (Stoller, 1993b).

Friends and neighbors are another source of information regarding symptoms (Edwardson, Dean, & Brauer, 1995). Friends are often age peers, and, given the prevalence of chronic conditions among elderly people, networks of friends and acquaintances often include fellow sufferers with whom to compare notes and share information (Ford, 1986; Strain, 1990). Women report that they have health-related conversations with friends and acquaintances more frequently than do men. Part of this gender difference reflects higher rates of marriage and the predominant reliance of married men on their wives, but it is also consistent with other research on social relationships that indicates men are less likely than women to discuss intimate and emotional matters with others. Larger networks that incorporate consultants from a broader range of sources are likely to provide more diverse information but to exert weaker influence than small dense networks (Strain, 1990; Furstenberg & Davis, 1984), a difference consistent with Granovetter's (1974) notion of the "strength of weak ties."

Discussions of lay consultation have often mirrored a medical model: People sought information about diagnosis and treatment from their informal networks. Explicit requests for information and advice constitute one type of lay consultation, but researchers have documented several types of health-related discussions. Some are casual conversations, in which people simply report health problems or seek reassurance or assessments of the situation (Edwardson et al., 1995; Rakowski et al., 1988; Strain, 1990).

Furstenberg and Davis (1984) characterize these conversations as "reporting" (p. 831), arguing that they are part of everyday interaction in close relationships. Although only one quarter of Furstenberg's respondents actively sought information and advice from their lay networks, many reported

> carrying on a steady stream of casual conversations with spouse, relatives of the same generation, and/or friends about their symptoms, their illnesses, and the things they were doing to treat them . . . . [They] seemed to use health simply as a form of social currency, something that one could talk about and exchange with other people. (1985, p. 110)

Cameron, Leventhal, Leventhal, and Schaefer (1993) concur that a desire to talk and inform others about a problem is often more important than a need for information.

Lay consultations have multiple consequences. The process of telling and retelling the story of one's illness can assist in information processing (Furstenberg & Davis, 1984). Discussions with age peers can provide reference points from which older people can assess their own health (Strain, 1990). Lay consultants can teach and reinforce patterns of self-care, validate or contradict people's interpretations of their symptoms, encourage or discourage professional consultation, provide reassurance, or simply listen to complaints and concerns, thus affirming the person's importance and supporting self-esteem (Dean, 1986; Furstenberg & Davis, 1984). Stoller (1993a) found that people with larger support networks are less likely than those with smaller support networks to interpret symptoms as serious medical problems. Several interpretations could account for this result. First, social support may buffer the negative effects of symptoms, actually reducing their perceived intensity. Second, members of support networks may assist respondents in meeting role obligations, thus reducing the visibility of incapacity. Finally, network members may also serve as lay medical consultants, redefining the older person's initial assessments or suggesting treatments to alleviate symptoms.

Not all older people discuss their symptoms with family and friends. Brody et al. (1985) documented a number of explanations for not telling anyone about symptoms, with the most common being that the symptom was "no big deal" because it caused minimal disruption, because the cause was known, or because it was a familiar occurrence. Other reasons for failure to report symptoms included acceptance of discomfort as a normal and expected part of aging, pessimism about possibilities for relief, a reluctance to bother professionals or to worry their families, lack of appreciation of the symptoms' significance, and cognitive deficits that impair their capacity to communicate their experiences. (p. 87)

Older people sometimes fail to report health problems to their adult children, because they don't want to burden them with unnecessary bad news (Strain, 1990). Furstenberg reports that older people did not feel obligated to report health problems to children except "in the case of serious illness or when some weighty course of action was contemplated, such as surgery, or when help might be needed" (1985, p. 115).

Lay consultation patterns are also influenced by type of disease. Research on lay consultation concentrates on the earlier stages of symptom experience, either for acute conditions or for an acute onset of a chronic disease (Fursternberg & Davis, 1984). Much of the illness experienced by elderly people, however, involves chronic conditions. As Alonzo explains:

Among the chronically ill who may experience repeated and frequent exacerbation of signs and symptoms, it may be difficult to continually inform family members that they are symptomatic. In addition, chronically diseased individuals may have an abundance of prescribed and nonprescribed medications and other treatment resources that must be gone through before they can declare themselves in need of additional social and medical resources. (1986, p. 1307)

Furthermore, repeated reports of similar symptoms not only fail to bring new information but can be seen as complaining or malingering (Schlesinger, 1993).

Decisions regarding disclosure of symptoms are most complicated in the context of conditions that are not visible. In contrast to cancer patients undergoing radiation or older people crippled by arthritis, many chronic conditions are not readily apparent to other people. Indeed, as we shall see, a major goal of management regimens is containment, which Alonzo defines as "keeping signs and symptoms at the level of side-involvement by suppressing them, disattending them, concealing or shielding them, so they may be integrated into the activity, role demands, and obligations of the situation" (1984, p. 501).

Lay Treatment Strategies

Lay treatments encompass a variety of responses, including advertised and folk remedies, physical actions, modifications of intake of food or drink, and psychological or spiritual interventions (Wykle & Haug, 1993). The majority of research on self-care in the presence of illness has emphasized use of medications, both over-the-counter preparations and medications prescribed by physicians during prior consultations. Despite this emphasis on medications, Dean (1992) argues that the majority of self-treatment involves other types of responses, including appliances (e.g., thermometers, enemas, heating pads) and homemade preparations (e.g., herb teas, baths, salves). Dean cautions that "limiting the concept of self-treatment to home appliances, herbal medications, and various forms of home concoctions is a way of approximating self-care to the medical model and may exclude some of the most beneficial forms of self-care" (1986, p. 275). She recommends that self-treatment be defined to include changes in activity (e.g., bed rest, changes in exercise level), avoidance behaviors (e.g, not stooping or lifting, not smoking or drinking, avoiding stressful situations, avoiding drafts), or changes in diet (e.g., increasing fluids, increasing bulk). Freer (1980) identified an additional category of "social nonmedical responses" (p. 858) to symptoms (e.g., spending time with family and friends, watching television, or going out for lunch).

Elderly people do not always intervene when they experience a symptom. Less attention has been directed to situations in which people decide that the best response to a symptom is no treatment, although a sizeable minority of people do not take any action, at least initially or in response to certain symptoms (Dean, Holst, & Wagner, 1983; Stoller, Forster, & Portugal, 1993). Decisions to do nothing about a symptom have often been conceptualized as "ignoring symptoms" or "delays in seeking medical care," but Dean (1986) argues that they should be conceptualized as a form of self-care. Krause concurs with this designation, "especially when the decision to do nothing is based on the belief that 'time cures' and that symptoms will improve on their own without intervention" (1990, p. 227). Decisions not to implement treatment strategies can also reflect one of the temporal procedures described by Leventhal and colleagues (1992). They argue that two temporal procedures operate at the onset of illness episodes. The first is a rule to "seek help for symptoms of sudden and/or intense onset" (p. 119). The second, which they describe as a "wait and see" rule, is most common during an initial phase of illness when symptoms are vague and of low intensity.

Correlates of Self-Treatment

Researchers have identified a number of correlates of self-treatment strategies. One factor is *properties of symptoms* themselves (Prohaska et al., 1987). Stoller, Forster, and Portugal (1993) found that older people whose symptoms caused much pain and discomfort or interfered a great deal with desired activities usually treated their symptoms in some way and, when selecting an intervention strategy, were more likely to use medications than were people whose symptoms were less problematic. Verbrugge (1987) argues that how miserable a person feels is a particularly important predictor for acute episodes.

Attributions of seriousness also influence symptom response. Based on their review of the literature, DeFriese and Woomert (1983, p. 67) conclude that "medical self-care skills are routinely performed for less serious conditions." Analyses of Stoller's health diary data (Stoller & Forster, 1994) revealed that older people who believed their symptoms were definitely serious or who expressed uncertainty regarding the potential seriousness of their symptoms were less likely to manage symptoms on their own and more likely to consult a physician than people who said their symptoms were not serious. Leventhal and colleagues (1992) also report that "older patients were less able to tolerate ambiguity and sought care to reduce it" (p. 132). They conclude that current cohorts of elderly people are more vigilant and more responsive to health threats than are middle-aged and younger people.

Perceptions of health at the time of symptom onset also influence self-treatment decisions, with more chronic conditions and lower levels of perceived health associated with both more self-care interventions and higher rates of physician consultation (Penning & Chappell, 1990). Causal interpretations appear to exhibit a less consistent impact on lay treatment decisions. Leventhal and Prohaska (1986) report that respondents who attributed symptoms to aging were more likely to say they would cope by (a) waiting and watching; (b) accepting the symptoms; (c) denying or minimizing the threat; or (d) postponing or avoiding medical attention (e.g., waiting to bring up the symptoms during their next scheduled medical appointment). Older people can apply palliative strategies to relieve problematic symptoms regardless of their presumed origin. Stoller, Forster, and Portugal

(1993) concluded that whether people ignore or treat symptoms appears to have less to do with their familiarity and causal attribution than whether the symptoms cause them pain or discomfort, interfere with desired activities, or might be indicative of a serious condition.

Gender is the most consistent sociodemographic variable differentiating patterns of self-care. Women are more likely than men to treat their symptoms (Dean, 1986; Rakowski et al., 1988), and women report a greater variety of self-care practices (Bishop, 1987; Rakowski et al., 1988). In contrast, men are more likely to ignore symptoms until they become serious enough to indicate a need for professional care (Dean, 1989b; Hickey, Rakowski, & Akiyama, 1991). Verbrugge (1985) reported that other sociodemographic characteristics did not emerge as consistent predictors of self-treatment for acute illness. For chronic conditions, however, she found that the propensity for taking actions to relieve symptoms was positively related to age and to education.

Differences in Response to Acute and Chronic Disease

Research on illness behavior has highlighted the importance of distinguishing between treatment for acute episodes and management of chronic conditions. Dean's finding that self-care in old age is more often palliative than curative (Dean, 1992) partially reflects the increased prevalence of chronic conditions in late life. Chronic conditions produce symptoms continuously or episodically over time (Ford, 1986). Because "chronically ill patients do not recover, [they] must maintain regimens over an extended period, often without any dramatic evidence of their effectiveness" (Furstenberg & Davis, 1984, p. 828). The basic task in managing chronic illness is containment, which extends beyond alleviating symptoms or managing medical crises (Clark et al., 1991). *Containment* involves carrying on daily activity in as normal a manner as possible (Rakowski et al., 1988, p. 279); avoiding situations or activities that aggravate symptoms or that emphasize the presence of illness (Alonzo, 1984), assessing the degree to which different roles and social settings will accommodate manifestations of illness, anticipating the ways other people will respond to compromised role performance, evaluating the social propriety and consequences to others of remaining in a situation despite compromised performances, and estimating the resources available to manage the impact and visibility of illness (Alonzo, 1989). Even asymptomatic periods do not relieve people with chronic conditions of self-treatment responsibilities. Schlesinger (1993) describes the ongoing management of chronic pain in the lives of the young and middle-aged women she studied:

> Even if (the pain) does go away, many of the women said they didn't know if they would ever trust it not to come back. Living with pain thus involves not necessarily being in pain, but still incorporating pain prevention activities into your life. (p. 264)

Self-Management Versus Self-Care

The prevalence of chronic conditions in old age also blurs the distinction between self-care and self-management that implements professional recommendations. People develop strategies for treating chronic conditions over a long period of time (Verbrugge, 1987). Old people who have lived with a chronic disease often "become very knowledgeable about the condition, including the medications and procedures that work best for them in enhancing mobility and comfort" (Haug, 1986, p. 245). This knowledge is synthesized from multiple sources, including past experience, the media, discussions with acquaintances with a similar condition, and previous consultations with lay and health professionals (Segall & Goldstein, 1989). In this sense, it is difficult to distinguish self-care that is instigated by older people themselves from self-care that is taught and perhaps monitored by health care professionals (Kart & Engler, 1994). Even self-care techniques initiated by formal providers can be modified over time as they are integrated into an ongoing regimen of care. Hunt and colleagues (1989) describe this process among the women they interviewed:

> Over time, medical diagnoses and recommendations were altered in ways that allowed them to fit in with the exigencies and constraints of the women's daily lives. . . . [Such] alterations of treatment behavior were commonly accompanied by a reinterpretation of the illness explanation that produced a coherent rationale for the customized regimen. (p. 953)

Self-Care Capacity

The experience of living with chronic illness can also enhance old people's belief in their capacity for self-care (Hickey et al., 1991). Indeed, Haug (1986, p. 245) suggests that old people "may come to believe, whether accurately or not, that [they] know more about the disease than the doctor."

Over half (55%) of the respondents to the Supplement on Aging of the Longitudinal Study on Aging (LSOA) indicated that they were doing an excellent or very good job in taking care of their health, and an additional 34% believed they were doing a good job (Kart & Dunkle, 1989). Part of this confidence reflects the prevalence of chronic conditions. Hickey (1986) explains that the

> chronic nature of many age-related symptoms suggests that minimal or no treatment may be as effective as seeking professional care. Lifelong personal experiences with illness and changes in their health may give older people considerable confidence in their own ability to treat symptoms, regardless of severity. (p. 30)

Several other correlates of capacity for care have been identified. Women are more likely than men to express confidence in their capacity for self-care (Kart & Engler, 1994), and people who perceive their health as excellent or very good assess their capacity for self-care more positively than people who believe they are in poor health (Kart & Dunkle, 1989). Krause (1990) suggests that confidence in the capacity for self-care varies according to perceived seriousness of the symptoms people experience. "Older adults may believe that they are capable of handling relatively minor symptoms on their own, whereas they may value the expertise and technology provided in formal care settings in those instances where symptoms become more severe or life threatening" (p. 237).

Mastering self-care strategies for chronic disease and learning to function despite disability can reinforce old people's feelings of mastery and competence (Heurtin-Roberts & Becker, 1993; Kart & Engler, 1994; Leventhal & Prohaska, 1986). Developing self-care abilities reduces dependence on formal health care providers and provides a sense of self-sufficiency (DeFriese & Konrad, 1993). Managing and modifying treatment regimens can provide a mechanism for asserting control over illness and health (Kart & Engler, 1994). Indeed, Haug (1986) describes the satisfaction an old person can gain from achieving independence, from "not having to lean on a physician, particularly one who dismisses complaints as due to old age" (p. 246).

Efficacy of Self-Treatment

Belief in one's capacity for self-care does not mean that an older person is responding to symptoms appropriately, and a significant issue in the self-care literature concerns the appropriateness or efficacy of lay management. Ten years ago, Brody reported that many older people lack adequate knowledge about aging and health. They often

> are unable to perform simple procedures basic to many treatment plans; fail to seek professional care when needed; do not follow prescribed treatment plans; are not aggressive enough in seeking information about their conditions or treatments from professionals; [and] misinterpret the signs and symptoms of pathology as expectable aspects of normal aging. (Brody et al., 1985, p. 173)

More recently, researchers have expressed less concern about inappropriate responses to symptoms. Dean argues that, although "lay care is often discussed in terms of its potential dangers while medical care is generally discussed in terms of its effectiveness, . . . the limited evidence available suggests that self-care decisions are generally appropriate and self-treatment helpful" (1992, p. 37). After reviewing the literature on self-care, Kemper, Lorig, and Mettler (1993) concluded that available studies "all point to the widespread use of self-care, the effectiveness of self-care education in reducing health care utilization, and the safety of self-care" (p. 37). Stoller and colleagues explored the issue of efficacy in their health diary study by assessing both the clinical appropriateness of decisions regarding management of symptoms (Stoller, Forster, Pollow, & Tisdale, 1993) and the accuracy of lay knowledge regarding lay treatments (Stoller, Forster, & Pollow, 1994). Their older respondents exhibited considerable knowledge regarding the potential risk (as assessed by clinicians) associated with many of the symptoms they reported. Over two thirds of the people presenting with urination problems, heart palpitations, chest pain, vision problems, swelling, weakness, fever, and shortness of breath and classified by a clinical panel as "at risk" agreed that their symptoms might be serious. These symptoms are often dramatic in their onset and impede a person's ability to pursue his or her usual activities. Except for fever or weakness, which often occur with acute conditions like cold or flu, they occur less commonly over the life course. Because these symptoms are, in fact, often the most clearly remembered antecedents to medical crises, they become part of the illness narratives which older people share among themselves (Kleinman, 1988). Given the relatively high prevalence of these serious conditions among the older population, awareness of the significance of these "warning signs" becomes part of the repertoire of lay knowledge.

Of greater clinical concern are situations in which old people dismiss potentially serious symptoms as trivial. Stoller, Forster, Pollow, and Tisdale (1993) found that underestimating the potential seriousness of symptoms was most common for nervousness, headache, depression, nausea, cough, sore throat or hoarse voice, fatigue, sleep difficulties, stomach pain, and constipation. In contrast to the symptoms for which her respondents assessed potential risk correctly, these are fairly common symptoms which people experience throughout the life course. Unlike the more dramatic symptoms discussed above, several of these symptoms are nonspecific and can be attributed to a wide range of conditions, including somatic responses to stressful situations.

Stoller, Forster, and Pollow (1994) also explored the content of old people's repertoires of lay knowledge concerning appropriate treatments for commonly occurring symptoms. Treatments recommended by respondents were evaluated by a panel of clinicians, who classified them as therapeutic, palliative, benign, conditionally harmful, or harmful. Perhaps their most striking result is the large proportion of people who identified treatments considered palliative or therapeutic. The prevalence of awareness of beneficial treatments is highest for those symptoms experienced most frequently (e.g., sore throat, headache, joint or muscle pain, and gas or indigestion.) Very few respondents mentioned treatments that were uniformly harmful. Over two thirds, however, mentioned treatments that could be harmful under certain conditions. Most often, conditionally harmful treatments reflected lack of awareness that a particular treatment was contraindicated among people with potentially complicating conditions. Other recommendations were considered conditionally harmful by the clinical panel because they placed older people at possible risk for adverse drug-drug or drug-alcohol reactions or because their effects could be disproportionately harmful among older people. In these cases, the error was not in the respondent's awareness of appropriate or, at least, nonharmful responses, but rather in failing to recognize risk factors. Many of these treatments may have been constructive responses to symptoms experienced by the respondents themselves. In offering advice to others, however, elderly people appear to generalize treatment strategies, failing to consider potentially complicating conditions under which some advice may be harmful.

The expectation that older respondents could be differentiated according to the quality of their lay knowledge was not supported. Stoller and colleagues found no evidence of perilous lay practitioners dispensing dangerous advice. Neither did they find lay health advisors who were the source of untainted wisdom. The majority of respondents offered a mixture of therapeutic, palliative, benign, and conditionally harmful advice. The best predictors of recommending any given category of treatment were the numbers of other types of treatments recommended. People who exhibited the broadest repertoires of lay knowledge were more likely to offer each type of treatment than people who exhibited more limited repertoires. People with broader repertoires of lay knowledge had higher levels of education and were more likely to emphasize responsibility for and control over their own health. Although they were no more likely than people offering a more restricted range of treatment recommendations to elicit general health information from other people or the media, they had experienced a larger number of symptoms, tended to consult a larger number of other people when they experienced symptoms and, to some extent, were more likely to serve as lay consultants for others.

THEMES IN UNDERSTANDING ILLNESS BEHAVIOR

This review of the literature has highlighted several issues which are essential components of our understanding of illness experience in late life. This section develops seven topics which merit continuing attention by researchers.

Illness Behavior as a Dynamic Process

Although symptom interpretation, lay consultation, and self-treatment are often studied separately (Strain, 1989; Verbrugge, 1987), illness behavior is a temporal process (Ford, 1986; Krause, 1990; Leventhal et al., 1992). Twaddle (1974) conceptualized the stages as a series of actions or decisions which can occur in various permutations and combinations. Not every illness episode will include each action or decision, and the order of the actions or decisions can vary. Therefore, a number of different illness behavior patterns are possible. As Ford explains, medical care is only one possible outcome in a

> complex process of assessment and decision-making which is shaped by culture, attitude, folk medical knowledge, personal biography, influence from social networks, present goals and perceptions of the costs and benefits of

entering the sick role, as well as by the inherent ambiguity of most symptoms themselves. (Ford, 1986, p. 130)

Leventhal and colleagues (1992) also emphasize illness behavior as an ongoing process, with individuals "constantly constructing, updating, or reconstructing representations of settings and feelings, generating and executing procedures for coping, evaluating or appraising outcome" (p. 115).

A few studies have examined illness behavior over time. Several investigators describe an illness "script" in which old people rely initially on their own resources and seek help from informal or formal consultants only when their actions fail to alleviate their symptoms (Davis et al., 1991; Weinert & Long, 1987). Strain (1989) distinguishes simultaneous actions from actions separated by time. Following this approach in a qualitative analysis of actions reported in health diaries, Stoller, Kart, and Portugal (1997) document 10 patterns of illness behavior over a 3-week reporting period: ignored all symptoms (6.0%), self-care only (13.9%), lay consultation on first day symptom(s) were reported (31.3%), lay consultation after period of self-care (18.1%), professional consultation after period of self-care (4.6%), self-care followed by lay consultation followed by professional consultation (2.7%), lay and professional consultation on same day after period of self-care (0.8%), lay consultation on first day followed by professional consultation (9.3%), lay and professional consultation on first day (4.4%), and professional consultation on first day (8.9%). Selection of a particular pathway was influenced by gender, availability of lay consultants, physician access barriers, and symptom characteristics, including respondent assessments of pain, interference with desired activities, and potential seriousness.

These studies represent only the initial steps in understanding the dynamic nature of self-care. Cameron and colleagues (1993) suggest that failure of self-care actions can lead to both changes in coping procedures and alterations in illness representations, but we still lack prospective data documenting the antecedents and consequences of these changes. Similarly, we know little about the impact of lay consultation on either illness representations or self-care strategies.

Lay Repertoires of Knowledge

Another theme is the importance of lay repertoires of knowledge in understanding illness behavior. Decisions about how to manage symptoms are grounded in people's interpretations of illness and disease and their knowledge about treatment strategies. Fitzpatrick (1984) sees the process of making sense of illness as both "selective and syncretic" (p. 18), with ideas drawn "selectively from a variety of different traditions and adjusted according to current concerns of the individual." One component of lay repertoires consists of traditional beliefs and practices which have been passed down for generations, most often by women through family networks (Wilkinson, 1987). These folk medical traditions co-exist with theories and practices grounded in scientific medicine (Mechanic, 1986). Traditional practices often represent the synthesis of healing practices from other cultures. They also reflect ecological habitat, including the availability and distribution of particular types of plants and herbs. Although continually revised and reconstructed, lay repertoires exhibit tenacity. New information is filtered through this previously synthesized knowledge, and is often modified or reworked to better conform to previous beliefs and to the exigencies of everyday life (Hunt et al., 1989). Leventhal and Prohaska (1986, p. 191) explain the persistence of these personally crafted ideas about disease:

> [An] older person may have lengthy personal history and substantial social support for various beliefs and practices, no matter how incorrect they may be. Moreover, many of these beliefs and practices may be self-reinforcing . . . , may have a direct effect on an individual's sense of control, reduce feelings of uncertainty and increase positive moods, no matter how useless they are for combatting colds, cardiovascular disease or cancer.

Shifting Boundaries Between Acute and Chronic Illness

A third theme is the distinction between responses to acute and chronic illness. Most of the literature on self-care is based on an acute orientation, with illness seen as emerging out of generally good health (Ford, 1986; Furstenberg & Davis, 1984; Levkoff et al., 1987). Although older people do experience acute episodes with more or less clearly defined boundaries, there is most often a context of one or more chronic conditions. Alonzo (1984) distinguishes among four types of illness situations which can occur independently or simultaneously: everyday illness, acute illness, chronic illness, and life-threatening illness.

Unlike acute conditions, chronic illnesses oscillate between periods of exacerbation and periods of quiescence. For acute episodes, people focus on relieving symptoms (Verbrugge, 1987). People experience chronic illness as continuous but perceive acute exacerbations that require application of self-care behaviors that have been crafted over time (Heurtin-Roberts & Becker, 1993; Rakowski et al., 1988; Verbrugge, 1987). The perceived onset of a chronic disease can be gradual, as in the case of cancer, or sudden, as in the case of heart attack or stroke (Furstenberg & Davis, 1984). Negative outcomes expand and accumulate over trajectories that vary in shape (Verbrugge & Jette, 1994). These trajectories unfold within a particular social context, with the meaning and impact varying with the demands and tolerance of the situation (Alonzo, 1989; Corbin & Strauss, 1985; Stoller, 1993a).

Living with chronic disease requires not only mastery of specific management strategies; it also demands crafting new meanings of illness. The meanings people develop surrounding chronic illness also determine how they respond to unfolding trajectories (Bury, 1991). Belgrave (1990) reports that the elderly women she studied spoke about their chronic conditions in different ways. Some focused on a concrete physical problem, describing characteristics of symptoms that made particular activities more difficult. Others described treatment regimens. Conditions such as heart attacks that involve an acute crisis were frequently conceptualized as an isolated past event. Women with few symptoms who were undergoing treatment programs that did not interfere with their lifestyle "spoke of their illness as an abstract medical condition that had little to do with them personally" (p. 487).

Patients bring order or coherence to the experience of chronic disease by creating narratives that incorporate commonsense representations (Baumann, Cameron, Zimmerman, & Leventhal, 1989; Leventhal, 1984) but place illness within the context of their particular biography (Williams, 1984). Kleinman (1988) believes that making and retelling these illness narratives is particularly prevalent among elderly people.

> They frequently weave illness experience into the apparently seamless plot of their life stories, whose denouement they are constantly revising. . . . [This] retrospective narratization can readily be shown to distort the actual happenings (the history) of the illness experience, since its *raison d'être* is not fidelity to historical circumstances but rather significance and validity in the creation of a life story. (pp. 49–50)

Although chronic conditions increase in prevalence in late life, both interpretations and coping strategies tend to be grounded in the experience of acute illness:

Most people encounter scores of common, everyday illnesses before they ever experience a serious disease. People essentially learn how to think and feel about and respond to illness by experiencing common, everyday colds, flu, muscle strains, etc. . . . They are the vehicles through which people learn to think about illness. (Lau, Bernard, & Hartmann, 1989, p. 196)

Alonzo (1986) reported responses learned in this way even among people experiencing life-threatening conditions. During the symptomatic period which precedes heart attacks, individuals tend to normalize symptoms and attempt to remain involved in their daily activities and current situation. "What is surprising is that individuals and lay others find it difficult to break out of a pattern of self-treatment typically used with other less life-endangering illnesses" (Alonzo, 1986, p. 1307).

The nature of chronic illness does not support a clear distinction between sick and well (Rakowski, 1986). The experience of chronic illness in everyday life teaches people that symptoms or physical problems are "an almost anticipated rather than extraordinary part of life" (Belgrave, 1990, p. 479). Long-term experience with chronic disease can enhance peoples' confidence in their ability to manage their conditions (Hickey, 1986) but at the same time can undermine confidence in "the dependability and adaptability of basic bodily processes that the rest of us rely on as part of our general sense of well-being" (Kleinman, 1988, p. 45). Eventually, in the case of severe degenerative disease, illness acts "like a sponge, [soaking] up personal and social significance from the life of the sick person" (Kleinman, 1988, p. 31).

Impact on Self-Concept

Different types of illness situations can have different effects on older people's self-concepts. Unlike episodes of acute illness, chronic conditions which are always present become part of one's identity (Blaxter, 1983). The relevance of illness for a person's self-concept reflects the intrusion of disease and management regimens on everyday life. For example, Belgrave reports that chronic disease "can limit one's life without greatly affecting self-concept if a slower-paced lifestyle is seen as appropriate for a woman's position in her life course and not as the result of physical problems" (1990, p. 496). This perspective is consistent with Alonzo's (1984, 1989) situational approach. Containment is a crucial step in minimizing the negative effects of disease on self-concept. Failure to contain the intrusion of disease on everyday life can lead to "inability to pursue usual activities, to discrediting by others, and to social isolation. . . . Restrictions of daily life reduce the opportunities to construct a valued self and lead to an all-consuming focus on illness and concern with the self as lost interests are not replaced" (Belgrave, 1990, p. 477). Thus, it is not so much the presence of illness that undermines self-esteem but rather the inability to contain health problems (Belgrave, 1990) and failure to demonstrate competence and independence (Levkoff et al., 1987).

The extent to which illness or disability undermines self-concept also varies by condition. The high prevalence of chronic illness in late life can mitigate the potentially isolating effect of many common diagnoses. As Belgrave explains, "the 'usualness' of physical problems may blunt their potential for stigma while at the same time providing a peer network of fellow sufferers" (1990, p. 476). Successful coping can even generate respect and admiration for the older person who is seen as "aging gracefully" (Stoller & Gibson, 1996). Trading effective coping for self-esteem is a delicate enterprise, however, because too much success can render's one's health problems invisible and undermine the legitimacy of future claims for support or other secondary gains (Schlesinger, 1993).

Although being old and experiencing chronic conditions is expected and acceptable, evidence of incompetence is socially devastating (Mitteness, 1987). Mitteness argues that age-related disorders like incontinence, confusion, and memory impairment result in strong negative sanctions, because they imply lack of social competence and signify "the beginning of the end." Norms regarding disclosure and response to incontinence are mediated by close ties to the sufferer. Mitteness (1987, p. 205) reports that "criticism and contempt were most often shown to the generalized, anonymous other, while sympathy was reserved for incontinent people who were friends or relatives." In the absence of very strong personal ties, incontinence could be mentioned only with self-deprecating humor, which diffused negative sanctions. Even in the context of close friendship, however, tolerance and support were conditional on effective coping:

> Efforts at control (rushing to bathroom) were noted with sympathetic humor. But smell and urine-stained clothing, seats or floors were not. Whenever smell and urine were mentioned, they were combined with criticism, anger, and contempt for the incontinent other. . . . The stigmatizing components of incontinence were smell and wetness. (Mitteness, 1987, p. 205)

Mitteness' insightful qualitative study of urinary incontinence indicates a potential link between the growing research on illness behavior in late life and the literature on disability and stigma across the life course. She reminds us that the "usualness" of certain chronic conditions within informal networks can mitigate their stigmatizing impact in old age, thus facilitating disclosure and access to informal resources. Some conditions, however, are viewed as more devastating, with assaults on self-concept less easily mitigated. More than mere age-related disorders, they become "symbols for the disintegration of order and polluting aspects of disorder, of (too old) old age;" that urinary incontinence is seen by most people as a "normal, irreversible part of the aging process" means that it is "in the future of not just a random few who become ill, but is the future of all of us" (Mitteness, 1987:213).

Self-Care and Minority Status

Disadvantaged minority group status is associated with poor health and poor health care. Although the number of physician visits does not currently differ by gender, race, or social class, disadvantaged elders are more seriously ill when they enter the medical care system than are more privileged elders (Van Nostrand, Furner, & Suzman, 1993). Some investigators suggest that an accumulation of negative encounters with the health care system over the life course reduces medical utilization in old age (Rosner, Namazi, & Wykle, 1987; Wallace, 1990) and encourages greater reliance on self-care (Haug, 1986; Wykle & Haug, 1993).

Researchers have documented some of these self-care strategies (Coulton, Milligan, Chow, & Haug, 1990; Haug, 1993; Rosner et al., 1988) and discussed ways in which traditional practices and folk medical wisdom are blended with scientific medicine (Mechanic, 1986). Wilkinson (1987) attributes cultural variation in healing practices to a combination of socioeconomic backgrounds and ethnic heritages, conceptions of illness and causes of disease, the distribution and types of plants and herbs, and the extent of absorption of scientific medicine into established family customs. For example, she describes traditional African American healing practices as "a functional synthesis of family healing patterns created from a blending of former African and European health maintenance customs with those of American Indians" (1987, p. 69). She attributes the similarity between Mexican and Native American folk medicine traditions to the similarity of habitats.

Davis and Wykle (chapter 8 in this volume), explore cultural beliefs about self-care among elderly African Americans. Yet, self-care practices among ethnic and racial minorities are still not well understood, and a number of questions remain for future investigators. For example, to what extent do differences in symptom management reflect economic barriers related to social class and/or psychological barriers related to discriminatory treatment across the life course? How do cultural differences in representations of illness and in repertoires of lay knowledge explain variation in strategies for coping with disease and disability? How do the countervailing effects of perceived susceptibility to disease and perceived efficacy of professional care influence symptom response among minority elders in poor health but with a lifetime of negative medical encounters (Haug, Akiyama, Tryban, Sonata, & Wykle, 1991)? To what extent do models of illness behavior based on the studies of White elders reflect the experiences of elders of color? Will research reflecting the lived experience of illness among elders of color transform existing frameworks for explaining illness behavior and self-care?

Methodological Issues

Interpretation of Age Differences

Several methodological issues must be considered in interpreting the research on self-care. The first, common to all gerontological research, involves interpretation of age differences, a problem made more difficult by the limited number of studies employing longitudinal designs (Krause, 1990). Differences due to aging per se need to be distinguished from those reflecting differences in "knowledge, attitudes, and beliefs about disease that are a function of the life history of individuals in a given age cohort" (Leventhal et al., 1992, pp. 121–122). A life-course perspective provides one approach for clarifying the ways in which people's location in the social system, the historical period in which they live, and their unique personal biographies shape the experience of health and illness in old age (Ory, Abeles, & Lipman, 1992; Stoller & Gibson, 1996). Kleinman suggests that older people use a life course perspective in presenting their medical histories, "weaving illness experience into the apparently seamless lot of their lives" (1988, p. 49). Changes in the medical care system can also produce cohort differences in health attitudes and behaviors. Haug, Wykle, and Namazi (1989) describe three cohorts with different experiences with medical care. First, there are those . . . born in 1912 or earlier, before medical discoveries of antibiotics and other technologies, when medical care could offer little more than amelioration of discomfort or surgery. Those . . . born in 1913 to 1927, are in the cohort that experienced the deprivations of the first W[orld] W[ar] and the Great Depression in their childhood or adolescence, when economic hardship made physical care a luxury to be used only in dire emergencies. Both these cohorts could contain many, particularly blacks, with a rural background, when few physicians were available. Finally, a middle aged cohort, born between 1927 and 1942, grew up in an age of medical miracles, when the belief in the efficacy of doctor's care was high. (1989, p. 173)

Although Haug and colleagues did not find direct support for their hypothesized cohort differences in either rates or types of care, it is possible that the impact of these differing experiences is mediated through other explanatory variables.

Data Collection Strategies

A number of decisions must be negotiated by researchers studying self-care: whether to record intentions or actual behavior, whether to gather data on behavior as it occurs or to rely on retrospective reporting, whether to elicit health information through an interviewer or ask respondents to record responses on their own; and whether to use a structured or unstructured format.

Whether questions focus on reported intentions or actual behavior can also influence results. Chappell, Strain, and Badger (1988) reported that individuals who actually experienced symptoms were more likely to report self-care as an initial response, whereas individuals who answered hypothetically were more likely to report immediate consultation with a professional. They conclude that "hypothetical responses in survey research minimize the importance of self-care as an initial response and overestimate frequency of professional contact" (1988, p. 97).

Most studies of lay response to illness are based on retrospective studies in which older people are asked to focus on an illness episode experienced in the past. Researchers warn that this data collection strategy leads to underreporting of short-term bouts of illness and low-grade but chronic conditions (Rakowski et al., 1988). Furthermore, "individuals may also retrospectively define past episodes as having been serious or not serious, depending on what long-term effects remain, rather than based on the discomfort or disruption of routine that occurred at the time of the episode" (Rakowski et al., 1988, p. 280).

Several researchers have used health diaries to elicit information about symptom experience on a daily basis. While health diaries minimize problems of retrospective data, these self-report strategies are not without limitations. Common symptoms may not be reported in health diaries because they are "taken for granted rather than being recognized and treated as illness" (Dean, 1986, p. 73) or because self-treatment has been "integrated into daily routines to such an extent that it is no longer spontaneously identified as symptom response" (Dean, 1986, p. 73). Both of these problems are more probable with symptoms of chronic conditions. In addressing the problem of bias in self-reports of symptoms, particularly in an unstructured format, Rosner, Namazi, and Wykle describe use of health diaries as a

> solitary activity which, by its very nature, encourages the individual to select from his or her life experience those research-related aspects which he/she perceives to be important to report. . . . (Problems) judged to be less serious may not be considered worthy of reporting under conditions where one must do one's recording. It takes disciplined effort and time to record such details on a daily basis. "Is it worth the bother?" may become the guide to selective reporting, paring away all but the self-determined essentials. (1992, pp. 263–264)

Sampling Issues

Studies of self-care in response to illness are also affected by sampling issues. Unless samples are very large, studies of actual symptom response most often tap common symptoms which are generally not potentially serious. However, if type of symptom and perceived seriousness account for many of the differences in illness response, these studies provide little variation to explain (Dean, 1986).

Length of the reporting period can also influence the amount of variation in symptom response. For example, Verbrugge (1987) concludes that

> In the short time frame of a day, there is great commonality in how men and women and age groups react to common bothersome symptoms. This is especially true for acute symptoms. Differences in attitudes, roles, and resources that separate the sex and age groups assert themselves in longer time frames

(e.g., in timing and sequencing of actions for symptom episodes, in long term management of chronic disease, p. 561).

Another methodological concern involves comparisons of results based on regional samples. Geographic regions vary on population density and other dimensions of the rural-urban continuum, economic resources, availability of medical care, race or ethnicity, geographic isolation and migration patterns, and regional culture, variables which influence lay interpretations of symptoms and treatment strategies. Few of the studies employing national samples have controlled for region. Researchers employing quantitative methodologies should be encouraged to report the statistical detail that would enable future investigators to merge the results of local or regional studies using techniques of meta-analysis. Qualitative studies should also provide sufficient information about the environmental and cultural setting to allow meaningful comparisons.

Specification of Models

Several scholars have raised concerns regarding specification of models explaining self-care behaviors. Reliance on multiple regression techniques can obscure the interrelationships among predictors (Wan, 1989). For example, in studies based on the health behavior model or the health belief model, indicators of illness experience are often

analyzed as parallel to social and psychological variables. Since they (i.e., need) account for most of the variance in utilization in regression procedures, social situational, and attitudinal variables are often discounted as relatively unimportant. The type of symptoms may be largely independent of factors in the social environment, but perceptions of the seriousness of the symptoms are shaped by social and psychological variables. Thus, variation due to social factors is already included in measures of the seriousness of reported symptoms" (Dean, 1986, p. 78).

Dean's summary of previously hypothesized models of illness behavior highlights the absence of the "complex interactions and feedback loops involved in the process of change over time" (1986, p. 79). Krause also raises the issue of misspecification, warning that illness behavior cannot be fully understood unless researchers "select appropriate data-analytic procedures that can best capture the theoretical specifications embedded in their models" (1990, p. 241).

IMPLICATIONS

Practice and Policy Implications

Research on self-care in late life has implications for both practitioners and policy analysts. From a practice standpoint, "understanding illness theories used by patients offers potential for improved communication, more appropriate therapeutic instruction, better treatment regimens, and enhanced adherence to medical advice" (Mechanic, 1986, p. 2). Beliefs about causation are implicated in psychological adjustment to illness and medical outcomes (Hampson, Glasgow, & Zeiss, 1994; Klonoff & Landrine, 1994). Knowledge about illness behavior can reduce the gap between lay and professional perspectives, between what Mishler (1984) describes as the voice of medicine and the voice of the life world. In certain situations, this gap presents risks to the older person. Attributing symptoms of potentially life-threatening disease to normal aging or exacerbations of previously diagnosed conditions can cause critical delays in treatment (Haug et al., 1989; Kart, 1981). Even when old people consult health professionals, communication is often impaired if the patient and practitioner attribute different meanings to the same symptom (Jones, Weise, Moore, & Haley, 1982). Practitioners can overestimate the clinical sophistication of patients who use or appear to use biomedical terms (Demers, Atamole, Mustin, Kleinman, & Leonardi, 1980).

Understanding lay meanings of illness and treatment strategies is also essential to ensuring compliance with recommended treatment. As Kleinman explains, "One of the core tasks in the effective clinical care of the chronically ill—one whose value it is all too easy to underrate—is to affirm the patient's experience of illness as constituted by lay explanatory models and to negotiate, using the specific terms of those models, an acceptable therapeutic approach" (Kleinman, 1988, p. 49). Treatments will be followed only when they are consistent with a patient's social construction of reality (Angel & Thoits, 1987). Mitteness (1987) warns that "the most elegant and effective therapeutic techniques can be sabotaged if one ignores the subtlety of the cultural constraints of illness" (p. 217). As we have seen, medical explanations and treatment recommendations are often modified into a customized regimen that reflects pre-existing beliefs about illness combined with the constraints of everyday life (Hunt et al., 1989).

Adherence to professionally prescribed treatment regimens is enhanced when the patient and the health care practitioner share common representations of the disease. In contrast, nonadherance or dropping out of medical care is most likely when discrepancies arise regarding causal models, treatment procedures, and outcome criteria (Leventhal et al., 1992). Several investigators have found that patients who attribute chronic disease to their own behavior are more likely to initiate changes in risk-related behavior and to adhere to management regimens (Afflect, Lennon, & Croog, 1987; Bar-On, 1986; Royer, 1995), although these studies have not focused explicitly on elderly patients.

Research on the social context of self-care also has implications for designing health education campaigns and self-care curricula (Stoller et al., 1994c; DeFriese & Woomert, 1983). Assessments of the efficacy of self-care can help educators target behaviors associated with potential risk. Understanding the meanings of health and illness can assist in customizing programs for particular groups (Weinert & Long, 1987). In designing health education materials, it is important to recognize that older people approach information with a repertoire of lay knowledge and beliefs through which new information is filtered and modified (Hunt et al., 1989).

The expanding literature on illness behavior demonstrates that lay persons provide the majority of illness care. There is no doubt that self-care minimizes short-term costs for medical care. The long-term consequences for both the individual and the medical care system hinge on the efficacy of self-care. Appropriate and timely self-care can reduce medical costs, protect the health care system from time demands of nonserious complaints, and result in a more rapid alleviation of symptoms (Haug et al., 1989; Kemper et al., 1993). On the other hand, attributing symptoms to old age or using inappropriate self-care strategies can delay access to medical care, with catastrophic consequences for life-threatening conditions for which early detection and treatment are essential (Haug et al., 1989; Kart & Engler, 1994). Even for less threatening conditions, ignoring potentially dangerous symptoms can result in higher medical costs in the long run (Wilkinson, Darby, & Mant, 1987).

Researchers have also demonstrated that successfully managing illness can enhance feelings of mastery and independence among older people (DeFriese & Konrad, 1993; Heurtin-Roberts & Becker, 1993; Kart & Engler, 1994). Learning what behaviors and what situations exacerbate symptoms can mitigate the potentially isolating effects of chronic illness. This emphasis on self-sufficiency and responsibility for one's own health is also consistent with current directions in preventive health and holistic medicine. A misplaced emphasis on individual responsibility for health, however, can result in blaming the victim. "A focus on life-style and the benefit of lay care cannot substitute for addressing structural and environmental factors which produce disease" (Dean, 1986, p. 282). Similarly, the ability to control and contain symptoms reflects the disease trajectory and situational demands as well as the self-care abilities of people experiencing the symptoms.

Directions for Future Research

This review has developed a number of themes for investigators. Future research should recognize the dynamic nature of illness behavior by examining the multiple paths old people follow in interpreting and treating illness. Symptom interpretation, self-care, lay consultation, and professional utilization are steps in a recursive process that unfolds over time as people come to understand and manage acute, chronic, and life-threatening illness in late life. These concerns underline the need for more panel studies.

Most research on illness behavior has focused on individual actors. Scholars have recognized that individual care in illness is embedded in family and extended networks, and researchers have documented patterns and correlates of consultation within lay referral networks. Less is known about either the content of these discussions or the norms governing disclosure. Under what conditions is it inappropriate to discuss health? When are symptom reports viewed as complaining? Under what conditions do elders fear negative sanctions or anticipate secondary gains if they disclose health problems? What treatment recommendations are exchanged during health-related discussions and what are the commonsense representations of illness that underlie these recommendations?

From a practical standpoint, continuing attention should be directed toward evaluating the efficacy of self-care practices and the appropriateness of consultation decisions. We need to know more about the ways in which people evaluate, integrate, and modify recommendations based on past experience and family tradition, discussions with family and friends, information gathered from the media, and regimens described by health care professionals or alternative healers. We need to evaluate the accuracy of lay repertoires of health information and the extent to which implementing lay treatment recommendations places people at risk either by harmful consequences or by delays in appropriate interventions.

Integration and synthesis must remain high on the agenda of future investigators. Previous work has not yet generated an adequate model of social behavior surrounding disease and illness. "Whether this lack of understanding results from the heterogeneity of the diagnostic categories studied, the difficulty and inadequacies in research methodology, the imprecision of the generic concepts, the tremendous variability of individual behavior, or all of the above is not fully known" (Alonzo, 1994, p. 50). Resolving the dilemma, however, requires a synthesis of understandings developed by scholars grounded in different disciplines and using multiple methodologies, with greater sensitivity to the subjective experience of illness and to measurement of latent variables and greater reliance on longitudinal data collection strategies.

REFERENCES

Afflect, G., Lennon, H., & Croog, S. (1987). Causal attribution, perceived benefits, and morbidity after a heart attack: An 8-year study. *Journal of Consulting and Clinical Psychology, 55,* 29–35.

Alonzo, A. (1979). Everyday illness behavior: A situational approach to health status deviations. *Social Science and Medicine, 13A,* 397–404.

Alonzo, A. (1984). An illness behavior paradigm: A conceptual exploration of a situational-adaptation perspective. *Social Science and Medicine, 19,* 499–510.

Alonzo, A. (1986). The impact of the family and lay others on care-seeking during life-threatening episodes of suspected coronary artery disease. *Social Science and Medicine, 22,* 1297–1311.

Alonzo, A. (August, 1989). *Health and illness and the definition of the situation: An interactionist perspective.* Paper presented at the annual meetings of the Society for the Study of Social Problems, Berkeley, CA.

Angel, R., & Thoits, P. (1987). The impact of culture on the cognitive structure of illness. *Culture, Medicine and Society, 11,* 465–494.

Backett, K.C., & Davison, C. (1995). Lifecourse and lifestyle: The social and cultural location of health behaviors. *Social Science and Medicine, 49,* 629–638.

Bar-On, D. (1986). Professional models vs. patient models in rehabiliation after heart attack. *Human Relations, 39,* 917–932.

Baumann, L., Cameron, L., Zimmermann, R., & Leventhal, H. (1989). Illness representations and matching labels with symptoms. *Health Psychology, 8,* 449–469.

Belgrave, L. (1990). The relevance of chronic illness in the everyday lives of elderly women. *Journal of Aging and Health, 2,* 475–500.

Bishop, G. (1987). Lay conceptions of physical symptoms. *Journal of Applied Social Psychology, 17,* 127–146.

Blaxter, M. (1983) The causes of disease: Women talking. *Social Science and Medicine, 17,* 59–69.

Brody, E., Kleban, M., & Oriol, W. (1985). *Mental and physical health practices of older people, A guide for professionals.* New York: Springer Publishing.

Bury, M. (1991). The sociology of chronic illness: A review of research and prospects. *Sociology of Health and Illness, 13,* 451–467.

Cameron, L., Leventhal, E., Leventhal, H., & Schaefer, P. (1993). Symptom representations and affects as determinants of care-seeking in a community-dwelling, adult sample population. *Health Psychology, 12*(3), 171–179.

Chappell, N. (1989). Health and helping among the elderly: Gender differences. *Journal of Aging and Health, 1*(1), 102–120.

Chappell, N. L., Strain, L. A., & Badger, M. (1988). Self-care in health and in illness. *Comprehensive Gerontology, 2,* 92–101.

Chrisman, N., & Kleinman, A. (1983). Popular health care, social networks and cultural meanings: The orientation of medical anthropology. In D. Mechanic (Ed.), *Handbook of health, health care and the health professions* (pp. 569–590). New York: Free Press.

Clark, N. M., Becker, M. H., Janz, N. K., Lorig, K., Rakowski, W., & Anderson, L. (1991). Self-management of chronic disease by older adults: A review and questions for research. *Journal of Aging and Health, 3*(1), 3–27.

Conrad, P. (1994). The experience of illness. In P. Conrad & R. Kern (Eds.), *The sociology of health and illness, critical perspectives* (3rd ed., pp. 135–137). New York: St. Martin's.

Corbin, J., & Strauss, A. (1985). Managing chronic illness at home. *Qualitative Sociology, 8*(3), 224–242.

Coulton, C. J., Milligan, S., Chow, J., & Haug, M. (1990). Ethnicity, self-care and use of medical care among the elderly with joint symptoms. *Arthritis Care Research, 8,* 19–28.

Davis, D. C., Hendersen, M. C., Boothe, A., Douglass, M., Faria, S., Kennedy, D. Kitchens, E., & Weaver, M. (1991). An interactive perspective on the health beliefs and practices of rural elders. *Journal of Gerontological Nursing, 17*(5), 11–16.

Davison. C., Frankel, S., & Smith, G. (1992). The limits of lifestyle: Reassessing fatalism in the popular culture of illness prevention. *Social Science and Medicine, 34,* 675–685.

Dean, K. (1986). Lay care in illness. *Social Science and Medicine, 22,* 275–284.

Dean, K. (1989a). Methodological issues in the study of health related behavior. In R. Anderson, J. Davis, I. Kickbusch, D. McQueen, & J. Turner (Eds.), *Research on health behaviour: Its application in health promotion.* Oxford: Oxford University Press.

Dean, K. (1989b). Self care components of lifestyles: The importance of gender, attitudes and the social situation. *Social Science and Medicine, 29,* 137–152.

Dean, K. (1992). Health-related behavior: Concepts and methods. In M. Ory, R. Abeles, & P. Lipman (Eds.), *Aging, Health and Behavior* (pp. 27–56). Newbury Park, CA: Sage.

Dean, K., Holst, E. & Wagner, M. (1983). Self-care of common illness in Denmark. *Medical Care, 21,* 1012–1032.

DeFriese, G., & Konrad, T. (1993, Fall). The self-care movement and the gerontological health care professional. *Generations, 20,* pp. 37–40.

DeFriese, G., Konrad, T. R., Woomert, A., Norburn, J. K., & Bernard, S. L. (1994). Self-care and quality of life in old age. In R. P. Abeles, H. C. Gift and M. G. Ory (Editors), *Aging and quality of life: Charting new territories in behavioral sciences research.* New York: Springer Publishing.

DeFriese, G., & Woomert, A. (1983). Self-care among the U.S. elderly. *Research on Aging, 5,* 3–23.

Demers, R., Altamole, R., Mustin, H., Kleinman, A., & Leonardi, D. (1980). An explanation of the dimensions of illness behavior. *Journal of Family Practice, 11,* 1085–1092.

Depner, C., & Ingersoll-Dayton, B. (1985). Conjugal social support: Patterns in later life. *Journal of Gerontology, 40,* 761–766.

Dill, A., Brown, P., Ciambrone, D., & Rakowski, W. (1995). The meaning and practice of self-care by older adults: A qualitative assessment. *Research on Aging, 71*(1), 8–41.

Edwardson, S., Dean, K., & Brauer, D. (1995). Symptom consultation in lay networks in an elderly population. *Journal of Aging and Health, 7,* 402–416.

Fitzpatrick, R. (1984). Lay concepts of illness. In R. Fitzpatrick, J. Hinton, S. Newman, G. Scambler, & J. Thompson (Eds.), *The experience of illness* (pp. 11–31). London: Tavistock.

Fleming, G., Giachello, A., Andersen, R., & Andrade, P. (1984). Self-care: Substitute, supplement or stimulus for formal medical services? *Medical Care, 22,* 950–966.

Ford, G. (1986). Illness behavior in the elderly. In K. Dean, T. Hickey, & B. Holstein (Eds.), *Self-care and health in old age* (pp. 130–166). London: Croom Helm.

Freer, C. (1980). Self-care: A health diary study. *Medical Care, 18,* 853.

Furnham, A. (1994). Explaining health and illness: Lay perceptions on current and future health, the causes of illness, and the nature of recovery. *Social Science and Medicine, 39,* 715–722.

Furstenberg, A. (1985). Older people's choices of lay consultants. *Journal of Gerontological Social Work, 19,* 21–34.

Furstenberg, A., & Davis, L. (1984). Lay consultation of older people. *Social Science and Medicine, 18,* 827–837.

Glasser, M., Prohaska, T., & Roska, J. (1992). The role of the family in medical care-seeking decisions of older adults. *Family and Community Health, 15*(2), 59–70.

Granovetter, M. (1974). The strength of weak ties. *American Journal of Sociology, 78,* 1360–1380.

Hampson, S. E., Glasgow, R. E., & Toobert, D.J. (1990). Personal models of diabetes and their relations to self-care activities. *Health Psychology, 9,* 632–646.

Hampson, S., Glasgow, R., & Zeiss, A. (1994). Personal models of osteroarthritis and their relation to self-management activities and quality of life. *Journal of Behavioral Medicine, 17*(2), 143–158.

Hansen, M., & Resick, L. (1990). Health beliefs, health care and rural Appalachian subculture from an ethnographic perspective. *Family and Community Health, 13*(1), 1–10.

Haug, M. (1986). Doctor-patient relationships and their impact on elderly self-care. In K. Dean, T. Hickey, & B. Holstein (Eds.), *Self care and health in old age* (pp. 230–250). London: Croom Helm.

Haug, M. (1993). The role of patient education in doctor-patient relationships. In J. Claire & R. Allman (Eds.), *Socio-medical perspectives on patient care.* Lexington: University Press of Kentucky, pp. 198–210.

Haug, M., Akiyama, H., Tryban, G., Sonata, K., & Wykle, M. (1991). Self care: Japan and the U.S. compared. *Social Science and Medicine, 33,* 1011–1022.

Haug, M., Wykle, M. & Namazi, K. (1989). Self care among older adults. *Social Science and Medicine, 29,* 171–183.

Heurtin-Roberts, S., & Becker, G. (1993). Anthropological perspectives on chronic illness: Introduction. *Social Science and Medicine, 37,* 281–283.

Hickey, T. (1986). Health behavior and self-care in late life: An introduction. In K. Dean, T. Hickey, & B. Holstein (Eds.), *Self-care and health in old age.* London: Croom Helm.

Hickey, T., Rakowski, W., Akiyama, H. (1991). Daily illness characteristics and health care decisions of older people. *Journal of Applied Gerontology, 10*(2), 169–184.

Hunt, L., Jordan, B., & Irwin, S. (1989). Views of what's wrong: Diagnosis and patients' concepts of illness. *Social Science and Medicine, 28,* 945–956.

Jones, R., Weise, H., Moore, R., & Haley, J. (1982). On the perceived meaning of symptoms. *Medical Care, 29,* 710–717.

Kart, C. (1981). Experiencing symptoms: Attribution and misattribution of illness among the aged. In M. Haug (Ed.), *Elderly patients and their doctors* (pp. 70–78). NY: Springer Publishing.

Kart, C., & Dunkle, R. (1989). Assessing capacity for self-care among the aged. *Journal of Aging and Health 1,* 430–450.

Kart, C., & Engler, C. (1994). Predisposition to self-health care: Who does what for themselves and why. *Journal of Gerontology: Social Sciences, 49*(6), S301–S308.

Kemper, D., Lorig, K., & Mettler, M. (1993). The effectiveness of medical self-care interventions: A focus on self-initiated responses to symptoms. *Patient Education and Counseling 21,* 29–39.

Kleinman, A. (1988) *The illness narratives: Suffering, healing and the human condition.* New York: Basic Books.

Klonoff, E., & Landrine, H. (1994). Culture and gender diversity in commonsense beliefs about the causes of six illnesses. *Journal of Behavioral Medicine, 17,* 407–418.

Krause, N. (1990). Perceived health problems, formal/informal support, and life satisfaction among older adults. *Journal of Gerontology: Social Sciences, 45*(5), S193–S205.

Lau, R., Bernard, T., & Hartmann, K. (1989). Further explorations of common-sense representations of common illnesses. *Health Psychology, 8*(2), 195–219.

Leventhal, E. (1984) Aging and the perception of illness. *Research on Aging, 6,* 119–135.

Leventhal, H., Leventhal, E., & Schaefer, P. (1992). Vigilant coping and health behavior. In M. Ory, R. Abeles, & P. Lipman (Eds.), *Health, behavior and aging* (pp. 109–140). Newbury Park, CA: Sage.

Leventhal, E., & Prohaska, T. (1986). Age, symptom interpretation and health behavior. *Journal of the American Geriatrics Society, 34,* 185–191.

Levin, L., & Idler, E. (1983). Self-care in health. *Annual Review of Public Health, 4,* 181–201.

Levkoff, S., Cleary, P,. & Wetle, T. (1987). Differences in the determinants of physician use between the aged and the middle-aged. *Medical Care, 25,* 1148.

Mathews, H., Lannin, D., & Mitchell, J. (1994). Coming to terms with advanced breast cancer: Black women's narratives from eastern North Carolina. *Social Science and Medicine, 38,* 789–800.

Mechanic, D. (1978). *Medical sociology: A comprehensive text* (2nd ed.). New York: Free Press.

Mechanic, D. (1986). The concept of illness behavior: Culture, situation and personal predisposition. *Psychological Medicine, 16,* 1–7.

Mishler, E. (1984). *The discourse of medicine: Dialectics of medical interviews.* Norwood: Ablex.

Mitteness, L. (1987). So what do you expect when you're 85?: Urinary incontinence in late life. In J. Roth & P. Conrad (Eds.), *Research in the Sociology of Health Care. Vol. 6.* Greenwich, CT: JAI Press.

Norburn, J. K., Bernard, S., Konrad, T. R., Woomert, A., DeFriese, G., Kalsbeek, W., Koch, G., & Ory, M. (1995). Self-care and assistance from others in coping with functional status limitations among a national sample of older adults. *Journal of Gerontology: Social Sciences, 50B,* S101–109.

Ory, M. R. Abeles, R., & Lipman, P. D. (1992). *Aging, behavior and health*. Newbury Park, CA: Sage.

Penning, M., & Chappell, N. (1990). Self care in relation to informal and formal care. *Ageing and Society, 10*(1), 41–59.

Prohaska, T. R., Keller, M. L., Leventhal, E., & Leventhal, H. (1987). Impact of symptoms and aging attributions on emotions and coping. *Health Psychology, 6*, 495–514.

Rakowski, W. (1986). Personal health practices, health status and expected control over future health. *Journal of Community Health, 11*, 189–203.

Rakowski, W., Julius, M., Hickey, T., Verbrugge, L., & Halter, J. (1988). Daily symptoms and behavioral responses. *Medical Care, 26*, 278–295.

Rosner, T., Namazi, K., & Wykle, M. (1988). Physician use among the old-old: factors affecting variability. *Medical Care, 26*(1), 982–991.

Royer, A. (1995). Living with chronic illness. *Research in the Sociology of Health Care, 12*, 25–48.

Schiaffino, K., & Cea, C. (1995). Assessing chronic illness representations: The implicit models of illness questionnaire. *Journal of Behavioral Medicine, 18*, 531–548.

Schlesinger, L. (1993). Pain, pain management and invisibility. *Research in the Sociology of Health Care, 10*, 233–268.

Segall, A., & Goldstein, J. (1989). Exploring the correlates of self-provided health care behavior. *Social Science and Medicine, 29*, 153–161.

Stoller, E. (1993a). Interpretations of symptoms by older people: A health diary study of illness behavior. *Journal of Aging and Health, 5*, 58–81.

Stoller, E. (1993b). Gender and the organization of lay health care: A socialist-feminist perspective. *Journal of Aging Studies, 7*, 151–170.

Stoller, E., & Forster, L. (1994). The impact of symptom interpretation on physician utilization. *Journal of Aging and Health, 6*, 5007–5534.

Stoller, E., Forster, L., & Pollow, R. (1994). Older people's recommendations for treating symptoms: Repertoires of lay knowledge about disease. *Medical Care, 32*, 847–852.

Stoller, E., Forster, L., Pollow, R., & Tisdale, W. (1993). Lay evaluation of symptoms by older people: An assessment of potential risk. *Health Education Quarterly, 20*, 505–522.

Stoller, E., Forster, L. , & Portugal, S. (1993). Self-care responses to symptoms by older people: A health diary study of illness behavior. *Medical Care, 31*, 24–41.

Stoller, E., & Gibson, R. (1996). *Inequality and the aging experience* (2nd ed.). Thousand Oaks, CA: Pine Forge.

Stoller, E., Kart, C., & Portugal, S. (1997). Explaining pathways of care taken by elderly people: An analysis of responses to illness symptoms. *Sociological Focus, 30*(2): 147–165.

Strain, L. (1989). Illness behavior in old age: From symptom awareness to resolution. *Journal of Aging Studies, 3*(4), 325–340.

Strain, L. (1990). Lay consultation among the elderly: Experiences with arthritis. *Journal of Aging and Health, 2*(1), 103–122.

Strain, L. A. (1996). Lay explanations of chronic illness in later life. *Journal of Aging and Health, 8*(1), 3–26.

Twaddle, A. (1974). The concept of health status. *Social Science and Medicine, 8,* 29–38.

Umberson, D. (1992). Gender, marital status and the social control of health behavior. *Social Science and Medicine, 34,* 907–917.

Van Nostrand, J., Furner, F., & Suzman, R. (Eds.). (1993). Health data on older Americans: United States, 1992. *Vital Health Statistics, Vol. 3.* Washington, DC: National Center for Health Statistics.

Verbrugge, L. (1985). Triggers of symptoms and health care. *Social Science and Medicine, 20,* 855–876.

Verbrugge, L. M. (1987). Exploring the iceberg: Common symptoms and how people care for them. *Medical Care, 25,* 539–569.

Verbrugge, L., & Jette, A. (1994). The disablement process. *Social Science and Medicine, 38*(1), 1–14.

Wallace, S. (1990). The political economy of health care for elderly blacks. *International Journal of Health Services.*

Wan, T. T. H. (1989). The behavioral model of health care utilization by older people. In M. Ory & K. Bond (Eds.), *Health care for an aging society.* New York: Springer Publishing.

Weinert, C., & Long, K. (1987). Understanding the health care needs of rural families. *Family Relations, 36,* 450–455.

Wilkinson, D. (1987). Traditional medicine in American families: Reliance on the wisdom of elders. *Marriage and Family Review, 11*(3/4), 65–76.

Wilkinson, I. F, Darby, D. N., & Mant, A. (1987). Self care and self medication: An evaluation of individual health care decisions. *Medical Care, 25,* 965–978.

Williams, G. (1984). The genesis of chronic illness: Narrative reconstruction. *Sociology of Health and Illness, 6*(2), 176–200.

Wykle, M., & Haug, M. (1993). Multicultural and social-class aspects of self-care. *Generations,* pp. 25–28.

CHAPTER 3

The Research Basis for the Design and Implementation of Self-Care Programs

Thomas Prohaska

Research in the field of self-care has progressed considerably in the past decade. While basic questions such as "What is self-care?" are still being discussed (Dean, 1989), we have now identified many of the most critical self-care behaviors leading to health promotion and delay of disability as well as many of the psychosocial and environmental factors associated with performance of self-care by older individuals. Similarly, the proliferation of self-care programs for older adults since the Self-Care Assessment of Community-Based Elderly study by DeFriese and Woomert (1983) has made it increasingly difficult to summarize the status of self-care programs for older adults. Although research about self-care among older adults is extensive, there are major gaps in our understanding of the process of self-care. Also, there are considerable numbers of older adults who would benefit from self-care programs but who are not being reached.

This chapter briefly discusses current theoretical perspectives, technology, treatments, and procedures used in self-care research and programs for older adults. Three areas of concern—gaps in our understanding of self-care—are discussed: the importance of conceptualizing self-care as a process of change; the lack of attention to recruitment, attrition, and reactivation of individuals into self-care practices; and the need to better understand the role of family, health, and symptom experiences in the process of self-care. Examples are also provided of how these concerns are being addressed. Finally, this chapter will provide some requisite skills and necessary antecedents to successful adoption and maintenance of appropriate self-care practices by older adults.

SELF-CARE AS A PROCESS OF CHANGE

Research and clinical investigations of self-care practices assume that the individual has some volitional control over his or her behavior and that self-care is largely a product of subjective perceptions and rational decision making (see chapter 5 in this volume for further discussion of risk perception models). This standpoint may explain why so much of the theory applied to self-care and health promotion behavior in older adults is based on one or more cognitive/rational decision-based models such as the health belief model (Janz & Becker, 1984; Maiman & Becker, 1974; Rosenstock, 1974) and Bandura's social cognitive theory (Bandura, 1977; 1989; Bandura & Adams, 1977).

Health Belief Model

As previously described in chapter 2, the health belief model assumes that individuals desire to avoid illness and that specific actions will prevent or reduce the threat of a specific disease or diseases. It posits that health practices are based on the beliefs or perceptions that an individual holds for a specific illness. This includes perceived susceptibility and severity of the disease, the perceived benefits and barriers associated with performing the health action and a trigger or cue to action, which serves as a stimulus to performing the health practice (Janz & Becker, 1984).

The concept of self-efficacy and outcome efficacy is based on the recognition that in order for individuals to engage in specific self-care activities, they must first believe that they have the necessary skills to perform the activity. Perception of competence is particularly important for complex behaviors, lifestyle behaviors, and long-term changes in self-care practices. Self-efficacy can be developed through a variety of sources of information: past performance, accomplishments, vicarious experiences, social and verbal persuasion, and physical or emotional arousal (Bandura, 1977, 1986). Outcome efficacy pertains to the belief that the specific behavior will lead to a desired outcome. More recently, the health belief model has been modified to accommodate perceptions of self-efficacy and outcome efficacy (Rosenstock, Strecher, & Becker, 1988). A more extensive discussion of theoretical approaches used to address key parameters in self-care with older adults can be found in chapter 5.

These models are frequently used in self-care program design and research and have met with some success with older populations. Typically, the development of self-care programs is guided by portions of these theoretical models or the combination of components from various models. For example, Buchner, Larson, and White (1987) examined the impact of postcard reminders on influenza vaccinations in community-residing elderly. The postcard served as a "cue to action," a component of the health belief model. Similarly, Clark et al. (1988) developed a self-management education program for older adults with heart conditions based, in part, on social learning theory. They designed a four-session program to foster problem-solving skills among older adults with difficulties associated with heart disease. Participants were provided opportunities to observe a credible role model manage their health problem (self-efficacy through vicarious social modeling) and to increase their belief that self-management would lead to better health (outcome efficacy).

While these health behavior models continue to be incorporated into self-care programs for older adults, limitations have emerged. Rimer (1990) noted that the health belief model has limited predictive value when there is little disagreement in the health beliefs. If there is no disagreement on the severity of a disease, then perceived severity as a factor looses its predictive value. Although these models do no worse than other cognitive models of behavior, at best they predict a small to moderate amount of the variance in self-care behaviors (Mullen, Hersey, & Iverson, 1987). The health belief model seems to be better at predicting the onset of a first-time behavior than it is at predicting continuation and termination of behaviors (Janz & Becker, 1984). While self-efficacy and outcome efficacy are important for an individual who is learning to perform specific health practices, efficacy is not an issue for the individual who is not even thinking about self-care. Another limitation with these theoretical perspectives is that the target behavior is often viewed as an all-or-none event. That is, the outcome behaviors are treated as either present or absent. Does the person smoke or not? Did the person receive the immunization or the mammogram? There is no discussion of the strength of the self-care activity, or the transition from nonperformance to performance and maintenance of the activity.

The Transtheoretical Model of Behavior Change

The transtheoretical model of behavior change (Prochaska & DiClemente, 1983; Prochaska, DiClemente, & Norcross, 1992) may be a useful perspective to address the shortcomings of other cognitive models. The basic construct of the transtheoretical model states that persons change behaviors by proceeding through stages. Rather than the presence or absence of a health practice, the stages of change model proposes that individuals move through a cycle of precontemplation, contemplation, preparation, action, and maintenance. Precontemplation is the stage at which there is no intention to change behavior in the foreseeable future (not thinking about or considering an exercise program). Contemplation is the stage in which people are aware that a problem exists and are seriously thinking about overcoming it (e.g., considering an exercise program but not making any plans). Preparation is the stage in which small steps are made to engage in the behavior but effective action has not yet been taken (e.g., purchase of exercise shoes). Action is the stage in which persons modify their behavior and participate in the activity in question. Maintenance is the stage in which the person stabilizes the behavior and it becomes routine. A relapse is viewed as a movement from one stage to a previous stage.

Using the transtheoretical model, self-care practices can be viewed in terms of readiness to adopt a behavior (precontemplation, contemplation, and preparation stages) and the strength of a practice once it is performed (action and maintenance stages). Self-care interventions can be designed to move the individual from one stage to the next. Given this stage approach, there are a number of ways self-care programs may be deemed successful by researchers and program evaluators. Any movement of an individual from one stage to the next can be considered a success. For example, a self-care program may be considered beneficial if it results in changing participants' intentions from not contemplating a change in their diet (precontemplation) to contemplating a change in diet in the near future (contemplation stage). Another advantage of this model is that it provides a framework for determining which psychosocial and perceptual factors are most critical for moving an individual from one stage to the next. One can determine the most salient components in the process of change from one stage to the next. For example, self-efficacy and outcome efficacy may be important in self-care behavior in general, but it may be most important in the successful transition from the contemplation to the action stage or from action to maintenance stage. This model not only allows us to determine *if* a psychosocial factor is important in adoption of self-care practices but also *when* it is important.

Although the transtheoretical model and the majority of the original research were designed to address addictive behaviors (i.e., smoking in younger populations), it has been recently applied to exercise activities in middle-aged and older adults (Barke & Nicholas, 1990; Gorely & Gordon, 1995; Marcus, Rossi, Selby, Niàura, & Abrams, 1992) and smoking cessation in older adults (Clark, Kvis, Prohaska, Crittenden, & Warnecke, 1995; Rimer et al., 1994). First, Barke and Nicholas (1990) have examined levels of participation in physical exercise activities among older adults based on the transtheoretical model of behavior change. They reported that the stages of change model significantly differentiated between older adults who were active participants of exercise programs and those who were not exercising. Second, Orleans, Rimer, Christinzio, Keintz, and Fleisher (1991) conducted a survey of 289 members of the American Association of Retired Persons who were currently smoking. They reported differences in perceptions held by smokers who were considering quitting smoking in the next year (contemplators) and smokers who had no intentions of quitting in the foreseeable future (precontemplators). Compared to precontemplators, contemplators reported more smoking-related symptoms, had stronger beliefs in the health harms of smoking and the benefits of quitting, reported a greater quitting self-efficacy and had higher ratings of the barriers in quitting smoking. Finally, application of the stages of change perspective has also been applied in a community-based smoking cessation intervention for older adults (Clark et al., 1995). It was found that older smokers who plan to quit smoking (contemplation) were more likely to have a greater concern about health effects of smoking and perceived a stronger desire by others for them to quit than smokers with no such plans (precontemplation).

Research and program interventions in self-care will continue to rely on cognitive/rational decision-based models of behavior. Krause (1990) noted that these models, along with the behavioral model of health service utilization (Wolinsky et al., 1983; Wolinsky & Johnson, 1991), are the foundation for a considerable portion of the self-care research for older adults. As Rimer noted, "The health belief model can best be improved through its continued use in the real world and through the development of interventions. It is likely to be most useful when combined with other models" (Rimer, 1990, p. 142). The study by Orleans et al. (1991) serves as a good example of how various models of self-care behavior can be combined and applied in the context of the transtheoretical model to create a useful framework for designing a smoking cessation intervention for older adults. It is likely that a greater proportion of research and program intervention in self-care of older adults will employ combinations of theoretical perspectives and will use the transtheoretical model of behavior change as a framework for examining components of these theories. What will evolve is a better understanding of how specific psychosocial factors influence self-care change and at what stages of change these factors are most critical.

One consequence of a model that stresses self-care as a process of change is that attention is focused on nonparticipants of self-care practices (precontemplators, contemplators). There has been a lack of attention paid to understanding those who are part of the target population for self-care programs and who would benefit from self-care programs but are not being reached. Are we targeting self-care programs to only the most motivated older adults? Issues of recruitment, attrition, and reactivation of older individuals into self-care practices will be examined in the next section.

SELF-CARE RECRUITMENT AND ATTRITION

By definition, self-help programs are only for motivated individuals who take the initiative to participate. Often we have little or no information on the older adult who refused to participate or, in the case of community-based programs, the characteristics of the older target population. At best, self-care programs compare baseline characteristics of those who drop out of the program to those who remain or complete the program. More attention needs to be directed at understanding recruitment and attrition in self-care programs.

Sources of Attrition

Addressing concerns of recruitment and attrition can begin with the process of identifying when (or at what stage) a person got lost on the path to adopting a self-care practice and identifying why the person was lost (e.g., unrecruited, relapsed). Understanding loss at recruitment and the sources of attrition are keys to program revision. The following are possible sources of attrition in self-help programs:

1. absence of exposure to the recruitment message
2. decision not to participate after exposure to the recruitment message
3. failing to register for the self-help program after making the decision to participate
4. dropping out between registration in the self-help program and the first session
5. not completing the program
6. never adopting the self-help practices learned in the program
7. relapse among those who adopted the self-help behaviors but did not maintain them

Clinical and community-based self-care programs with older adults often address program attrition (4 through 6), with almost no attention to recruitment (1 through 3), and little attention to relapse at the maintenance stage (7). Many self-care programs rely primarily on the individual's self-motivation to participate. The result of this passive recruitment approach is that we have little knowledge of the factors associated with unsuccessful recruitment (1 through 3). Without active and aggressive recruitment, however, the very people who could benefit the most by participation in the program often decide not to participate. Older adults who are concerned about their ability to perform the self-care practice, those who see no utility in the practice, and those who may not be concerned about their health and how the neglect or misuse of self-care activities might adversely affect it, may be less likely to participate. In short, we know little about those who are in the stages of precontemplation and contemplation who do not move to the preparation stage (enroll in the self-care program).

Factors Affecting Participation

Recent research in self-care with older adults has raised the issue of identifying the unrecruited population (Buchner & Pearson, 1989; Mills et al., 1996; Wagner, Grothus, Hecht, & LaCroix, 1991). For example, Wagner et al. (1991) compared health status and life-style characteristics of participants and nonparticipants in a health promotion program for seniors from a group health cooperative (HMO). Compared to participants, older HMO members who did not participate in the health promotion program were more likely to have lower family income, less formal education, and poorer self-ratings of health. Clark et al. (1995) examined factors associated with recruitment attrition in a community-based smoking cessation program.

They compared perceptions and beliefs about smoking in older adults from the target community to a group of older adults in the target community who registered for the self-help television-based smoking cessation program. Compared with older smokers in the target population who were planning to quit someday, those who registered for the smoking self-help program perceived greater severity of lung cancer in terms of impact on their life and burden to their family, had greater concern about the health effects of smoking and were more determined to quit. Morey et al. (1989) compared older veterans who agreed to participate to those who decided not to participate in an exercise program and found that those who refused to volunteer for the program had more chronic diseases and used more medications than did participants. Similarly, Gecht, Connell, Sinacore, and Prohaska (1996) found that older persons with arthritis were more likely to participate in an exercise program if they believed that their joint pain and stiffness would decrease if they exercised. Combined, these studies suggest that in order for self-care programs to reach older adults who do not usually participate in such programs, an effort has to be made to educate this reluctant population and to address their concerns and lack of motivation. Recruitment should become more proactive and must assist the older adult to overcome the initial barriers to participation.

Adherence Rates

Although we have more information on attrition rates for older adults who enter self-care programs than we have on recruitment rates, the lack of both standard outcome measures and common points of measurement for self-care practices makes it difficult to compare attrition across programs and behaviors. Evaluation of adherence and self-care behavior maintenance is dependent on the target behavior, the time frame chosen, and the rigor of the self-care program.

It is a problem to decide at what point in the self-care process attrition should be measured. An example of the consequences of this is illustrated by Rubenstein, Josephson, Nichol-Seamans, and Robbins, (1986) in their study of a community-based health screening program for older adults. A comprehensive health screening program was provided in a freestanding community senior center. Of the clients screened, 54% had at least one health problem deemed serious enough to be referred to a physician for further evaluation. Of the clients referred to the physician, 70% reported following through with the recommendation. Among the clients who saw a physician for a specific referred problem, 38% actually received some kind of treatment for that problem. Thus, of all the clients who participated in the screening, 15% received treatment from a physician for a problem detected during the screening. This study provides insight into sources of attrition between the use of health screening services and physician follow-up (e.g., attrition between screening and follow-up and between follow-up and treatment). Reporting attrition at each stage of the process provides a useful tool for program revision. An exploration of the older target population who did not participate in the screening (recruitment attrition) would have made this study even more informative.

Relevance of Stage Theory

In some cases attrition is due to decisions to no longer participate in the self-care program, while in others attrition may not be a matter of choice, such as when older adults report quitting exercise because of exacerbation of arthritis symptoms (Gecht et al., 1996). Reasons for attrition at the action stage may be very different than reasons for attrition at the maintenance stage. A person who relapses at the action stage of adopting a self-care practice may have very different needs for reactivation than one who relapses at the maintenance stage. All these important distinctions have yet to be fully addressed by research. A systematic effort to examine when and why the attrition occurred and to tailor programs to meet the needs of the older person who relapses is necessary. Optimal program compliance efforts should concentrate on minimizing the number of participants who choose to drop out (relapse prevention) as well as trying to reengage those who had to drop out and are able to return to a program of self-care (reactivation).

Targeting Older Adults in Recruitment Efforts

A key to maximizing recruitment, minimizing attrition, and increasing overall success of self-care programs is to focus on a targeting strategy that addresses the needs and circumstances of the older population. Target strategies can be based on the presence of specific illnesses or chronic conditions in the target population (e.g., persons diagnosed with diabetes), the presence of a health risk factor (e.g., hypertension), a behavioral risk factor (e.g., smoking), demographic characteristics, and the setting in which the self-care intervention is delivered (e.g., community-wide, clinic, senior center). While the advantages and disadvantages of these approaches and classifications to self-care have been discussed (see Rakowski, 1992, for a review), there are two recent trends in targeting self-care programs for older adults worthy of further discussion.

Inclusion of Physically Frail Older Adults

The first trend in targeting older adults in self-care programs is to not exclude individuals from programs solely on the basis of frailty and poor health status. Rakowski (1992) and others have noted that disease prevention and health promotion are not reserved for the well elderly. Since 80% of those age 60 and older have one or more chronic conditions and comorbidities (Guralnik, LaCroix, Everett, & Kovar, 1989) few elderly would be eligible if we were to focus solely on the well elderly. Frail older adults in nursing homes and those with significant physical impairment and multiple symptoms have demonstrated positive health outcomes with health promotion interventions (Fiatarone, et al. 1990; Hickey, Wolf, Robins, Wagner, & Harik, 1995; Perkins, Rapp, Carlson, & Wallace, 1986). While health care practitioners continue to open their exclusion criteria to admit frail older populations into self-care health promotion programs, there is a risk that older adults in poor health will self-select out of many of these self-care programs (Prohaska & Glasser, 1994). The positive approach of targeting physically frail older adults in self-care programs should be extended to self-care programs for the cognitively impaired. (See chapter 2 for a further discussion of the role of symptom experiences in self-care activities by older adults.)

Settings Frequented by Older People

The second trend in targeting self-care programs is the emphasis on designing and implementing the programs in settings where concentrations of older persons can be found. Programs for older adults are most effective in settings where access to significant proportions of this group is assured. Health promotion programs, therefore, should be linked to and integrated with other community resources, such as health services, counseling, adult education, senior centers, transportation, information and referral, and family-oriented services (Dorfman, 1991).

Physician-based self-care programs in medical clinics and health care settings have particular merit for older individuals. Older adults are readily accessible through medical office and health clinic settings. Adults age

55 and older average four or more visits per year, primarily to physicians in general practice or internal medicine (Van Nostrand, Miller, & Furner 1993). Orleans et al. (1991) reported that three fourths of older persons (age 50 to 74 years) who smoked had at least one health care visit in the previous year. Another advantage of physician-based health promotion and self-care programs for older adults is that many hold physicians in high regard, accept their authority, and do not challenge recommendations made by health professionals (Haug, 1979).

While there are merits for self-care programs for older adults in health care settings, doctor/patient interactions with older patients rarely include discussions of the patient's health practices and issues of health promotion (Greene, Hoffman, Charon, & Adelman, 1987; Lavizzo-Mourey & Diserns, 1989). Orleans et al. (1991) reported that only 42% of older persons who smoked reported receiving medical advice to quit smoking in the past year. Medical clinics and health maintenance organizations have had considerable success with self-care management programs for the treatment of chronic illness such as diabetes (Gilden, Hendryx, Casia, & Singh, 1989) and heart disease (Clark et al. 1988). However, if self-care health promotion programs in health care settings are going to continue to expand, negative attitudes and beliefs of health care professionals toward health promotion and self-care for older adults will have to be addressed.

Self-care programs have had success targeting other settings with concentrations of older adults. Examples of these include exercise programs in nursing homes (Perkins et al., 1986), smoking cessation programs and exercise programs in the persons' homes (Clark et al., 1995; King, Haskell, Taylor, Kraemer, & DeBusk, 1991; Mills et al., 1996), self-care and health promotion programs in senior centers (Watkins & Kligman, 1993) and in church settings (Kumanyika & Charleston, 1992; Ransdell, 1995; Sutherland, Hale, & Harris, 1995). Targeting strategies will continue to identify new populations and new resources for self-care program development. For example, Prohaska, Glasser, and Newman (1992), reported that mall-walking clubs offered older adults a year-round opportunity to participate in a self-care walking program. They found that older adults had participated in mall-walking activities for years with little need for other resources.

The two trends for targeting presented here suggest a continued effort to bring self-care programs to increasingly larger numbers of older adults. Generalizations from setting to setting are difficult, as each has its own unique characteristics. For example, over 15% of the older population participate in senior center activities and may represent a more active and less frail population of older adults than might be expected in the general older population (National Center for Health Statistics [NCHS], 1986). More self-care programs could target the frail older population by combining self-care interventions with other community-based health services. For example, the Chicago Department on Aging is currently providing health education and health promotion programs in the areas of nutrition, medication management, and self-directed exercise/physical therapy to homebound frail older adults eligible for community-based, long-term care services (Peters, Baldyga, & Prohaska, 1994).

States and regions currently have no method of knowing the extent and focus of self-care efforts from one region to another or the success of these programs in targeting and treating specific populations of older adults. Coordination across self-care programs is minimal. States currently monitor health practices with the Behavioral Risk Factor Survey, but survey results will not tell us why the behavioral health risk factor exists. It is unlikely that the survey can be used to evaluate the success of a specific program or inform us as to the type and level of self-care programs in a specific area. Only a coordinated effort to document target groups will assure that all groups of older adults will have access to self-care programs.

The targeting strategies discussed above focus on characteristics of the older individual and settings appropriate for self-care programs. However, the older individual engages in self-care practices in the context of his or her environment. It is well recognized that the family is a critical component of self-care behavior in older adults. Self-care programs and targeting strategies have come to recognize the importance of family and friends in self-care practices. The next section will examine how family influences the process of self-care.

FAMILY IN THE PROCESS OF SELF-CARE

What is the role of family in self-care activities and how do they facilitate or inhibit the self-care process in older adults? The role of family in self-care practices of older adults can be viewed from multiple perspectives. Family members and significant others are the first and often the only point of communication by an older individual about health concerns and advice on self-care. Family members can act as gatekeepers to the formal health care system. That is, they can facilitate or impede access to health care services for their older relatives. The doctor/older patient interaction may include a third person in the medical encounter who often is a family member or friend. The social support network, comprised of family and friends, is also a resource which can moderate the effect of health threats and therefore has an indirect effect on self-care. And finally, family members serve to facilitate and reinforce self-care practices by their older relative.

Role of Family in Health Discussions

Research by Brody and her colleagues (Brody & Kleban, 1981, Brody, Kleban, & Moles, 1983) demonstrated that a family member is usually the first and often the only person with whom older individuals will discuss health problems and symptom experiences. Rakowski, Julius, Hickey, Verbrugge, and Halter (1988) noted that a large proportion of day-to-day symptom experiences of older adults go unreported to anyone, including family members. Similarly, Prohaska, Funch, and Smith-Blesch (1990) found that 19% of older adults diagnosed with cancer of the colon or rectum did not talk with any lay person about their symptoms. Findings from these studies suggest that while family may be more aware of the specific day-to-day health concerns of older adults than health professionals, they may not be fully aware of the older persons self-care needs.

Role of Family in Seeking Medical Care

Family and friends are also involved with communication of health concerns of their older relative during the process of accessing medical care. Research on doctor/older patient interactions has recognized that the medical encounter will frequently involve the triad of physician, elderly patient, and patient's companion (Adelman, Greene, & Charon, 1987). The third person accompanying the older patient on the medical visit is usually a family member. Between 20% and 37% of the medical visits by older patients include a family member or friend (Glasser, Prohaska, & Roska, 1992; Greene, Adelman, Charon, & Hoffman, 1986; Prohaska & Glasser, 1996). Similarly, Prohaska et al. (1990) examined frequency of companions on medical visits and found that it increased significantly with the age of the patient.

Researchers have begun to examine the triad of doctor, older patient, and companion to determine the role of the third person (family) on the self-care process leading to the medical encounter and self-care activities subsequent to the medical encounter. Prohaska et al. (1990) reported that older adults accompanied on the medical visit experienced longer mean patient delays (time between the onset of the first symptom and medical contact) than those who were not accompanied, although the differences were not significant. Glasser et al. (1992) reported that family members accompanying the older person to the medical visit were involved in the decision to seek care. Prohaska and Glasser (1996) have also examined the self-care activities and the role of the third person subsequent to the medical encounter. They found that the role of the companion in the triad extends beyond the medical encounter. The third person in the triad may be a caregiver with considerable involvement in the medical decision-making process as well as influence on the older patient's self-care and adherence to medical recommendations after the medical encounter.

Family Members and Self-Care Activities

Research on patterns of the third person role in the medical encounter provides some insight into the role of family in the self-care process of older adults. There is general agreement that most older adults account for their own health and engage in self-care activities. There is also agreement that for some older adults, self-care is not an option and family members and others will take the role of caregiver and take varying degrees of responsibility for the health and well-being of the older person. Older adults, responsible for their own self-care, do not necessarily shift to total care from family members and others, especially if the health problem is a chronic progressive disease. The time between total self-care (or primary self-care) and major dependence on caregivers may be a matter of years and may include movement from one to the other form of care.

However, there is a transition process in which older adults share responsibility for their health care activities and health care decisions, especially if the other person is the spouse. In over 30% of the instances where an older adult was accompanied to the doctor, the medical care decision process and self-care activities prior to the medical encounter were based on discussion, negotiation, and mutual decision making (Glasser et al., 1992; Prohaska & Glasser, 1996). This stage might be referred to as "shared care." Shared care represents a stage in life when health care decisions and health care activities are a joint venture between the older person and the informal caregiver (family). It is a time of shared decision making concerning when, if, and even how formal medical care should be used.

Another means by which family influence self-care is through their support and assistance in helping the older adult perform self-care practices. Interventions and studies of self-care have demonstrated the importance of family support in the development and maintenance of self-care practices. For example, Clark et al. (1995) found that older smokers were more likely to register for a self-help smoking cessation program if persons close to the older smoker desired him or her to quit. Similarly, Rimer et al. (1994) reported that older adults who had quit smoking stated that family and friends were a strong positive influence and a primary reason for their quitting attempts. The role of the spouse for optimizing self-care has also been reported in self-care diabetes education programs for older adults. Gliden et al. (1989) reported that, compared to program participants with low family involvement with patient care, involvement of the spouse in diabetes education maximized the beneficial effects of the program, including improvements in knowledge, psychosocial functioning, and metabolic control.

Although families may provide support and assistance in helping the older adult perform self-care practices, there are potentially negative consequences of family involvement in self-care activities of the older relative. Wortman and Conway (1985) noted that support providers such as family members may hold misconceptions about illness and may offer inappropriate self-care advice. For example, well-intentioned family members may recommend rest and inactivity for their older relative in need of regular exercise. Family members who accompany their older relative during the medical encounter may take the role of the antagonist, undermining the physician's recommendations to the older patient (Adelman et al., 1987). However, the majority of older patients who are accompanied to the medical visit by family view the family member as positive and essential to the medical visit (Prohaska & Glasser, 1996).

Evolution of Family Roles and Their Benefits

Families have a long-term involvement with the self-care activities of their older members. They serve as a point of communication and a source of advice for the older relative who is developing self-care behaviors. Family members are also very involved with the interaction of the older adult and the medical care system; they may be gatekeepers to health services as well as being actively involved in the doctor/older patient interaction. The role and responsibilities of family and friends in self-care activities is continuously being redefined as the older individual moves from independence to frailty and dependence. Finally, family play a role in the process of developing and maintaining self-care behaviors. Self-care programs that examine family support find that it is often—but not always—beneficial, promoting adoption of self-care practices. Additional research is needed to more fully define the role of family in the self-care process. In turn, self-care programs should incorporate these defined roles into more comprehensive programs reflecting the context in which self-care activities are performed.

Clearly, incorporating the family in self-care interventions and programs would facilitate performance of self-care practices. However, programs should also include the basic components of behavior change found to be successful in health education/health promotion programs. The final section addresses some common components of health education/health promotion programs which are frequently incorporated into successful self-care programs for older adults.

COMMON COMPONENTS OF
SUCCESSFUL SELF-CARE PROGRAMS

Self-care programs have considerable variability in the target behaviors, the intervention strategy, theory guiding program content, and outcome measures. Even with this considerable variation, interventions that are successful in helping older adults adopt and maintain self-care practices tend to share common characteristics. Rather than present an exhaustive list of successful program characteristics, this section discusses four common components as a foundation based on general principles of health education/health promotion. These include:

- provision of information on issues associated with the self-care practice
- methods to motivate the older individual to adopt and maintain the self-care behaviors
- collection of meaningful and timely feedback
- methods to maintain the self-care practice

Providing information to increase knowledge has been and will continue to be a fundamental component of behavior change. Information dissemination is more than basic awareness of risk factors and appropriate self-care practices. It must include information to help the individual estimate personal risk. National and regional surveys have shown that older adults are generally knowledgeable about behavioral risk factors (Prohaska, Leventhal, Leventhal, & Keller, 1985; Thornberry, Wilson, & Golden, 1986). However, "The potential for misinterpretation of personal risk based on research identifying health risk behaviors is great for practitioners and older individuals alike" (Prohaska & Clark, 1994, p. 57). The message will constantly need repeating as there are new cohorts of older adults who may not be aware of specific risk factors. Also, new information will have to be provided as health care professionals continue to refine our knowledge about appropriate self-care practices.

While knowledge is necessary for behavior change, it is not sufficient. Education and information will have limited value in developing self-care practices without attention to motivation. Motivation is either an implied or a stated component of most cognitively based models of behavior change (e.g., health belief model, social cognitive theory). Self-care programs often build in motivation. It may be as simple as praise or a gold paper star placed next to the name of nursing home participants who meet daily distance requirements for stationary bike riding (Perkins et al., 1986), or as complex as observing and identifying with a role model who successfully copes with a serious heart condition. (Clark et al., 1988). Interventions designed to maximize motivation for older adults enrolled in self-care programs should be extended to motivating older individuals to participate in these programs.

Meaningful and timely feedback on the consequences of self-care practices is another common component to successful behavior change interventions. This is related to the concept of outcome efficacy (Bandura, 1977, 1989) in that the expectation that specific behaviors will reduce the threat of a disease and will result in achieving a specific goal. For example, if older adults perceive that quitting smoking will result in a noticeable change in their endurance or physical health, a lack of improvement could change outcome efficacy and a relapse may occur. Self-care practice may also discontinue if the feedback received is aversive. For example, Ary, Toobert, Wilson, and Glasgow (1986) reported that negative physical reactions were among the reasons for nonadherence to recommended exercise and insulin injections for patients with diabetes.

The final component to successful interventions in health behavior change and self-care is attention to environmental factors that continue to support the self-care activity. The probability of a self-care *practice* becoming a self-care *habit* is greatly increased if the individual continues to be reinforced for the behavior. If not, extinction is likely. Fortunately, many self-care practices have consequences that reinforce the practice. That is, the practice has positive consequences which can be observed by the individual. Self-care interventions should include methods to teach participants how to monitor these improvements and to link them to the self-care practice.

As emphasized in chapter 2, self-care is a social phenomenon. The family can contribute to maintaining self-care practices in the older adult. As discussed earlier, family and friends play an important role in the onset, progression, and termination of self-care practices. Interventions should provide methods for family to reinforce self-care practices in older adults to assure maintenance of the behavior.

FUTURE DIRECTIONS IN SELF-CARE

This chapter has discussed theoretical perspectives, technology, treatment, and procedures in self-care research and programs for older adults. It has stressed the importance of addressing self-care as a process of change and the need to focus attention on nonparticipants of self-care programs. It proposes that research should take a broader public health perspective in community-based programs by comparing characteristics of the target population and participants of the self-care program. Progress in bringing more older adults into self-care programs by increasingly including those who are in poor health and by providing self-care programs in appropriate community settings was also noted. Together these topics suggest future trends in self-care research and intervention programs.

The first likely trend is that a greater proportion of research and program intervention in self-care will employ the transtheoretical model as a framework for designing and evaluating these programs. Other theoretical perspectives will continue to be used in combination with this model. With a process of change approach to self-care behavior and the continued use of cognitively based and other models of behavior, research is likely to focus on identifying factors associated with the movement of the older adult from one stage of the self-care practice to the next. This should result in development of self-care programs with guides and interventions tailored to move the older adult from one stage to the next. The Clear Horizons self-help smoking cessation guide for older adults is an example of this trend (Rimer et al., 1994).

Another possible trend in self-care research may be increasing attention to nonparticipants and more aggressive approaches to recruitment, retention, and reactivation. Self-care programs could be designed to address special populations such as older adult smokers who have recently relapsed. The recent trend to bring self-care programs to community settings should also be encouraged. It is hoped that more self-care programs will target older adults in public housing, rural areas, and other locations where programs are not traditionally located. Finally, self-care programs should continue to examine the role of individuals who influence self-care practices, including family members, friends, and health professionals. There is a need to better understand when and under what circumstances family members are an asset or liability to the older adult in the self-care process. Interventions could be designed to incorporate defined support roles into more comprehensive programs reflecting the context in which self-care activities are performed.

REFERENCES

Adelman, R., Greene, M., & Charon, R. (1987). The physician-elderly patient-companion triad in the medical encounter: The development of a conceptual framework and research agenda. *The Gerontologist, 27,* 729–734.

Ary, D., Toobert, D., Wilson, W., & Glasgow, R. (1986). Patient perspective on factors contributing to nonadherence to diabetes regimen. *Diabetes Care, 9*(2), 168–172.

Bandura, A. (1977). Self-efficacy: Toward a unifying theory of behavioral change. *Psychological Review, 84*(2), 191–215.

Bandura, A. (1986). *Social foundations of thought and action.* Englewood Cliffs, NJ: Prentice Hall.

Bandura, A. (1989). Human agency in social cognitive theory. *American Psychologist, 44,* 1175–1184.

Bandura, A., & Adams, N. (1977). Analysis of self-efficacy theory of behavioral change. *Cognitive Therapy and Research, 1,* 287–308.

Barke, C., & Nicholas, D. (1990). Physical activity in older adults: The stages of change. *Journal of Applied Gerontology, 9*(2), 216–223.

Brody, E., & Kleban, M. (1981). Physical and mental health symptoms of older people: Who do they tell? *Journal of the American Geriatrics Society, 29,* 442–449.

Brody, E., Kleban, M., & Moles, E. (1983). What older people do about their day-to-day mental and physical health symptoms. *Journal of the American Geriatrics Society, 31,* 489–498.

Buchner, D., Larson, E., & White, R. (1987). Influenza vaccination in community elderly: A controlled trial of postcard reminders. *Journal of the American Geriatrics Society, 35,* 755–760.

Buchner, D., & Pearson, D. (1989). Factors associated with participation in a community senior health promotion program: A pilot study. *American Journal of Public Health, 79,* 775–777.

Clark, M., Kviz, F., Prohaska, T. Crittenden, K., & Warnecke, R. (1995). Readiness of older adults to stop smoking in a televised intervention. *Journal of Aging and Health, 7,* 119–138.

Clark, N., Rakowski, W., Wheeler, J., Ostrander, L., Oden, S., & Keteyian, S. (1988). Development of self-management education for elderly heart patients. *The Gerontologist, 28,* 491–498.

Dean, K. (1989). Conceptual, theoretical and methodological issues in self-care research. *Social Science and Medicine, 29*(2), 117–123.

DeFriese, G., & Woomert, A. (1983). Self-care among U.S. elderly. *Research on Aging, 5,* 3–23.

Dorfman, S. (1991). Health promotion for older minority adults: A review. (PF4722(991) D14493). Washington, DC: The National Resource Center on Health Promotion and Aging, American Association of Retired Persons.

Fiatarone, M., Marks, E., Ryan, N., Meredith, C., Lipsitz, L., & Evans, W. (1990). High-intensity strength training in nonagenarians. *Journal of the American Medical Association, 263,* 3029–3034.

Gecht, M., Connell, K., Sinacore, J. & Prohaska, T. (1996). A survey of exercise beliefs and exercise habits among people with arthritis. *Arthritis Care and Research, 9,* 82–88.

Gilden, J., Hendryx, M., Casia, C. & Singh, S. (1989). The effectiveness of diabetes education programs for older patients and their spouses. *Journal of the American Geriatrics Society, 37,* 1023–1030.

Glasser, M., Prohaska, T., & Roska, J. (1992). The role of family in medical care-seeking decisions of older adults. *Family and Community Health, 15,* 59–70.

Gorley, T. & Gordon, S. (1995). An examination of the transtheoretical model and exercise behavior in older adults. *Journal of Sports & Exercise Psychology, 17,* 312–324.

Greene, M., Adelman, R., Charon, R. & Hoffman, S. (1986). Ageism in the medical encounter: An exploratory study of the doctor-elderly patient relationship. *Language Communication, 6,* 113–124.

Greene, M., Hoffman, S., Charon, R., & Adelman, R. (1987). Psychosocial concerns in the medical encounter: A comparison of the interactions of doctors with their old and young patients. *The Gerontologist, 27, 2,* 164–168.

Guralnik, J., LaCroix, A., Everett, D., & Kovar, M. (1989). *Advance data, aging in the eighties: The prevalence of comorbidity and its association with disability.* Hyattsville, MD: U.S. Department of Health and Human Services.

Haug, M. (1979). Doctor patient relationships and the older patient. *Journal of Gerontology, 34,* 852–860.

Hickey, T., Wolf, F., Robins, L., Wagner, M., & Harik, W. (1995). Physical activity training for functional mobility in older persons. *The Journal of Applied Gerontology, 4,* 357–371.

Janz, N., & Becker, M. (1984). The health belief model: A decade later. *Health Education Quarterly, 11,* 1–47.

King, A., Haskell, W., Taylor, C., Kraemer, H., & DeBusk, R. (1991). Group-vs home-based exercise training in health older men and women: A community-based clinical trial. *Journal of the American Medical Association, 266, 11,* 1535–1542.

Krause, N. (1990). Illness behavior in late life. In R. Binstock & L. George (Eds.), *Handbook of aging and the sciences* (3rd ed., pp. 227–243). San Diego, CA: Academic.

Kumanyika, S., & Charleston, J. (1992). Lose weight and win: A church-based weight loss program for blood pressure control among black women. *Patient Education and Counseling, 19,* 19–32.

Lavizzo-Mourey, R., & Diserens, D. (1989). Preventive care for the elderly. In R. Lavizzo-Mourey, S. C. Day, D. Diserens & J. A. Grisso (Eds.), *Practicing prevention for the elderly* (pp. 1-10). Philadelphia: Hanley & Belfus.

Maiman, L., & Becker, M. (1974). The health belief model: Origins and correlates in psychological theory. *Health Education Monograph, 2,* 336–353.

Marcus, B., Rossi, J., Selby, V., Niaura, R., & Abrams, D. (1992). The stages and process of exercise adoption and maintenance in a worksite sample. *Health Psychology, 11,* 368–395.

Mills, K., Stewart, A., King, A., Roitz, K., Sepsis, P., Ritter, P., & Bortz, W. (1996). Factors associated with enrollment of older adults into a physical activity promotion program. *Journal of Aging and Health, 8,* 96–113.

Morey, M., Cowper, P., Feussner, J., DiPasqual, R., Crowley, G., Kitzman, D., & Sullivan, R. (1989). Evaluation of a supervised exercise program in a geriatric population. *Journal of the American Geriatrics Society, 37,* 348–354.

Mullen, P., Hersey, J., & Iverson, D. (1987). Health behavior models compared. *Social Science and Medicine, 24,* 973–981.

National Center for Health Statistics (1986). *Aging in the eighties. Age 65 years and over. Use of community services.* (Preliminary data from the Supplement on Aging to the National Health Interview Survey, United States 1984 Advanced Data from Vital and Health Statistics, No. 124. DHHS Pub. No. PHS 86-1250). Hyattsville, MD: U.S. Public Health Service.

Orleans, C., Rimer, B., Cristinzio, S., Keintz, M., & Fleisher, L. (1991). A national survey of older smokers: Treatment needs of a growing population. *Health Psychology, 10,* 343–351.

Peters, K., Baldyga, W., & Prohaska, T. (1994, November). *Building a model health promotion program under Title III-F: The university as a service provider.* Paper presented at the 47th annual meeting of the Gerontological Society of America, Atlanta, GA.

Prochaska, J., & DiClemente, C., (1983). Stages and processes of self-change in smoking. Toward an integrative model of change. *Journal of Consulting and Clinical Psychology, 5,* 390–395.

Prohaska, J., DiClemente, C., & Norcross, J. (1992). In search of how people change: Applications to addictive behaviors. *American Psychologist 47, 9,* 1102–1114.

Prohaska, T., & Clark, M. (1994). The interpretation-and misinterpretation-of health status and risk assessments. *Generations, 18,* 57–60.

Prohaska, T. Funch, D., & Smith-Blesch, K. (1990). Age patterns in symptom perception in illness behavior among colorectal cancer patients. *Behavior, Health and Aging, 1,* 27–39.

Prohaska, T., & Glasser, M. (1994). Older adult behavior change in response to symptom experiences. *Advances in Medical Sociology, 4,* 141–162.

Prohaska, T., & Glasser, M. (1996). Patients' view of family involvement in medical care decisions and encounters. *Research on Aging, 18,* 52–69.

Prohaska, T. Glasser, M., & Newman, S. (1992, November). *Participants and consequences of mall-walking programs for older adults.* Paper presented at the annual meeting of the Gerontological Society of America, Washington, DC.

Prohaska, T., Leventhal, E., Leventhal, H. & Keller, M. (1985). Health practices and illness cognition in young, middle aged, and elderly adults. *Journal of Gerontology, 40,* 569–578.

Perkins, K., Rapp, S., Carlson, C., & Wallace, C. (1986). A behavioral intervention to increase exercise among nursing home residents. *The Gerontologist, 26,* 479–481.

Rakowski, W. (1992). Disease prevention and health promotion with older adults. In M. Ory, R. Abeles, & P. Lipman (Eds.), *Aging, health, and behavior* (pp. 239–275). Newbury Park, CA: Sage.

Rakowski, W., Julius, M., Hickey, T., Verbrugge, L., & Halter, J. (1988). Daily symptoms and behavioral responses: Results of a health diary with older adults. *Medical Care, 26,* 278–296.

Ransdell, L. (1995). Church-based health promotion: An untapped resource for women 65 and older. *American Journal of Health Promotion, 9,* 333–336.

Rimer, B. (1990). Perspectives on intrapersonal theories in health education and health behavior. In K. Glanz, F. Lewis, & B. Rimer (Eds.), *Health behavior and health education: Theory, research and practice* (pp. ???). San Francisco: Jossey-Bass.

Rimer, B., Orleans, C., Fleisher, L., Cristinzo, S. Resch, N., Telepchak, J., & Keintz, M. (1994). Does tailoring matter? The impact of a tailored guide on ratings and short-term smoking-related outcome for older smokers. *Health Education Research, 9,* 69–84.

Rosenstock, I. (1974). The health belief model and prevention health behavior. *Health Education Monograph, 2,* 354–386.

Rosenstock, I., Strecher, V., & Becker, M. (1988). Social learning theory and the health belief model. *Health Education Quarterly, 15,* 175–183.

Rubenstein, L., Josephson, K., Nichol-Seamons, M., & Robbins, A. (1986). Comprehensive health screening of well elderly adults: An analysis of a community program. *Journal of Gerontology, 41,* 342–352.

Sutherland, M., Hale, C., & Harris, G. (1995). Community health promotion: The church as partner. *The Journal of Primary Prevention, 16,* 201–216.

Thornberry, R., Wilson, W., & Golden, P. (1986). Health promotion and disease prevention: Provisional data from the National Health Interview Survey: United States, Jan.–June 1985. In R. Thornberry, (Eds.), *Advance data from vital and health statistics* (No. 119. DHHS Pub. No. (PHS) 86-1250). Hyattsville, MD: National Center for Health Statistics.

Van Nostrand, J., Miller, B., & Furner, S. (1993). Selected issues in long-term care: Profile of cognitive disability of nursing home residents and the use of informal and formal care by elderly in the community. In J. Van Nostrand, S. Furner, R. Suzman (Eds.), *Health data on older Americans: United States, 1992. Vital Health Statistics, 3,* 143–186.

Wagner, E., Grothus, L., Hecht, J., & LaCroix, A. (1991). Factors associated with participation in a senior health promotion program. *The Gerontologist, 31,* 598–602.

Watkins, A., & Kligman, E. (1993, January-February). Attendance patterns of older adults in a health promotion program. *Public Health Reports,* pp. 86–91.

Wolinsky, F., Coe, R., Miller, D. Pendergrast, J., Creel, M., & Chavez, M. (1983). Health service utilization among the noninstitutionalized elderly. *Journal of Health and Social Behavior, 24,* 325–337.

Wolinsky, F., & Johnson, R. (1991). The use of health services by older adults. *Journal of Gerontology, 46,* S345–357.

Wortman, C., & Conway, T. (1985). The role of social support in adaptation and recovery from physical illness. In S. Cohen & S. L. Syme (Eds.), *Social support and health.* Orlando, FL: Academic.

CHAPTER 4

Evaluating Psychosocial Interventions for Promoting Self-Care Behaviors Among Older Adults

William Rakowski

THE CLASSIFICATION OF INTERVENTION RESEARCH

What are the salient dimensions along which existing research on self-care can be categorized? At risk of oversimplification, intervention studies may be grouped in regard to seven general domains. Complexity arises because many choices exist within each of the seven domains. It is the combination of these options across domains, in any single study, that produces the extreme diversity often found in the literature. The seven general domains are:

- the disease/illness/functional limitation that is the "problem focus" of study
- the health practice(s) that are the target of intervention
- the outcome variable(s) that are being monitored to judge progress toward alleviating the problem
- the duration of time over which the outcome variable(s) are being monitored after the intervention ends
- specification of the population being targeted by the intervention

- the setting or "channel" in which the intervention is delivered
- the specific techniques used to deliver the intervention

These domains, and the options within them, are not completely orthogonal to each other. Some intervention techniques are not feasible or practical in combination with particular populations, or in certain settings. However, a truly comprehensive research program on older adult self-care could produce a phenomenal range of studies.

One needs to look only at the smoking cessation literature in the general population to see the diversity of interventions that can be generated on a single type of health-related practice. Some investigators become specialists in a "channel" of delivery (e.g., physician offices, retirement communities, hospitals) and experiment by varying intervention techniques, population target groups, and outcome variables; others specialize in intervention modalities (e.g., motivational interviewing, interactive video, self-help books) and by varying some of the seven domains cited above.

Self-Care in the Causal Chain

Fundamental to the design of any intervention is having a conceptual scheme for the role which self-care has in a causal chain-of-events for that intervention. Is the self-care practice itself the outcome of the study? Or, is self-care seen as being a necessary intermediate step, but still an antecedent to other outcomes that are being assessed as the eventual target? In either case, the essential first step is justifying why the self-care activity is important to influence at all. Because intervention is a planned attempt to produce behavior change, and persons are being asked to invest their time and other resources to achieve the change, there must be sufficiently convincing theoretical or empirical evidence for making the recommendation.

Figure 4.1 provides a simple scheme which may help to organize an investigator's perspective regarding how a particular self-care study fits into the larger context. The position of self-care in the diagram is important. When self-care is the dependent variable, it is used as the outcome of several antecedents. The causal chain-of-effect is straightforward. As such, the task is to understand better the factors which account for the variance of the self-care practice. However, when self-care is the target of the intervention and other dependent measures are used, the causal chain is expanded, and self-care becomes only one of several factors potentially influencing the outcome.

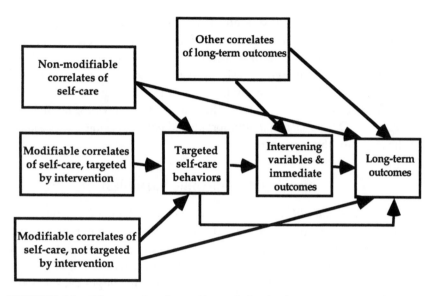

FIGURE 4.1 Diagram showing self-care behavior in a presumed causal chain of effect between antecedent variables, intervening variables, and long-term outcomes. The expected effect of intervention on self-care practices must be understood in the broader context of all potential influences on the longer-term outcome variables, not only impact on the self-care practices themselves.

When should a particular self-care practice, or a group of highly correlated practices, be used as the primary dependent measure for an intervention study? Or, stated differently, when is the self-care behavior itself sufficient as the sole outcome variable? This is a difficult question. A primary or sole focus on self-care as the outcome would seem to be appropriate only in circumstances where the self-care practice has been previously established to be related to longer-term health consequences.

For example, epidemiologic evidence has established a causal relationship between smoking, morbidity, and mortality. Smoking cessation has been linked to better health status relative to continuing to smoke. Moreover, there are no established medical risks from smoking cessation, although there are withdrawal phenomena which are well known to those who try to quit. Therefore, validated smoking cessation is accepted as a sufficient end point. The additional implication is that positive health benefits will accrue subsequently. Other examples are Pap testing and screening mammography, at least within certain age groups of women. At present, obtaining these tests is considered sufficient outcome. As a result, "self-care interventions" for these health practices have the objective of providing strategies to increase performance rates of the behavior.

Some persons might argue, however, that self-care behavior is not a sufficient outcome variable. Cost implications of the intervention and broader quality-of-life issues deriving from the intervention may also be included as outcomes. Questions about appropriate and necessary outcome variables set the stage for the next section.

Choosing the Outcome Variables

What outcomes *should* self-care be expected to influence? The answer is not static. Interventions to address (or to redress) a problem evolve over time, as a body of expertise grows and intervention technology is refined. It is probable that the selection of outcome variables will also change over time, and will relate to the placement of self-care in a larger causal chain.

The list of potential dependent variables for an intervention study is long, and can include:

- mortality rates and/or survival time
- morbidity rates and/or the severity of illness events
- rates of occurrence of longer-term sequelae to initial illness events
- side effects and complications of the intervention
- speed of recovery after an illness event
- health service utilization indicators
- functional health status
- cost of health care
- health-related knowledge
- health-related attitudes
- influence on the performance of health practices other than the one(s) specifically targeted
- overall life satisfaction or effect on other personality domains
- productivity or contribution to society
- effects on other areas of life such as family interactions, social connectedness, or the strain put on personal finances or related resources
- general quality of life and/or illness-specific quality of life

Each of the above categories of outcome variables can itself be operationalized by any number of specific indicators. It is important to be realistic in specifying the outcome variables for any given self-care intervention, relative to the existing body of knowledge and the state of intervention technology. For example, it may be most realistic initially to expect that change in a self-care practice (e.g., home blood pressure monitoring) will favorably influence attitudinal and self-concept variables, and perhaps a utilization variable such as delay/nondelay of responding to a symptom of illness. Investigating the effects of intervention on parameters such as long-term sequelae, impacts on family members or social connectedness, community-level morbidity rates, and cost of care may well need to wait for improved technology or for interventions targeted at special risk populations where such outcomes are reasonable.

One recommendation is that self-care interventions for older persons should avoid the temptation to include a panoply of outcomes for the sake of trying to make up for lost time. When multiple outcome indicators are used, the investigator should attempt to lay out a priority order, which may mean that effects on mortality, morbidity, and cost of care are not always the top priority. Similarly, the scientific review community should not expect self-care interventions to include a comprehensive set of outcomes, as it is likely that self-care interventions in certain populations or for certain illnesses will not be a panacea across a wide range of outcomes.

There is a corollary to this caution. Not all types of self-care interventions or self-care behaviors will directly influence specific outcomes such as survival time/mortality, cost-of-care indexes, or long-term morbidity. Will this place certain types of self-care studies at a disadvantage in competitive funding? Will certain types of self-care practices (e.g., dental flossing, breast self-exam, checking hot water temperature in one's residence) be seen as inherently less deserving of research support because their impact on cost and mortality indexes might not be as significant as other self-care activities (e.g., smoking cessation, physical activity, blood pressure monitoring)? There is a need to support basic social and behavioral research on self-care even if the self-care practice does not promise to yield front-page headlines.

Presence of a Suitable Comparison Group

The results of self-care interventions, as with any intervention, need to be evaluated and understood relative to a standard of comparison. In the initial phases of intervention research on a health practice, outcomes are compared against two standards. One of these is the outcome of "usual care" when the intervention has a clinical setting; the other is the "natural history" which results when self-care practices are left to occur as they normally would in the population. Epidemiologic data are crucial for determining the base rates when natural history is used as the comparison group.

As intervention research on a topic matures there is a shift in the nature of the comparison or control groups that are used. At some point, either usual care or natural history will be superceded by intervention techniques that appear to be the current gold standard. This standard will then set the criterion to be surpassed or, at least, matched by new intervention strategies. At the same time, it is important not to focus solely on success rates (e.g., percent who lost weight, percent who begin to exercise, reduction in medical claims). There may be other criteria for judging success, such as whether the new intervention outperforms the existing gold standard, or reaches a different population group (e.g., the rural as opposed to the urban; persons who usually are lost to attrition).

Dosage of Intervention Delivered and Received

Process evaluation is the general term that denotes collecting data that document the delivery of the intervention. Process evaluation can also include analysis of how the project met its proposed intermediate goals on a hypothesized causal chain leading from the intervention through intermediate outcomes to longer-term outcomes.

Process evaluation is straightforward and simple in one way, but potentially difficult to achieve in another. Interventions need to provide enough opportunities for contact with the procedures and materials to allow participants to receive a sufficiently intense exposure, that will in turn result in initial self-care behavior change. Therefore, self-care intervention research proposals should make a cogent case for the dose of intervention being delivered relative to the demands of the behavior to be changed, and should then document the delivery of that dose during project implementation.

An assessment of immediate or short-term program impact becomes a "process variable" which can be used to help understand why longer-term outcomes are or are not achieved. The degree to which initial behavior change is maintained over successive follow-ups then becomes a longer-term outcome of the intervention. It is especially important to use process evaluation in self-care intervention studies because the kinds of health-related practices involved must be transferred from the research/training setting to everyday life. Studies that fail to show an effect for self-care intervention will need to determine whether the failure was at the level of theory, selection of dependent measures, choice of intervention strategies, or project implementation.

Table 4.1 provides types of information which could be collected in self-care intervention studies, in order to help document the dosage of intervention that an individual received. The list is not intended to be comprehensive—other information may be well suited to a given study. Nor does Table 4.1 deal with how the data are obtained (e.g., patient exit interviews, chart review, interviews with collaterals, charting attendance, ratings by on-site observers). Instead, the purpose is to stimulate thinking about process evaluation to document intervention delivery. A thorough discussion and example of process evaluation, even though not grounded in aging research, can be found in a description of the Multicenter Child and Adolescent Trial for Cardiovascular Health (CATCH: Stone, McGraw, Osganian, & Elder, 1994).

A second, but less straightforward issue in process evaluation has to do with the packaging or decomposition of the intervention. Specifically, into

**TABLE 4.1   Information That Can Be Monitored During
               Process Evaluation**

- Do participants demonstrate increased knowledge about the topic as a result of the intervention? (Assessed immediately at the end of the intervention)
- Do participants demonstrate increased behavioral skills as a result of the intervention? (Assessed immediately at the end of the intervention)
- Did participants engage in the expected activities during the supervised intervention sessions?
- What was the attendance rate for each participant during regularly scheduled sessions?
- Were materials distributed as planned by intermediaries, such as health care providers, senior center directors, or housing site supervisors?
- How much individual attention did program participants receive from program leaders during the intervention?
- Do participants report that they were able to have their questions answered to their satisfaction?
- To what extent did participants practice on their own between regularly scheduled sessions?
- To what extent do participants recall materials such as posters, flyers, materials sent in the mail, and programs or public service announcements that appeared on TV/radio?
- Were there changes in the setting(s) while the program was being delivered (e.g., termination of original staff and addition of new staff; change in administrative head of unit; movement of the program to other rooms; change in time of day when the program was offered)?

how many small units of analysis should the intervention activities and the target self-care practice be broken? The relevant question asks what level of intervention delivery analysis or behavior analysis is necessary given the current state of self-care interventions and the level of data that is considered essential to move the field forward.

THE EVOLUTION OF QUESTIONS ADDRESSED BY INTERVENTION

Generally, intervention research begins with a series of "efficacy studies" that investigate the impact of intervention in well-controlled settings, and with participant samples who pose no unusually difficult challenges. The objective is to determine if the intervention works under circumstances of good resources, a motivated group of participants, and good control over intervention delivery.

After efficacy has been demonstrated, other generic questions take priority. Table 4.2 lists some of the questions that underlie the development or maturation of intervention studies on a particular topic. Broadly speaking, these questions address the several ways of categorizing intervention research that were presented earlier in the chapter. Research projects always face the challenge of following currently accepted and well-validated procedures versus introducing modifications that, although not yet well tested, seem reasonable on conceptual grounds or on the basis of other professional experience. Each study should be careful to specify what its new approaches are, since it is these new features which help to answer the questions posed in Table 4.2.

INDIVIDUALIZED VERSUS STANDARD INTERVENTIONS

It seems safe to say that individualized, tailored, or personalized interventions have often been treated with skepticism in the scientific community. The perspective traditionally taken on individualized intervention has been that such packages carry too high a risk of leading to unstandardized, and therefore nonreplicable, studies. Following a standard protocol and ensur-

TABLE 4.2   The Progression of Questions Often Posed by a Series of Increasingly Targeted Intervention Studies

Efficacy study

- Can an intervention effect be demonstrated in well-controled settings, with adequate resources and current technology, with samples that present no special challenges (e.g., extensive comorbidities)?

Effectiveness studies

- Is it possible to extend the intervention to settings and individuals with the same characteristics as in the basic efficacy study, but in greater numbers and without the same close degree of supervision?
- How do participant characteristics influence the effectiveness of the intervention?
- Can the duration of time over which benefits persist be extended?
- What is the maximum benefit that can be expected from the intervention when resources are highly concentrated?
- What is the minimum intervention that can be provided while still achieving a sufficient level of benefit?
- Can the intervention be transferred to settings other than the one(s) in the original research? What other intervention delivery channels can be used?
- Can the intervention be successfully extended to persons at higher or lower levels of risk, relative to the original sample?
- Are there secondary benefits from the intervention, or costs and risks to the intervention?
- Can additional behavioral outcomes be added to the basic design, without diluting the impact that was found in the original efficacy studies?

ing the potential for replication are two of the long-standing cornerstones of systematic scientific investigation.

Because we know so little about where, when in life, and from whom self-care practices are learned and how they are sustained over time, it is inappropriate to presume that a single intervention will work equally well with everyone. This is true even if the single intervention is a multicomponent package. Usually, the premise is that at least some pieces of the package will be relevant for the individual and will stimulate behavior change. The challenge is to find an acceptable middle ground between nomothetic and idiographic intervention strategies.

There now may be a defensible basis for such studies. The traditional "soft spot" of personalized interventions was the absence of an objective means by which the personalization would occur. The process seemed to be too subjective and variable from participant to participant. Recently, tailored interventions have become more explicitly guided by behavioral science theory, such as the "stage-matched" interventions guided by the transtheoretical model of behavior change (see chapter 3). These interventions classify individuals into discrete groups by predetermined algorithms based upon their readiness to adopt a new behavioral practice, and then apply a predefined set of constructs to organize interventions targeted to each stage of readiness. These constructs have been validated in prior studies as being salient to the respective stages of readiness.

Interventions can be organized by "expert systems" which follow preestablished decision rules to take information from a participant interview (or other database) and create a personalized package. Persons with different background characteristics receive different packages according to a theory-guided methodology, while persons with the same baseline characteristics receive the same intervention package. Personalization does not need to mean that a person's intervention package is completely unique, subjectively determined by the intervention agents, and nonreplicable. Therefore, the prospects for tailored, personalized interventions are promising.

RANGE OF DISEASES/CONDITIONS IN EXISTING STUDIES

Self-care interventions have been conducted to address several different health problems. Included are: arthritis (Calfas, Kaplan, & Ingram, 1992; Ettinger et al., 1997; Lorig & Holman, 1993; Lorig, Mazonson, & Holman, 1993); cancer (Atwood, Aickin et al., 1992; Atwood, Buller et al., 1991; Rimer et al., 1992; Weinrich, Weinrich, Stoomberg, Boyd, & Weiss, 1993), cardiovascular disease (Applegate et al., 1992; Clark et al., 1992; Dodge, Clark, Janz, Liang, & Schork, 1993; Mayeda & Anderson, 1993); diabetes, often with an emphasis on dietary management (Gilden, Hendryx, Clar, Casia, & King, 1992; Glasgow et al., 1992; Litzelman et al., 1993); falls and injury prevention (Reinsch, MacRae, Lachenbruch, & Tobis, 1992; Stevens et al., 1991/92); smoking cessation (Hill, Rigdon, & Johnson, 1993; Kviz, Crittenden, Clark, Madura, & Warnecke, 1994; Rimer et al., 1994; Vetter & Ford, 1990); and urinary incontinence in women (Burns, Pranikoff, Nochajski, Desotelle, & Harwood, 1990; Fantl, Wyman et al., 1991;

Wells, Brink, Diokno, Wolfe, & Gillis, 1991) and in men (Burgio, Stutz-man, & Engel, 1989).

There have also been self-care interventions stimulated more by the desire to promote and sustain wellness and general functioning than to address a specific illness (Brice, Gorey, Hall, & Angelino, 1996; Elder, Williams, Drew, Wright, & Boulan, 1995; Fries, Bloch, Harrington, Richardson, & Beck, 1993; Fries, Harrington, Edwards, Kent, & Richardson, 1994; German et al., 1995; Slymen, Drew, Wright, Elder, & Williams et al., 1992; Vickery, Golaszewski, Wright, & Kalmer, 1988; Wagner, Grothaus, Hecht, & LaCroix, 1991).

One observation about these studies is important. Although the above studies have been classified as applicable to self-care, the articles did not all describe themselves as "self-care studies" or as part of a broader picture of self-care research. Thus, there was no overarching model or well-defined body of literature on self-care to which the individual articles were intending to contribute.

AN OVERALL IMPRESSION OF APPARENT SUCCESS

Demonstration of Effect

For the most part, interventions to foster self-care skills have had effects on the studies' primary outcome measures. Consequently, there is reason for optimism that a systematic program of funded studies will build on that base and lead to even more effective strategies.

Success has not been universal, however, nor should an unqualified degree of success be expected. For example, Wells et al. (1991) studied pelvic muscle exercise to deal with urinary incontinence. Six months of pelvic muscle exercise did result in greater pelvic muscle strength relative to a group who received a 4-week medication protocol; but the two groups did not differ on other outcomes (self-reported urine control and wetting; urine control when told to cough). Similarly, Nelson et al. (1984) found positive effects of general self-care intervention on skills, confidence, and lifestyle change; but there were no effects on physician visits, hospital stays, or quality of life. Elder et al. (1995) found that gains observed after 1 year were not maintained in a 3-year follow-up.

Reinsch et al. (1992) reported that a falls prevention program which employed exercise training and class-based instruction did not reduce risk of falling. The comparison condition was a discussion group that discussed health-related, but not fall-related, topics. Topp, Mikesky, Wigglesworth, Holt, and Edwards et al. (1993) investigated dynamic resistance strength training as it affected gait velocity and balance. The comparison group was a contact-only control. The exercise group demonstrated greater strength of knee extensors and flexors after the 12-week program. However, they did not show improvement on the gait and balance measures. Finally, in the area of diabetes education, using a comprehensive package targeting diet and exercise, Glasgow et al. (1992) found improvements for caloric intake and fat intake. However, no evidence was found for impact on fiber intake or for exercise.

Mixed findings such as these require explanation, and to the authors' credit they most often do not overlook this detail. For example, Topp et al. (1993) suggest that a different dependent variable—changes in postural sway or center of gravity—might have been a preferable variable (p. 506). Glasgow et al. (1992) suggested that fiber intake was already close to the recommended level—leaving little room for improvement—in contrast to the higher levels of percent calories from fat. They also offered the post hoc possibility that quality of life was not measured with the most appropriate index, and that self-efficacy, mood, and exercise may have been at ceiling level. Haber (1986) posited that the lack of effect in his project to lower blood pressure might have been due to recruiting participants with widely divergent blood pressures, thereby producing too diverse a sample both in motivation for change and the need for change.

A central issue is the degree to which causal pathways have been speci-fied *before* the intervention. Benson et al. (1989) provided an a priori clas-sification of their outcomes into expected "direct" and "indirect" effects of the intervention. Their study showed a greater impact on direct effects (i.e., those outcomes with an immediate causal linkage to the intervention) than on indirect outcomes (i.e., those outcomes which were farther removed along a causal pathway). This type of prior specification of a hierarchy of outcomes would be a very helpful addition to the literature.

Length of Follow-Up

Immediate postprogram assessment and short-term evaluations are a common element of intervention studies. However, several interventions on self-care practices have looked at outcomes over longer durations. Evaluation at 3 to 6 months has been common (Applegate et al., 1992; Glasgow et al., 1992; Rimer et al., 1992; Rose, 1992; Vetter & Ford, 1990; Wells et al., 1991). Brice et al. (1996) had a 9-month outcome analysis, and 1-year follow-up periods have been noted in several studies (Atwood et al., 1992; Benson et al., 1989; Calfas et al., 1992; Fries et al., 1994; Hill et al., 1993; Reinsch et al., 1992).

Longer periods for outcome assessment have also been used. Gilden et al. (1992) utilized an 18-month follow-up in their diabetes education project. Fries and colleagues have employed a 2-year follow-up (Fries et al., 1992) and a 30-month follow-up (Fries et al., 1993). The falls intervention conducted by Stevens et al. (1991/92) also used a 2-year period, as did the smoking cessation study of Rimer et al. (1994). Elder et al. (1995) had a total of 3 years of follow-up. The hypertension intervention reported by Morisky, Levine, Green, and Smith (1982) found effects over both 2-year and 5-year follow-ups. Finally, the arthritis interventions by Lorig and colleagues have covered between 20 months and 4 years of follow-up (Lorig et al., 1993; Lorig et al., 1985).

It is important to note that long follow-up (e.g., 2 years or more) is not a prerequisite for the acceptability of an intervention. The decay of an effect between 6 months and 1 year does not necessarily mean that the intervention is ineffective. Duration of program impact must be evaluated relative to the dosage of the intervention. Is a 1- or 2-year impact a reasonable expectation? Or, is 6 months a sufficient duration? Just as there is a need to place self-care in a causal framework, it is also important to place a temporal framework on the outcomes that can be expected.

An important consideration in self-care research involves the duration of the intervention period itself. Self-care interventions are often delivered in multiple sessions, such as a series of didactic seminars or a sequence of home visits. However, the period can be much longer. For example, German et al. (1995) report an intervention period of 2 years, and Ettinger et al. (1997) conducted their intervention over 18 months. In such studies, even an immediate postprogram evaluation covers the effect of activities that have occurred over a notable length of time. These reports illustrate that the intervention phase of self-care studies can be as long as needed to deliver the required dose of the intervention.

VARIATIONS IN SELECTED COMPARISON/CONTROL GROUPS

Varieties of Groups

Some studies have used "usual care" or a "no contact" control (e.g., Applegate et al., 1992; Clark et al., 1992; Fantl et al., 1991; Gilden et al., 1992;

Glasgow et al., 1992; Hopkins, Murrah, Hoeger, & Rhodes, 1990; Stevens et al., 1991/92). Other investigators have used a delayed intervention, "wait list," control in order to allow some examination of whether effects would be replicated (e.g., Brice et al., 1996; Emery & Blumenthal, 1990; Fries et al., 1993; Glasgow et al., 1992).

Other studies have used comparison groups involving some type of exposure to materials, activities, or an accepted medical regimen. Rimer et al. (1992) used low-cost mammography plus posters and materials in retirement communities, and, in an earlier study, used a program on physical fitness as the comparison for a training package specifically directed at cancer control (Rimer, Keintz, & Fleisher, 1986). Nelson et al. (1984) compared a lecture/demonstration on foot care and hypertension with the established multiple-session general self-care intervention. Reinsch et al. (1992) also used a general health-related discussion group as the control for their falls prevention intervention, while Calfas et al. (1992) used a similar control strategy in their study of osteoarthritis self-care. Topp et al. (1993) used a two-session driver education course as the control for their dynamic resistance training intervention. The use of health-related control groups on topics not directly related to the intervention is a reasonable place to begin as some protection against an attention/contact "placebo" effect. Also any trends in the control group are helpful for estimating secular change as a reference point for power calculations in subsequent projects.

Kviz et al. (1994) compared groups of smokers who engaged a "buddy" in the course of a smoking cessation program versus those who had not. Enlisting a buddy for support was one of the features of the program package and not an intervention characteristic that was intentionally manipulated. Benson et al. (1989) used a comparison group based on friendship networks. That is, persons who volunteered for their program were asked to list one to three friends somewhat like them in age, gender, and socioeconomic status. The comparison group was selected from these lists of friends. Rimer at al. (1992) selected their mammography comparison group to simulate Medicare's partial reimbursement of screening.

Wells et al. (1991) employed recipients of a standard drug treatment as the comparison group for their pelvic muscle intervention training. Weinrich et al.'s (1993) controls received the existing American Cancer Society slide/tape/handout package on colorectal cancer. Rice et al. (1989) employed existing literature as the baseline for their study on recall of medical information. The intervention then consisted of modifying the text by restructuring the content. Rimer et al. (1994) contrasted three programs in a test of smoking cessation: Clearing the Air, Clear Horizons, or Clear Horizons plus two counselor calls. These last four studies are instances where the comparison groups used an already existing package, which had been developed either for medical treatment or by a professional organization for educational purposes. Most intervention studies with older persons have not used a gold standard in a comparison group against which a new methodology is being tested. This is very likely due to the fact that there are as yet no clearly developed gold standards for interventions with older persons.

The comparison groups used in intervention studies have been appropriate choices given the state of intervention research and techniques in those areas of aging. However, there is ample room for research to establish standards for the amount of change that can be expected under "natural conditions" or "usual care." Such information is, of course, extremely useful for a priori calculations of power and the determination of necessary sample size. At present, we have very little basis for judging how large the effects of a potentially new self-care intervention should be in order to outperform a no-contact or a usual care comparison. Similarly, there is ample opportunity for the initial development and subsequent refinement of interventions to become the current gold standard against which new techniques are compared.

To the extent that the maturity or developmental stage of an area of intervention is judged by the control/comparison groups that are used, self-care interventions for older persons, in most areas, would be judged as being at an early phase of development. However, intervention reports are becoming progressively more detailed, with increasing methodological and technical sophistication.

Number of Groups in the Design

The designs of interventions on self-care behaviors have often been set up as two-group comparisons. Because so many interventions have employed usual care or no-contact controls, it is possible that studies with older persons are not examining a very diverse range of techniques or methodologies. This comment takes nothing away from well-conceived and well-conducted two-group designs, which are consistent with the tradition of straightforward clinical trials. Perhaps it is time for more three- and four-group designs, which allow researchers to vary characteristics of the intervention.

Although less frequent, there have been studies with older persons that used three or four groups. Haber (1986) used a four-group design, varying both yoga versus exercise and one versus three meetings per week. Weinrich et al. (1993) had a four-group design that used the American Cancer Society colorectal program with or without adaptation to aging. The second variable was presence or absence of older persons as peer educators in the program. Hill et al. (1993) also used a four-group design for their smoking cessation study: behavioral training only, behavioral training plus nicotine gum, behavioral training plus exercise, and exercise only.

Gilden et al. (1992) used a three-group design, in which the two intervention groups were a 6-week diabetes education session, and the 6-week program plus 18 additional months of social support. Atwood et al. (1992) report a four-group design based on assignment to a high versus low dietary fiber intervention, as well as a high versus low dietary fat intervention. Emery and Blumenthal (1990) used a three-group design of aerobic exercise, yoga, and a waiting list control. Burns et al. (1990) contrasted Kegels exercises, biofeedback, and a no-treatment control. Ettinger et al. (1997) contrasted two exercise regimens with a health education comparison group to examine effects on pain and mobility indexes.

CONCEPTUAL MODELS GUIDING THE INTERVENTION

While there is a plethora of theories about behavior and behavior change (see chapter 5), most self-care intervention research has been atheoretical. This section will highlight articles that provide what seem to be especially strong examples for explaining the rationale underlying the experimental intervention. Included here are Weinrich et al.'s (1993) project on colorectal screening, which provided good detail to explain the peer modeling element of the intervention. The falls intervention report by Stevens et al. (1991/92) gives a very thorough presentation of its elements and their integration, as does the smoking cessation report by Rimer et al. (1994). Atwood et al. (1992) devote a substantial space to explain how the Health Behavior in Cancer Prevention model formed the basis of their dietary intervention for colorectal cancer prevention. Finally, although there was no single explicit theory cited by Glasgow et al.'s (1992) diabetes intervention, it is a fine example of a well-explained set of interventions, outcome measures, and process evaluation measures.

Lorig, Lubeck, Kraines, Seleznick, and Holman (1985) and Lorig, Mazonson, and Holman (1993) explain the basis of their intervention in self-efficacy theory. Clark and colleagues (1992) provide a sound explanation of the self-regulation principles which underlay the activities comprising their Take PRIDE heart disease self-management program. The publication of a series of articles by a research team often provides the best opportunity for the theoretical basis of the intervention to be explained. In addition to those authors cited above, the reader is directed to the publications by Fries and colleagues (1992, 1993, 1994), and to the reports by Rimer and colleagues (1992, 1994).

There has been no preeminent theory guiding self-care interventions with older persons. Peer or group support has been relied upon frequently, as well as the desire to encourage a sense of self-efficacy among participants. Principles of incremental goal setting have been employed across the successive sessions of an intervention. Self-regulation has been an implicit requirement in many interventions that require continuing practice between formal training sessions (e.g., urinary incontinence, heart disease management, exercises for arthritis). There is no reason to expect that any one or small set of theories will dominate self-care intervention. It is likely that the combination of the intervention implementation setting, the target behavioral objectives, and the intended audience will highlight the importance of selected theoretical principles.

Interventions are, by nature, attempts to meet the needs of an intended audience. They are, therefore, at least implicitly guided by the philosophy of matching the program to the intended audience. A key challenge lies in assembling the proper set of constructs to accomplish that match. It is also important to remember the difference between constructs that explain behavior as it currently exists and constructs that explain behavior change. Reports by Fries and colleagues (1992, 1993, 1994), and by Rimer et al. (1994) can be consulted for examples of research which had individualized the intervention.

OUTCOME MEASURES EMPLOYED IN EVALUATING PROGRAM EFFECTIVENESS

Most interventions with self-care practices have used a wide range of outcome variables. Some have used a limited number of outcomes, relative to the potential variety that were listed earlier in this chapter. Weinrich et al. (1993) simply employed the return of a completed occult stool test within about six days as their measure of effectiveness, while Hill et al. (1993) used quit rates at three points of follow-up. Clark et al. (1992) used the subscales of the Sickness Impact Profile as the outcome of their heart disease self-management intervention. Vickery, Golaszewski, Wright, and Kalmer (1988) looked specifically at service utilization and cost; Atwood et al. (1992) used adherence to the study protocol during the intervention phase in their project on fat and fiber intake. Fries et al. (1993) examined health risk appraisal scores and cost data specifically in their broad-based self-care intervention. Rimer et al. (1992) targeted their analysis at the effects of intervention on mammography-related beliefs and screening utilization. The FICSIT meta-analysis addressed time to the first episode of falling as the primary outcome variable (Province et al., 1995), and the intervention by Tinetti et al. (1994) also used the incidence of any falls as the outcome measure.

Some reports have used several more dependent measures, but within a single domain. For example, Emery and Blumenthal (1990) had between 15 and 20 indicators of perceived change in several psychosocial domains as a part of their project with exercise and yoga groups. Applegate et al. (1992) focused their analysis on weight loss, 24-hour urine sodium excretion, and systolic and diastolic blood pressure as outcomes of a hypertension control intervention. Morisky et al. (1982) analyzed medication-taking, appointment-keeping, weight status, and blood pressure status (under control/not controlled) in their study of hypertension management. Ettinger et al. (1997) used multiple indicators relevant to pain and mobility associated with osteoarthritis; Elder et al. (1995) examined status on several indicators of diet and physical activitiy.

Other studies have used outcomes from several different categories of variables. For example, Nelson et al. (1984) examined knowledge, self-care skills, lifestyle change, health service use, health status, and quality of life. Glasgow et al. (1992) used several measures specifically relevant to diabetes control (e.g., fasting blood glucose, glycosylated hemoglobin), but also assessed diabetes-related self-efficacy, problem solving, diabetes-related quality of life, and general mood state. Lorig and colleagues (1985, 1993) have looked at knowledge, disability, depression, self-efficacy, pain, physician visits, and estimated cost of health care. Calfas et al. (1992) assessed not only arthritis-specific perceived well-being, but also general well-being, depression, and social support.

It is important to document the impact of intervention as accurately as possible. Therefore, a broad inventory of potential outcomes can be important. At the same time, it is equally important to avoid falling into the trap of believing that "more is better" in regard to how many outcomes to include. The possible effects of self-care interventions must not be oversold or overpromised. The expected causal chain of the intervention must be realistic and guide the selection of outcome measures.

Some intervention reports with multiple outcomes have given an a priori statement of a priority order among their dependent measures. For example, Fantl et al. (1991) noted that the number of urinary incontinence episodes was the primary outcome, while two other indicators of bladder control and incontinence-related quality of life were secondary outcomes. Similarly, Benson et al. (1989) termed some outcomes as expected *direct* effects of their general self-care intervention, and several others as possible *indirect* effects. Reinsch et al. (1992), for their intervention to prevent falls, cited falls and injury as the primary outcomes, while strength, balance, fear of falling, and perceived health were the secondary outcomes. Stevens et al. (1991/92) indicate several attitude and knowledge variables as intermediate outcomes toward behavioral goals of falls prevention.

Priority specification can be helpful in self-care intervention, especially as it reflects a presumed causal chain within which the self-care practice is located. On the one hand, intervention studies with random assignment to groups might be expected to have a fairly straightforward causal pathway—in the event that all else is held equal by randomization. On the other hand, using measures that represent several different categories of outcomes begs the question of whether any one intervention could possibly affect outcomes to an equal degree at so many levels.

Finally, a comment can be made about the use of cost-related outcome measures. By and large, most self-care studies with older persons have not used the cost of care as an outcome. There are some important exceptions (Burton et al., 1995; Fries et al., 1993; Fries et al., 1994; Leigh et al., 1992; Lorig et al., 1993; Vickery et al., 1988). Except for Burton et al., these studies have reported a favorable impact on costs for the self-care intervention. Burton et al. reported no appreciable impact on cost of services, in the context of a "modest" benefit of the intervention program (Burton et al., 1995, p. 391).

Two features of these studies are worth noting. First, most of these interventions (Fries et al., 1993; Fries et al., 1994; Leigh et al., 1992; Vickery et al., 1988) relied extensively on mail as opposed to face-to-face contact.

Rimer et al. (1992) also used mailed materials, though in conjunction with several other strategies, including a group-based educational session. Therefore, seeing a cost savings for the intervention group is impressive because the intervention had several other components that added to the otherwise low cost of mailed materials. Second, these studies have all contrasted a self-care intervention with a no-contact control. It remains for additional research to examine whether different versions of self-care interventions are superior to one another on the cost dimension, in circumstances when something other than a no-contact control is employed.

POPULATION GROUPS REPRESENTED IN INTERVENTION

There have been limited studies looking at self-care in traditionally underserved and disenfranchised social groups, such as racial and ethnic minorities, persons of low income and low education, rural residents, and residents of the inner city. However, with the exception of the Exploratory Centers for Minority Aging and Health Promotion (NIA, 1996), there has been a lack of attention to systematic self-care research in any subgroup in the population.

The regulations regarding representation of women and minorities in NIH-funded research should guarantee that a wide range of groups are represented in intervention studies. However, there is still a risk of small numbers, so that some specially targeted initiatives may be necessary to have enough persons to conduct conclusive trials. Interestingly, self-care interventions with older persons are well positioned to avoid the errors of omission that have occurred in other lines of investigation.

The Socially Isolated Elderly

It is undoubtedly the case that intervention study samples have some biases. Perhaps most generally, persons who have been in self-care interventions have somehow been connected to traditional recruitment sources such as hospitals and physician offices, senior centers and nutrition sites, residential complexes, older adult organizations like AARP, newspapers, television, and radio, retiree groups, and health fairs. They may have had to make the effort to respond to advertisements in the media asking for volunteers.

Geographic Region

Self-care studies have been conducted across the country. However, the samples for the individual studies have been local or regional within a state. This should come as no surprise in the absence of a well-funded source for supporting multisite intervention trials. One exception is the Arthritis Self-Management Program (ASMP) which was developed by Lorig and colleagues over several years. The ASMP has been adopted as a national model training program not only by the U.S. Arthritis Foundation, but also in Canada, Australia, and New Zealand. Another exception is the Staying Healthy After 50 Program (Simmons, 1989), which was developed as a follow-up to the original Dartmouth Self-Care for Senior Citizens Program (Nelson et al., 1984). This program was adopted by the AARP and the Red Cross, and was implemented nationally. A third case is the smoking cessation project by Rimer et al. (1994), which recruited nationally through the AARP publication *Modern Maturity*. Multisite trials present challenges and should not be undertaken until methodologies are well tested. The FICSIT trials for falls and injury prevention (Province et al., 1995), and the National Institute on Aging–funded Centers for Minority Aging and Health Promotion (NIA, 1996) are movements in this direction. They are not multisite trials, such as the earlier Systolic Hypertension in the Elderly project, but they are vehicles for building a research program and developing expertise across the country.

Educational Level

As a general rule, persons with less than a high school education have not been a prominent part of intervention study samples. This is probably a function of the above-mentioned tendency for self-care interventions to focus on older persons who were routinely connected to health care and social organizations, as well as those who were willing to reply to solicitations in the media asking for volunteers.

For example, the Bank of America retiree study (Fries et al., 1993; Leigh et al., 1992) reported an average educational level of 13 years. Clark et al.'s (1992) heart disease self-management intervention noted that 77% of participants had graduated high school. Lorig et al.'s (1985, 1993) arthritis intervention projects had samples with an average education of 13 to 14.6 years. Wells et al.'s (1991) incontinence study indicated that 64% had partial college to graduate-level education, which was only slightly lower than

Fantl et al.'s (1991) figures of 68% to 75% in their incontinence project. Rimer et al.'s mammography project (1992) indicated that 74% had completed high school. The hypertension intervention by Applegate et al. (1992) reports an average education of 12–13 years. Emery and Blumenthal (1990) note that all of their participants had at least a high school education. Atwood et al.'s (1992) dietary/colon cancer trial reported recruiting participants in an upper socioeconomic status retirement community.

There are some exceptions to this trend. Nelson et al.'s (1984) general self-care intervention reported an average education of about 10.5 years. Their study reported some positive outcomes, as noted above. Morisky et al.'s (1982) hypertension report indicates that average education was 7.4 years for persons aged 65+, compared to 9.8 years for the comparison group of persons aged 18–64. Intervention outcomes were positive for both age groups. Rose's (1992) heart disease prevention program was conducted with persons who had an average education of between 10 and 10.5 years. Several knowledge and behavioral differences were found between the intervention and control groups after four months.

Weinrich et al. (1993) reported an average educational level of 7.8 years for their study using elderly educators in colorectal screening programs. They did find an effect of intervention on the rate of return of completed stool tests. An interesting facet of this study was the stratification of meal sites based upon percent of African American elderly. Sites with over 50% African American membership were assigned an elderly peer educator who was also African American, whereas sites with over 50% White elderly were assigned a White peer educator. Litzelman et al. (1993) reported an average educational level of just under 10 years for a diabetes control program. Again, several positive intervention outcomes were observed.

While not specifying educational level exactly, Haber's (1986) blood pressure control study was conducted with low-income older persons from federally subsidized housing. This project did not achieve its desired outcome, although Haber discusses process- and sampling-related reasons that may have affected the intervention. Reinsch et al. (1992) indicate that all of the senior centers in their falls prevention intervention were from low socioeconomic areas of Orange and Los Angeles counties. They did not find evidence of program impact, but also discuss reasons not related to education issues. Their interventions were conducted in either Spanish or English, as the particular senior center required.

At this point, it does appear that self-care interventions with lower education populations can be effective, presuming that the intervention activities are well planned and delivered in the proper dose. The reports by Nelson et al. (1984), Morisky et al. (1982), Weinrich et al. (1993), Litzelman et al. (1993), and Rose (1992) are encouraging. Those by Haber (1986) and by Reinsch et al. (1992) are not. However, these latter two articles suggest that there were important problems with implementation. In the case of Haber (1986), difficulties appear to exist in the peer leadership element of the intervention (i.e., little leadership existed to sustain the program over time), as well as in recruiting persons with blood pressures that were too widely divergent (i.e., blood pressures that were initially close to, and perhaps even below, the minimum level for defining hypertension). In the case of Reinsch et al. (1992), problems appeared to exist in the types of activities that were used in the intervention (i.e., an exercise program that was not sufficient to produce strength/balance benefits) and in intervention dose via the educational groups (i.e., meeting only once a week).

Racial and Ethnic Minorities

As might be expected, the above discussion of educational level is closely related to the representation of persons of color in the intervention studies. Morisky et al.'s (1982) hypertension project was conducted with a sample of elderly who were 90% African American. As noted, they reported positive outcomes. Weinrich et al.'s (1993) colon cancer project had a virtual 50-50 split between African American versus White elderly. Also as noted, this team, which found a positive impact, used a racial matching procedure for their peer educators. Roberts et al. (1989) conducted the Staying Healthy After 50 program in Hawaii, with an emphasis on sites that had higher percentages of Japanese and Filipino elderly. A positive impact was reported in the sample that tended to have at least a high school education.

Rose's (1992) heart disease prevention program comprised about 67% African Americans, and all 14 peer educators were African American women. Litzelman et al.'s (1992) diabetes program was 76% African American. As noted above, benefits were found in both programs. The blood pressure project by Haber (1986) had 91% African American and 6% Hispanic subjects. Reinsch et al.'s (1992) falls intervention did not fully indicate racial composition, but did note that three of 16 senior centers were predominantly Hispanic. As reviewed above, these two projects experienced important procedural problems that interfered with validity.

Carefully designed projects do have the potential to benefit the self-care skills of older persons from racial and ethnic groups. Many guides exist for working with these populations, and they should be consulted when preparing research protocols and intervention materials (see MAHP, 1996).

Males in Intervention Samples

Self-care interventions may be one area where it is important to try and oversample men. Some studies have been done only with men or only with women, often due to the recruitment source (e.g., the Veterans Administration) or to the highly gender-related prevalence of a problem (e.g., stress incontinence, breast cancer). A minority of the projects did not report on the gender composition. However, when both sexes have been included, the percentage of men is often low. As with other demographic groups, although the percentage may mirror rates in the population, their numbers may not be sufficient for detailed analyses.

In many studies, fewer than 40% of the participants were male, including Calfas et al.'s (1992) osteoarthritis study, Kviz et al.'s (1994) report on smoking cessation, Glasgow et al.'s (1992) diabetes intervention, and German et al.'s (1995) preventive services demonstration. Less than 20% male participation was found in Rose's (1992) heart disease program, Morisky et al.'s (1982) hypertension sample, the Staying Healthy After 50 interventions conducted by Benson et al. (1989) and by Roberts et al. (1989). Other projects do have 40% or more male participation, such as Topp et al.'s (1993) strength-training project, Hill et al.'s smoking cessation trial (1993), Atwood et al.'s (1992) colon cancer project, the Bank of America retirees study (Leigh et al., 1992; Fries et al., 1993) Applegate et al.'s hypertension study (1992), and Clark et al.'s (1992) heart disease education project.

Relatively low percentages are not as critical if there are large overall samples. However, many studies do not have large numbers of participants. Approximately half of the reviewed projects had total samples under 200, and many of those were under 150; some under 100. Information regarding sample size calculation was often missing. With small samples, it is extremely difficult to do sufficiently powerful comparisons to examine even a main effect of the intervention, let alone gender comparisons.

Unit of Assignment and Unit of Analysis

Much of the current self-care intervention research presumes that individuals are both the unit of assignment and the unit of analysis. Interestingly, Vickery et al. (1988) used households, rather than individuals, as the unit of analysis when looking at health care utilization and cost data. Virtually all other self-care interventions have used the individual as the unit of analysis, regardless of the way in which randomization to experimental/comparison groups was done (i.e., by sampling unit or by individual).

Rimer et al. (1992) analyzed mammography data at the individual level. However, they also included covariates in the final analytical model to account for differences between the four experimental and four control retirement communities. Given the limited number of units for randomization, this was an appropriate and helpful way to adjust the final outcome data.

Within the research community, there are calls for greater attention to issues of unit of assignment versus unit of analysis (Teresi, Lawton, Ory, & Holmes, 1994). This can be a formidable consideration when conducting research in schools, worksites, and medical care offices. Such considerations also can lead to rather substantial research budgets, in order to recruit the requisite number of settings that serve older adults, such as housing units and senior centers.

PROCESS EVALUATION

Process evaluation is still not a major feature of most publications that report self-care interventions for older persons. Some reports, however, do discuss the process of program implementation (e.g., Lichstein, Riedel, & Grieve, 1994; Simmons, 1989). These discussions of implementation are often very insightful and helpful for the planning of future programs. Other investigations (e.g., Vickery et al., 1988) report on participant recall or use of the intervention materials. It is in making an empirical linkage between the independent concepts of "process evaluation" and "outcome evaluation" that the literature is weak. The reader may be told about the process of implementing a program, but it is not clear how process influenced outcome.

Even here a distinction is necessary. Many articles publish not only the basic, unadjusted results comparing the intervention groups, but also conduct one or both of two types of additional analyses. One type is to stratify within the experimental and control groups by some other variable (e.g., age, gender, baseline severity), and then conduct outcome analyses relative to these stratification groups. The second type of analysis is multivariate, and estimates an intervention effect that is not confounded by other variables.

The additional purpose of these multivariate models is to try to identify other important variables that predict change over time, independent of the intervention. Persons who do not respond to the intervention then become high-risk groups who might be the focus of subsequent, more specifically targeted interventions.

These analyses are certainly important, but they do not qualify as process evaluation. Analyses which use the primary outcome measure as the dependent variable and simply introduce sociodemographic or health status factors as covariates are not looking at the implementation of the program. Rather, they examine "effect modifiers" defined by sociodemographic or psychosocial characteristics of the participants. Process evaluation is based on an analysis of characteristics of the program, the implementation of the program, and the possibility that persons with different background characteristics receive different doses of what was supposed to be a uniform intervention.

As an example, Glasgow et al. (1992) specified several process measures, "through which the intervention was hypothesized to operate" (p. 65). Analyses were reported for these measures (self-efficacy, mood, social desirability, problem solving); analyses were also reported for the primary outcomes as a function of intervention/control group membership. However, no linkage was made between change on the process variables and change on the outcome variables.

There are instances in the literature which can be viewed as examples of process evaluation. Rimer et al. (1986) provide perhaps the earliest instance of studying how program implementation characteristics (e.g., number of participants at the group session, questions asked by participants during the session, participant ratings of satisfaction with the intervention) were associated with the achievement of project goals. In a subsequent study of mammography within retirement communities, Rimer and colleagues (1992) reported on the association of screening rate with participation versus nonparticipation in the group educational session.

Atwood et al. (1991) have reported specifically on the newsletter component of their multifaceted intervention for colon cancer prevention. Wells et al. (1991) reported on the association between pelvic muscle exercise frequency per day (i.e., the self-care practice targeted in the intervention), and indexes of urinary incontinence. Kviz et al.'s (1994) report on smoking cessation focuses on the process of enlisting a buddy for support, as recommended in their intervention. German et al. (1995) provided a dose-response analysis of adherence to the intervention and achievement of outcomes, showing a positive association.

Future studies of self-care intervention with older adults should give more explicit attention to process evaluation. A main objective should be to assess the degree to which the intervention is made available as planned. If longer term follow-up is planned, another process variable to be assessed is the degree to which participants learn the content and skills contained in the intervention. Finally, participant retention can be an indicator of process. For example, does an intervention that requires several recontacts or substantial participant self-monitoring between sessions result in greater attrition compared to the minimal contact control group?

The most often missing type of analysis in the gerontology literature is *process-to-outcome* evaluation. This type of analysis looks at the degree to which differential exposure among participants to intervention characteristics is functionally related to individual differences on status for outcome variables. These analyses are important, after the primary outcome analysis, in order to determine whether or not there is a dose to response association between participation and benefit. Because of the potential for attrition due to dropping out, an "intention to treat" criterion may result in an underestimate of intervention benefit to the participants. A dose-response analysis (restricted to the intervention group) can help to demonstrate the validity of the association. Dose-response analyses can also be conducted in the control group, and can help to document the effects of secular trends on the outcome variables that may have overshadowed an intervention effect.

CONCLUSION

The nascent field of self-care intervention with older persons is rapidly developing and potentially vast. Whereas the results of studies to date are promising, the field of self-care intervention with older persons is prepared to move toward a more systematic program of study. As this development occurs, attention should be given to the following points which are critical for moving the field forward.

- Process evaluation should be an important part of future intervention studies, particularly in regard to documenting the dose of the intervention that was delivered, its receipt by the intended population, and conducting process-to-outcome evaluation when possible.
- Multigroup designs should be encouraged, which will allow for the

manipulation of some elements in a package of intervention activities and materials, to contrast the effectiveness-of-delivery options.

- Interventions should be based on a presumed causal chain of effect, in which the self-care practice is identified in the broader picture of primary and secondary outcomes, and in the context of other important influences on those outcomes.

- Self-care studies should be careful to specify their primary and secondary outcomes. The use of more outcome measures is not necessarily better, and can lead to complications in interpretation when results are not uniform across outcomes. A priority order, based on a presumed causal chain of effect, will help prevent this difficulty.

- Programs of research by a team of investigators, extended over time and multiple projects, will provide the strongest basis on which to examine the benefits of self-care intervention, and to identify the best strategies to employ. Some examples of this type of resource now exist in gerontological literature.

- Peer support may be a useful avenue to manipulate in future intervention research. It has a justified basis in social learning theory, and also seems to be a salient dimension for older persons. Similarly, self-regulation is implicit in virtually any behavior change, and its principles are likely to be increasingly visible in self-care studies with older persons.

- The use of persons as the unit of analysis in most self-care interventions may change, as projects become larger to include more aggregated units of assignment and statistical methodologies become more sophisticated. As larger units are used as a basis for recruitment, theoretical constructs guiding the intervention are also likely to broaden to incorporate change at the family, organizational, and community levels.

- Tailored or personalized interventions are likely to become more prominent. Guided by behavioral theory, they will provide standard and replicable methodologies for delivering intervention packages that are optimally matched to salient characteristics of program participants. However, behavior change theory should recognize the role of contextual and environmental factors on changing individual-level behavior and on maintaining the change.

- Recruitment, retention, and the composition of intervention group samples will be issues of continuing importance. They will undoubtedly be the subject of individual literature reviews in the future. However, it will also be helpful to try and move the field toward consensus on points such as acceptable rates of retention.

- As aging becomes a more prominent theme across disciplines, it will be important to look for older adults who were recruited into samples with a broader age span. Subanalysis of outcomes by age group, or the reporting of age by treatment interactions, can also yield important information, presuming that there are a sufficient number of older persons to warrant these approaches.
- The term *self-care intervention* naturally raises the image of interventions in which individuals have primary responsibility for behavior change. The current self-care literature with older persons reflects this type of program. A still unanswered question is the degree to which interventions can be designed with elements that allow us to move "upstream" and address basic social, biological, and environmental causes that lead to premature decline in functional status requiring remedial self-care intervention. Is there a place for self-care studies that focus on the organization or the community as the target of intervention?

REFERENCES

Applegate, W. B., Miller, S. T., Elam, J. T., Cushman, W. C., Derwi, D. E., Brewer, A., & Graney, M. J. (1992). Nonpharmacologic intervention to reduce blood pressure in older patients with mild hypertension. *Archives of Internal Medicine, 152,* 1162–1166.

Atwood, J. R., Aickin, M., Giordano, L., Benedict, J., Bell, M., Rittenbaugh, C., Rees-McGee, S., Sheehan, E., Buller, M., Ho, E.E., Meyskens, F.L., Jr., & Alberts, D. (1992).The effectiveness of adherence intervention in a colon cancer prevention field trial. *Preventive Medicine, 21,* 637–653.

Atwood, J. R., Buller, M. K., Sheehan, E. T., Benedict, J. A., Giordano, L., Alberts, D. S., Earnest, D., & Meyskens, F. L., Jr. (1991). Acceptability, satisfaction and cost of a model-based newsletter for elders in a cancer prevention adherence promotion program. *Patient Education and Counseling, 18,* 211–221.

Benson, L., Nelson, E. C., Napps, S. E., Roberts, E., Kane-Williams, E., & Salisbury, Z. T. (1989). Evaluation of the Staying Healthy After Fifty educational program: Impact on course participants. *Health Education Quarterly, 16,* 485–508.

Brice, G. C., Gorey, K. M., Hall, R. M., & Angelino, S. (1996). The STAYWELL program—Maximizing elders' capacity for independent living through health promotion and disease prevention activities. *Research on Aging, 18,* 202–218.

Burgio, K. L., Stutzman, R. E., & Engel, B. T. (1989). Behavioral training for post-prostatectomy urinary incontinence. *The Journal of Urology, 141,* 303–306.

Burns, P. A., Pranikoff, K., Nochajski, T., Desotelle, P., & Harwood, M. K. (1990). Treatment of stress incontinence with pelvic floor exercises and biofeedback. *Journal of the American Geriatrics Society, 38,* 341–344.

Burton, L., Steinwachs, D. M., German, P. S., Shapiro, S., Brant, L. J., Richards, T. M., & Clark, R. D. (1995). Preventive services for the elderly: Would coverage affect utilization and costs under Medicare? *American Journal of Public Health, 85,* 387–391.

Calfas, K. J., Kaplan, R. M., & Ingram, R. E. (1992). One-year evaluation of cognitive-behavioral intervention in osteoarthritis. *Arthritis Care and Research, 5,* 202–209.

Clark, N. M., Janz, N. K., Becker, M. H., Schork, M. A., Wheeler, J., Liang, J., Dodge, J. A., Keteyian, S., Rhoads, K. L., & Santinga, J. T. (1992). Impact of self-management education on the functional health status of older adults with heart disease. *The Gerontologist, 32,* 438–443.

Dodge, J. A., Clark, N. M., Janz, N. K., Liang, J., & Schork, M. A. (1993). Non-participation of older adults in a heart disease self-management project. *Research on Aging, 15,* 220–237.

Elder, J. P., Williams, S. J., Drew, J. A., Wright, B. L., & Boulan, T. E. (1995). Longitudinal effects of preventive services on health behaviors among an elderly cohort. *American Journal of Preventive Medicine, 11,* 354–359.

Emery, C. F., & Blumenthal, J. A. (1990). Perceived change among participants in an exercise program for older adults. *The Gerontologist, 30,* 516–521.

Ettinger, W. H., Burns, R., Messier, S. P., Applegate, W., Rejeski, W. J., Morgan, T., Shumaker, S., Berry, M. J., O'Toole, M., Monu, J., & Craven, T. (1997). A randomized trial comparing aerobic exercise and resistance exercise with a health education program in older adults with knee osteoarthritis: The Fitness Arthritis and Seniors Trial (FAST). *Journal of the American Medical Association, 277,* 25–31.

Fantl, J. A., Wyman, J. F., McClish, D. K., Harkins, S. W., Elswick, R. K., Taylor, J. R., & Hadley, E. C. (1991). Efficacy of bladder training in older women with urinary incontinence. *Journal of the American Medical Association, 265,* 609–613.

Fries, J. F., Bloch, D. A., Harrington, H., Richardson, N., & Beck, R. (1993). Two-year results of a randomized controlled trial of a health promotion program in a retiree population: The Bank of America Study. *The American Journal of Medicine, 94,* 455–462.

Fries, J. F., Fries, S. T., Parcell, C. L., & Harrington, H. (1992). Health risk changes with a low-cost individualized health promotion program: Effects at up to 30 months. *American Journal of Health Promotion, 6,* 364–371.

Fries, J. F., Harrington, H., Edwards, R., Kent, L. A., & Richardson, N. (1994).

Randomized controlled trial of cost reductions from a health education program: The California Public Employees' Retirement System (PERS) Study. *American Journal of Health Promotion, 8,* 216–223.

German, P. S., Burton, L. C., Shapiro, S., Steinwachs, D. M., Tsuji, I., Paglia, M. J., & Damiano, A. M. (1995). Extended coverage for preventive services for the elderly: Response and results in a demonstration population. *American Journal of Public Health, 85,* 379–386.

Gilden, J. L., Hendryx, M. S., Clar, S., Casia, C., & Singh, S. P. (1992) Diabetes support groups improve health care of older diabetic patients. *Journal of the American Geriatrics Society, 40,* 147–150.

Glasgow, R. E., Toobert, D. J., Hampson, S. E., Brown, J. E., Lewinsohn, P. M., & Donnelly, J. (1992). Improving self-care among older patients with Type II diabetes: The "Sixty Something . . ." study. *Patient Education and Counseling, 19,* 61–74.

Haber, D. (1986). Health promotion to reduce blood pressure level among older blacks. *The Gerontologist, 26,* 119–121.

Hill, R. D., Rigdon, M., & Johnson, S. (1993). Behavioral smoking cessation treatment for older chronic smokers. *Behavior Therapy, 24,* 321–329.

Hopkins, D. R., Murrah, B., Hoeger, W. W. K., & Rhodes, R. C. (1990). Effect of low-impact aerobic dance on the functional fitness of elderly women. *The Gerontologist, 30,* 189–192.

Kviz, F. J., Crittenden, K. S., Clark, M. A., Madura, K. J., & Warnecke, R. B. (1994). Buddy support among older smokers in a smoking cessation program. *Journal of Aging and Health, 6,* 229–254.

Leigh, J. P., Richardson, N., Beck, R., Kerr, C., Harrinton, H., Parcell, C. L., & Fries, J. F. (1992). Randomized controlled study of a retiree health promotion program: The Bank of America study. *Archives of Internal Medicine, 152,* 1201–1206.

Lichstein, K. L., Riedel, B. W., & Grieve, R. (1994). Fair tests of clinical trials: A treatment implementation model. *Advances in Behavioral Research and Therapy, 16,* 1–29.

Litzelman, D. K., Slemenda, C. W., Langefeld, C. D., Hays, L. M., Welch, M. A., Bild, D. E., Ford, E. S., & Vinicor, F. (1993). Reduction of lower extremity clinical abnormalities in patients with non-insulin-dependent diabetes mellitus: A randomized, controlled trial. *Annals of Internal Medicine, 119,* 36–41.

Lorig, K., & Holman, H. (1993). Arthritis self-management studies: A twelve-year review. *Health Education Quarterly, 20,* 17–28.

Lorig, K., Lubeck, D., Kraines, R. G., Seleznick, M., & Holman, H. R. (1985). Outcomes of self-help education for patients with arthritis. *Arthritis and Rheumatism, 28,* 680–685.

Lorig, K. R., Mazonson, P. D., & Holman, H. R. (1993). Evidence suggesting that health education for self-management in patients with chronic arthritis has sustained health benefits while reducing health care costs. *Arthritis and Rheumatism, 36,* 439–446.

Mayeda, D., & Anderson, J. (1993). Evaluating the effectiveness of the "Self-CARE for a Health Heart" program with older adults. *Journal of Nutrition for the Elderly, 13*(2), 11–22.

Morisky, D. E., Levine, D. M., Green, L. W., & Smith, C. R. (1982). Health education program effects on the management of hypertension in the elderly. *Archives of Internal Medicine, 142,* 1835–1838.

National Institute of Aging, Exploratory Centers for Minority Aging and Health Promotion: Description of projects. Supported by National Institute on Aging, Office of Research on Minority Health, National Institute of Health, November, 1996.

Nelson, E. C., McHugo, G., Schnurr, P., Devito, C., Roberts, E., Simmmons, J., & Zubkoff W. (1984). Medical self-care eduation for elders: A controlled trial to evaluate impact. *American Journal of Public Health, 74,* 1357–1362.

Province, M. A., Hadley, E. C., Hornbrook, M. C., Lipsitz, L. A., Miller, J. P., Mulrow, C. D., Ory, M. G., Sattin, R. W., Tinetti, M. E., & Wolf, S. L. (1995). The effects of exercise on falls in the elderly: A preplanned meta-analysis of the FICSIT trials. *Journal of the American Medical Association, 273,* 1341–1347.

Reinsch, S., MacRae, P., Lachenbruch, P. A., & Tobis, J. S. (1992). Attempts to prevent falls and injury: A prospective community study. *The Gerontologist, 32,* 450–456.

Rice, G. E., Meyer, B. J., & Miller, D. C. (1989). Using text structure to improve older adults' recall of important medical information. *Educational Gerontology, 15,* 527–542.

Rimer, B., Keintz, M. K., & Fleisher, L. (1986). Process and impact of a health communications program. *Health Education Research, Theory and Practice, 1,* 29–36.

Rimer, B. K., Orleans, C. T., Fleisher, L., Cristinzio, S., Resch, N., Telepchak, J., & Keintz, M. K. (1994). Does tailoring matter? The impact of a tailored guide on ratings and short-term smoking-related outcomes of older smokers. *Health Education Research, Theory and Practice, 9,* 69–84.

Rimer, B. K., Rensch, N., King, E., Ross, E., Lerman, C., Boyce, A., Kessler, H., & Engstrom, P. F. (1992). Multistrategy health education program to increase mammography use among women ages 65 and older. *Public Health Reports, 107,* 369–380.

Roberts, E., Takenaka, J. I., Ross, C. J., Chong, E. H., Tulang, J. I., & Napps, S. E. (1989). Hawaii Asian-American response to the Staying Healthy After Fifty program. *Health Education Quarterly, 16,* 509–527.

Rose, M. A. (1992). Evaluation of a peer-education program on heart disease prevention with older adults. *Public Health Nursing, 1992, 9,* 242–247.

Simmons, J. J. (Ed.). (1989). Staying healthy after 50: Experiences in creating and disseminating a health promotion program. *Health Education Quarterly, 16,* 45–550.

Slymen, D. J., Drew, J. A., Wright, B. L., Elder, J. P., & Williams, S. J. (1992). Compliance with a 12-month assessment in an elderly cohort participating in a preventive intervention study: The San Diego Medicare Preventive Health project. *International Journal of Epidemiology, 21,* 701–706.

Stevens, V. J., Hornbrook, M. C., Wingfield, D. J., Hollis, J. F., Greenlick, M. R., & Ory, M. G. (1991–1992). Design and implementation of a falls prevention intervention for community-dwelling older persons. *Behavior, Health, and Aging, 2,* 57–73.

Stone, E. J., McGraw, S. A., Osganian, S. K., & Elder, J. P. (Eds.). (1994). Process evaluation in the multicenter Child and Adolescent Trial for Cardiovascular Health (CATCH). *Health Education Quarterly, 2*(Supplement), S3–S142.

Teresi, J., Lawton, M. P., Ory, M., & Holmes, D. (1994). Measurement issues in chronic care populations: Dementia special care. *Alzheimer Disease and Associated Disorders, 8,* S144–S183.

Tinetti, M. E., Baker, D. I., McAvay, G., Claus, E. B., Garrett, P., Gottschalk, M., Koch, M. L., Trainor, K., & Horwitz, R. I. (1994). A multifactorial intervention to reduce the risk of falling among elderly people living in the community. *New England Journal of Medicine, 331,* 821–827.

Topp, R., Mikesky, A., Wigglesworth, J., Holt, W., & Edwards, J. E. (1993). The effect of a 12-week dynamic resistance strength training program on gait velocity and balance of older adults. *The Gerontologist, 33,* 501–506.

Vetter, N. J., & Ford, D. (1990). Smoking prevention among people aged 60 and over: A randomized controlled trial. *Age and Ageing, 19,* 164–168.

Vickery, D. M., Golaszewski, T. J., Wright, E. C., & Kalmer, H. (1988). The effect of self-care interventions on the use of medical service within a Medicare population. *Medical Care, 26,* 580–588.

Wagner, E. H., Grothaus, L. C., Hecht, J. A., & LaCroix, A. Z. (1991). Factors associated with participation in a senior health promotion program. *The Gerontologist, 31,* 598–602.

Weinrich, S. P., Weinrich, M. C., Stromberg, M. F., Boyd, M. D., & Weiss, H. L. (1993). Using elderly educators to increase colorectal cancer screening. *The Gerontologist, 33,* 491–496.

Wells, T. J., Brink, C. A., Diokno, A. C., Wolfe, R., & Gillis, G. L. (1991). Pelvic muscle exercise for stress urinary incontinence in elderly women. *Journal of the American Geriatrics Society, 39,* 785–791.

CHAPTER 5

Enhancing Self-Care Research: Exploring the Theoretical Underpinnings of Self-Care

Elaine A. Leventhal, Howard Leventhal, and Chantal Robitaille

T he excellent literature reviews in this volume's preceding chapters tell us about factors affecting older people's responses to their symptoms (Stoller, chapter 2), make suggestions as to how we might structure programs to improve self-care behaviors (Prohaska, chapter 3), and give us criteria for evaluating effectiveness of such self-care programs (Rakowski, chapter 4). The data generated from the descriptive studies reported in these reviews are important for setting health policies and practice requirements. They are also important for the development of theory as they direct investigators to important research questions.

The purpose of this chapter is to review major theoretical approaches underlying self-care processes. Drawing on key elements from other models, the authors present a self-regulation approach to self-care and explore the implications of this model for improving clinical practice.

An understanding of theoretical underpinnings is important for several reasons. First, in the absence of theory, it will be difficult to understand failures of replication and to reconcile contradictory findings. Theory plays a critical role by helping us to identify contextual factors that can moderate outcomes and produce apparently contradictory findings. Contextual factors include sociocultural factors (e.g., socioeconomic status, level of education) and personal factors (e.g., gender, personality). An important personal factor and one we are particularly interested in is age. In many if not most studies, age is treated as a variable that has direct effects on outcomes such as use of medical care, disease rates, and mortality. Our approach treats age as a contextual factor (i.e., as a factor that affects outcomes such as medical care, disease rates, and mortality) because age is associated with changes in the meaning ascribed to symptoms, beliefs about the utility of medical care, and immunological changes that affect ability to fend off pathogens. Thus, age is treated as a moderator of the variables comprising our process model of self-care. Theory also specifies the appropriate operations for the creation and assessment of variables and allows us to determine whether replication failures are due to shortcomings of theory (i.e., to misconstructions of the process underlying behavior) or to deficits in establishing the operations for the creation and measurement of independent and dependent variables.

Second, theory is critical for devising interventions and changing behavior. Understanding the process underlying health-damaging and health-promoting behaviors allows us to establish conditions to weaken the former and strengthen the latter. Thus, although it is important to identify these types of behaviors, the individuals performing them, and where they take place, this knowledge alone is insufficient to devise educational or therapeutic interventions for behavioral change. Theory is critical for the practice as well as for the study of self-care.

THEORY AND THE SELF-CARE PROCESS

Once we accept the importance of theory in self-care research, we must ask, "Which theory should we use?" Should we work with one of the currently popular theories, such as the health belief model (Becker & Maiman, 1975; Rosenstock, 1966), the theory of planned behavior (Ajzen, 1988), or social learning theory (Bandura, 1969), or should we elaborate a model of our own? This is not an easy question to answer. The use of constructs derived from social learning theory (e.g., self-efficacy) is reasonable for situations involving the replacement of undesirable, automatic behaviors with healthy, but complex and difficult to learn behaviors. Examples of this type of situation include smoking cessation (DiClemente, Prochaska, & Gibertini, 1985), the adoption and maintenance of a cardiovascular fitness exercise program (McAuley, Lox, & Duncan, 1993), and the management of chronic swelling, stiffness and pain of arthritis (Lorig, Chastain, Ung, Shoor, & Holman, 1989). By contrast, the use of constructs from the health belief model and the theory of planned behavior such as risk perception, social norms relating to the execution of a behavior, and motivation to avoid exposure to threat information, are likely relevant for studies concerned with the adoption of behaviors that demand little personal skill, such as mammography screening or participation in genetic testing (Lerman, Rimer, & Engstrom, 1991).

It is appropriate to select a theoretical model by evaluating its fit to the problem. Descriptive data can be of help with this task; they define the problem and help establish the parameters with which the theory must cope. A key question, therefore, is whether the parameters defined by descriptive studies of self-care can be matched to the constructs of existent models. This question is of special importance for evaluating models that combine risk perception constructs with constructs for the acquisition of behavioral skills.

The Attributes of the Self-Care Process

What are the key attributes of self-care behaviors and how might they influence our choice of theory? Self-care refers to a complex domain of behavior defined by multiple parameters. These include:

- *Acquisition status:* Does self-care refer to a behavior that is to be discarded or a behavior that is to be acquired?
- *Disease specificity:* Is the behavior relevant to a specific disease (e.g., a cause of cancer) or is it generic (e.g., health damaging)?
- *Motivation:* Is the target population motivated to engage in the desired behavior?
- *Prevention orientation:* Is the behavior designed to prevent a prospective disease threat or detect and cure an existent one?
- *Private versus social:* Is the behavior private, performed alone and without social support, or public, performed by many people and open to social support or social inhibition?
- *Response repertoires:* Does cessation or initiation of the behavior require practice and the acquisition of new skills, or is it well within existent response repertoires?
- *Timeline of response:* Is the behavior a one time affair and/or performed over a limited time frame, or does it require a long-term commitment?

- *Range and evolution of possible behaviors:* Is the behavior one of several behaviors comprising a treatment regimen that evolves over time?

If each of these eight parameters is treated as a dichotomous variable, they will generate a matrix of 256 cells. As several of the cells are complex, (e.g., the behavior can be a single action or one of several acts, the behavior(s) in the regimen may or may not change over time), the matrix may be larger still. And it takes only a little imagination to add still other dimensions by means of questions such as: "Is the behavior driven by a health concern, a disease concern, or neither?" "Do self-care practices change over the life span?" The matrix created by descriptive parameters soon defies understanding.

Do Existent Theories Address the Parameters of the Self-Care Process?

How well do existent theoretical models address the parameters of self-care? We will address that question with respect to each of two sets of models: (a) those designed to deal with risk perception, such as the health belief model (Rosenstock, 1966) and the theory of reasoned action (Ajzen & Fishbein, 1980) and (b) those designed to deal with changes in behavior and acquisition of skills, that is, learning approaches such as social learning theory (Bandura, 1969) and cognitive behavior therapy (Meichenbaum, 1977).

Modeling Risk Perception

The health belief model approaches risk perception from a utility framework: a probability factor (i.e., the perception of vulnerability to a disease threat) times a value factor (i.e., the perceived severity of the threat) defines the strength of motivation for action (Rosenstock, 1966). The specific action chosen is a function of the costs and benefits of each of the responses available for avoiding or controlling the threat.

The concepts in the theory of reasoned action are essentially similar to those of the health belief model. The dependent measure, *intention* to perform a specific health promotive response (or to eliminate a response that threatens health), is the sum of the product of the probabilities relating the response to personal values or utilities. Personal values include factors such as the desire to avoid a disease threat and the perceived costs and benefits of the response. The theory also includes a social influence factor. Each response has a social value which is the product of the individual's perception of other persons' opinions about the response (a normative factor) multiplied by the importance of these other persons. The two sets of values, personal and social, are summed to predict intention and the response that has the highest positive value will be selected.

Models of Skill/Behavioral Competence

Models for skill acquisition and perceived competence in performance derive from learning theory. Cognitive behavior therapy (Meichenbaum, 1977), the most pervasive of such models, includes constructs such as self-monitoring, an observational procedure to detect the cues (occasions) for the elicitation of undesired responses and occasions for performing desirable responses. Homework assignments are prescribed to ensure the practice of desired responses and to assure appropriate expectations regarding the outcome of these new responses, which constitutes the reward for their performance.

Practice on cue and the reception of reward are key elements of most learning frameworks. The learning approaches add two other important constructs: *modeling* and *self-efficacy* (Bandura, 1977). Modeling refers to learning by observation while self-efficacy refers to confidence in one's ability to perform specific responses. Neither the cognitive nor the social learning framework includes formal constructs to assess risk as seen in the risk perception models.

Do Integrations Address the Deficits?

Prior research (Leventhal, 1970; Leventhal & Watts, 1966; Leventhal, Watts, & Pagano, 1967) and common sense suggest that self-protective action depends upon the combination of risk perception with action plans and skills. Risk perception defines the problem and/or goals for performance, while action plans and skills provide the map and response competencies for performance. The obvious need for the combination has led investigators to incorporate action constructs, such as self-efficacy, into both the health belief model (Rosenstock, Stretcher, & Becker, 1988) and the theory of reasoned action (which was renamed the theory of planned behavior) (Ajzen, 1988). Consider, for example, the case of a 55-year-old male who adopted a low fat diet instead of an exercise program to prevent heart disease. An analysis of his decision from the perspective of the revised health belief model might find that he was motivated to take preventive action because he felt vulnerable to heart disease and believed heart disease to be life threatening. Because he did his own cooking but had never engaged in vigorous activity, he felt he was able to make the dietary change (self-efficacy present), but unable to engage in exercise (lack of self-efficacy for exercise). He made the choice even though he believed both actions were equally effective for the prevention of heart disease. While these integrations appear to be steps forward, they fail to resolve a host of problems.

First, none of these commonly used models addresses the role of emotional factors in changing risky behaviors and adopting healthy actions. Given the potential impact of emotions such as fear, depression, and anger upon health behaviors and health, this omission clearly needs to be rectified.

The second problem concerns the modeling of risk or perceived vulnerability. Many persons make all-or-none judgments when assessing likelihoods, either because they can not or will not make graded judgments. More important, perhaps, asking for risk judgments during an interview fails to assess the database that subjects access when they actually perform a risky or healthy behavior. For example, the conditions during an interview in which subjects report on the likelihood that they will avoid smoking are very unlikely to include the specific sights, odors, and sounds that provoke this behavior.

In addition to ignoring emotional factors and continuing to rely on probabilistic judgments to predict action, the combined models ignore at least five other dimensions relevant to the self-care process:

- They do not provide substantive constructs to capture the way different diseases create feelings of vulnerability.
- They do not deal with the perceived causes of disease and the relationship of perceived cause to the selection of preventive and/or treatment behavior.
- They do not address issues related to the perceived time course of disease and treatment.
- They do not provide ways of conceptualizing changes in the perception of threat and appropriateness and success of treatment(s) over time.

In our judgment, incorporating the self-efficacy construct from social learning theory into either the health belief model or the theory of reasoned action does not compensate for either model's deficiencies because the deficits reside in the way the models conceptualize the risk perception process. Self-efficacy does not address these issues. It attempts to account for phenomena such as willingness to act in the face of barriers or persistence in the acquisition of skills such as those developed in smoking cessation or weight reduction programs. Individuals in these programs have already decided to participate in treatment because they believe they are at risk (Leventhal, Baker, Brandon, & Flemming, 1989). The analysis of self-care behaviors, however, requires constructs that address the decision to initiate and to sustain care. These constructs must be applicable to widely varying environments, from those where risks are remote and preventive behaviors are called for, through those where appropriate procedures for controlling highly ambiguous cues must be selected, to those where prescribed treatments are initiated and performed.

A model of self-care also needs to account for the contribution of individual differences to the self-care process. The data for such factors are often confusing and sometimes contradictory. For example, the elderly display both more positive and more negative self-health behaviors than their younger counterparts (e.g., they are more careful about diet but less likely to exercise) (Prohaska, Keller, Leventhal, & Leventhal, 1987). They are more likely to utilize health care (Prohaska et al., 1987), yet they are less likely to adhere to hypertension medication regimens (Morrell, Park, Kidder, & Martin, 1997). The self-regulation model we will propose will help explain such contradictions because it accounts for motivation and integrates risk perception with response performance.

SELF-REGULATION: A FRAMEWORK
FOR THE COMMON SENSE OF SELF-CARE

To resolve the above problems, the model of self-care must satisfy the following conditions: First, it must capture the individual's representation of the environment, that is, his or her view of a potential or current health risk. This representation and its features define the problem as perceived and understood by the individual. Second, the model must specify the procedures used to identify and defend against the risk, and procedures for evaluating response outcomes. In sum, the individual is a problem solver who selects procedures to control risks on the basis of their perceived or psychological connection to the representation. Third, the model must represent the emotional reactions accompanying the process of recognizing, representing, and coping with threat, and the interactions among the affective and cognitive domains. Fourth, the problem-solving process, that is, the representation of the threat and procedures for its management, must be nested within and integrated with contextual factors that generate and modify the self-regulation process. Contextual factors include facets of the individual's personal make-up (e.g., age, perceptions of vulnerability to disease, etc.), and features of the sociocultural context in which she or he resides. Finally, the model needs to allow for a wide range of motives and behaviors not directly related to health that may affect the self-care process.

The self-regulation model below is designed to meet these objectives. To illustrate the power of the model we also present research findings and make suggestions for further studies.

A Self-Regulation Model for the Analysis of the Self-Care Process

Figure 5.1 presents a simplified view of a self-regulation model that we have been using for the past 30 years to understand how people explain and manage somatic events. It is a general framework for the analysis of the representation and management of health threats whether the information about the threat is first conveyed by a somatic experience, contact with another person, or a media event. Figure 5.1 illustrates two parallel tracks of processing. The upper track represents the individual's phenomenal reality, that is, the world as perceived by the actor. The lower track represents the generation of emotional responses that accompany phenomenal reality (Leventhal, Diefenbach, & Leventhal, 1992; see also Leventhal, 1970, for an earlier version). For example, with respect to symptom processing, the upper track refers to the individual's construction of a representation of a somatic sensation, that is, the transformation of a sensation to a symptom (Leventhal & Leventhal, 1993). This is followed by the generation of action plans and procedures for managing the symptom, and ends with the appraisal of anticipated and actual response outcomes. Outcome appraisals are judgments of the degree to which the execution of a particular plan meets expectations. These evaluations include estimates of the barriers and facilitators to the performance of a procedure during planning, the gains and losses experienced during response performance, and judgments of the efficiency and effectiveness of the procedure for reaching the expected outcome. The feedback from these

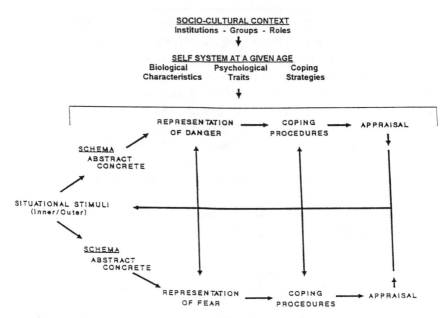

FIGURE 5.1 A model of the process involved in the representation, coping, and appraisal of symptoms and associated emotional responses. Emotional reactions can be generated by the symptom itself (e.g., pain), by the representation of a symptom (e.g., a cancer vs. injury), by the appraisal of coping, and by extraneous life stressors. The system is dynamic and changes over time with new information from coping, from the social environment, and from the cultural context. These inputs can affect every component in the model.

appraisals can lead to emotional reactions, reevaluation and changes in coping procedures, and changes in the representation of the disease threat and the criteria for evaluating outcomes.

The lower arm of the model depicts the possible emotional reactions to the threat and the coping strategies and outcome appraisals involved in the regulation of emotional reactions. The model suggests that the emotional responses are elicited in parallel by the same stimuli that create awareness of the threat (e.g., urethral bleeding, a lump in the breast or abdominal pain), or by other steps in the problem-solving process. Thus the emotional response will change in response to alterations in the meaning assigned a somatic stimulus as well as in response to success or failure in coping with it. Processing in each of the tracks can be initiated and moderated by social information such as comments from a family member about one's appearance, a physician's diagnosis or report on one's health status, and health messages in mass media.

The processing of somatic information extends over time, though not in the unidirectional manner implied by Figure 5.1. As an illness episode unfolds, the somatic sensations and their meaning will change as will plans, response procedures, and outcome appraisals. A variety of stage models have been proposed to define temporal patterns or typical sequences for such change. For example, our group has differentiated three such stages: (a) an appraisal stage which begins when an individual first notices a somatic change or is exposed to information about an illness threat and evaluates the significance of the information for the self (see Misovich, Fisher, & Fisher, 1997); (b) an illness phase, which is the interval beginning with the decision that one is ill and during which one might try a variety of self-care procedures prior to calling for medical assistance; and (c) a utilization phase, the interval beginning with the call for assistance to the point of contact with the care system (E. Leventhal, Leventhal, Schaefer, & Easterling, 1993; Safer, Tharps, Jackson, & Leventhal, 1979). Several similar models (see Alonzo, 1980; Caccioppo, Anderson, Turnquist, & Petty, 1985) extend the stages into treatment and recovery. Studies show that different aspects of the representation and different coping strategies are salient at different stages. For example, fear of treatment and avoidance strategies tend to come into play after the decision that one is ill has been made. Thus they are more salient during the "illness"stage than during the appraisal stage (E. Leventhal et al., 1993; Safer et al., 1979).

While stage models are helpful in simplifying our view of illness episodes, it is important to recognize that the temporal elaboration does not proceed in a simple, forward direction. The cues reminding us of the possibility or presence of an illness threat will enter and exit awareness due to changes in somatic symptoms (Easterling & Leventhal, 1989), the occurrence of disease in friends and relatives, and social and media information pointing to correlates and causes of disease. These cues or reminders activate the associative links connecting concepts of the self to concepts of disease. The result is a sense of personal vulnerability. As most illnesses wax and wane, there will be considerable back and forth movement in the self-regulation processes. Unfortunately, the definitions given to a stage suggest that it is a period of time in which specific processes take place (e.g., DiClemente et al., 1991). A stage is defined, however, by the processes themselves. For example, while the same procedures, such as using an over-the-counter medication, may be active during the appraisal and illness stages, the questions and appraisal criteria will differ; in the former the question will be whether the procedure identifies the symptom as a sign of illness; in the latter, whether the procedure can control or cure the illness. Indeed, in many instances it will be difficult to define clear boundaries between the stages.

The Content of Representations and Self-Care

The self-regulation model stimulated research that identified specific attributes of illness representations. To date, five attributes have been conceptualized: identity (i.e., symptoms and labels), time line (Meyer, Leventhal, & Gutmann, 1985), consequences (Croyle & Jemmott, 1991), causes, and controllability (Lau & Hartmann, 1983). This list may not be exhaustive (see Skelton & Croyle, 1991) and several of these attributes will undergo further differentiation. Studies showed how these attributes affect patients' adherence to prescribed medical regimens, that is, how self-care moderated prescribed care. Because many illnesses can be grouped as acute (flu, head colds, etc.), cyclic (allergies), or chronic (diabetes, arthritis, cancer), the model suggests that we will find combinations of these attributes, or psychological patterns or schemata, that correspond to these classifications. As acute conditions are most common, we can also expect that the initial representation of most illnesses will be as acute diseases, regardless of their actual chronicity.

A basic proposition of the self-regulation model is that representations are coded both abstractly (propositionally) and concretely (perceptually). Attributes are represented in the mind as labels and perceptual experiences, and the two are symmetrically linked. Thus we found, somewhat to our surprise, that perceptual experiences generate a representation of an illness for the self that differs from that based solely on abstract knowledge. Conflict between what we say we "know," and what we "feel," occurs across a wide range of conditions. Reactions to antidepressant medication provide an excellent and unstudied example. Depressed persons are told, and they know, that it will take 2 to 3 weeks before they will experience any benefit from their medication. Within hours or days, however, they feel symptoms such as dry mouth and fatigue, but they do not feel benefits in elevations of positive mood. Because they can feel the drug working, their "felt" time is discrepant with their conceptual time (i.e., 3 weeks), raising doubts about the efficacy of their treatment.

Temporal expectations are linked to every attribute of the representation and to every procedure for the avoidance and control of the threat. We have ideas about how long it should take for a disease to develop and how long it should take for a treatment to work. As these ideas are generally concordant with past experience with acute disease, it is no wonder that we do less than we might to take long-term preventive action. Thus, our temporal expectations are often inappropriate for the prevention and control of chronic illnesses. If we believe that lung cancer hits at a later age, we may think that we don't have to worry about it now, or if we think that heart disease can be cured, why bother with prevention. Another example is the apparently contradictory beliefs about breast cancer that have been reported among some older women. While there is agreement that early detection and treatment is important, some older women also state that cancer is untreatable and always fatal. The contradiction appears to reflect a differentiation of the early and later stages of the disease. The early stages of disease are understood as an acute condition, hence as "noncancer," while the later stages are understood as chronic and fatal, hence "cancer" (Gregg & Curry, 1994). Beliefs of this sort affect the perceived rationality and utility of engaging in self-care behaviors at different points in the history of a life-threatening disease.

Emotional Reactions and Self-Care

Emotional reactions such as fear, anger, and depression are commonly reported in response to the threats of disease and the pain and discomfort associated with both disease and its treatment (Johnston & Wallace, 1990). The self-regulation model suggests that the nature of the emotional experience will vary as a function of the representation of the threat (e.g., the level of threat and fear will be greater when illness is seen as life threatening, uncontrollable, and immediate). The model also predicts that emotion can have direct effects upon the representation of the threat, making it appear more severe. Emotion can also affect the procedures for threat management by inhibiting worthwhile self-care behaviors that are perceived as bringing one closer to the threat and encouraging both appropriate and potentially inappropriate self-care behaviors that are seen, accurately or not, as leading away from and preventing the threat (Millar & Millar, 1995).

Whether the emotional experience in response to a health threat is fear, depression, anger, or simple distress will reflect attributes of the representation such as its timeline, perceived controllability, and consequences. Fear and anxiety will be likely responses to the worsening symptoms of a disease that is painful and difficult to control. This fear may turn into depression following repeated failure of control efforts (Abramson, Seligman, &

Teasdale, 1978). The reciprocal relationship among representations, coping procedures, and emotional experience can have a direct effect on symptom experience. The intensity of the pain experience will increase when emotional distress is amplified in response to loss of control over a pain-provoking noxious stimulus (Baron & Logan, 1993).

The inhibition of self-care preventive behaviors was shown in our early studies of fear communications, although the inhibitory effects appeared only for some self-care behaviors, for a subset of study participants and for a relatively brief duration (Leventhal, 1970). More recent studies have found fear-motivated avoidance to be more salient when somatic sensations are identified as signs of potentially serious physical illness, that is, during the stage of illness delay (E. Leventhal, Easterling, Leventhal, & Cameron, 1995; Safer et al., 1979). It is likely that action is inhibited during this time frame, while the individual contemplates possible consequences, such as pain, surgery, and loss of function associated with the treatment of potentially serious diseases.

Finally, negative affect induced by life stress can have complex effects on self-care decisions, sometimes increasing and sometimes decreasing decisions to seek medical care for new symptoms. Cameron, Leventhal, and Leventhal (1995) found that life stressors affected care seeking for older subjects only when symptoms were ambiguous. When new symptoms were ambiguous and unclear as indicators of illness, life stress encouraged care seeking only when the stressors had been present for 3 weeks and longer (40% sought care). If the life stress was of recent onset, however, ambiguous symptoms were interpreted as signs of stress and few subjects sought care (20%). On the other hand, when symptoms were clear indications of medical problems, older subjects sought care whether or not they were experiencing other sources of life stress. These findings make clear the complexity of care-seeking decisions.

The Contribution of the Self-Regulation Perspective

The self-regulation model has addressed several of the five concerns ignored by prior models. The substantive constructs in the model, concepts such as identity (symptom and label) and timeline (acute and chronic) represent key attributes of illness representations that people use to formulate goals and to guide and evaluate both self-selected and professionally recommended treatment. These conceptual units allow one to understand and to predict what procedures an individual is likely to adopt to manage a disease threat and how consistently and effectively they are likely to be used. Perceptions of cause—a less studied construct—will also affect the selection of self-care procedures.

The model also addresses the ever-evolving nature of the self-regulation process. Representations of a disease change over time, as do the procedures adopted for its control. Further, self-regulation theory recognizes that emotional processes have a direct role in the self-care process. This role is both inhibitory (e.g., active and present negative emotions can undermine self-efficacy) and motivating (e.g., negative emotions can activate procedures that resolve a disease threat in order to reduce emotional distress).

Self-Regulation Occurs in Context

The context for self-regulation includes both the personal characteristics of the individual and sociocultural factors. Both sets of factors can have direct and indirect effects. Direct effects can be seen when social factors motivate specific self-care procedures (e.g., a person may seek expert advice for a symptom because of the urging of a spouse, or a person may adopt a self-care procedure to meet social expectations of attractiveness). Personal and sociocultural factors act indirectly when they influence self-care behaviors because they affect the representation of a disease threat, the perceived availability and utility of procedures for treatment and prevention, the criteria used for evaluating treatment outcome, and/or the evaluation of treatment outcome.

Personal Factors: The Self-Relevance Switch

The representation and procedures associated with the management of a potential disease threat change in character when that threat moves from an abstraction (i.e., something one has read or heard about in the mass media), to an event that has personal relevance to oneself. This transition is especially important for behaviors designed to prevent future, currently imperceptible threats, although it has not received a great deal of discussion in prior expositions of our self-regulation approach (e.g., Leventhal et al., 1992; Leventhal, Meyer, & Nerenz, 1980). Our theoretical and empirical efforts have focused upon issues of self-management in response to ongoing illnesses, that is, cases where somatic changes (i.e., symptoms and signs) define the personal relevance of the health problem. Understanding the factors responsible for the transition to personal relevance is crucial for both the development of theory and practice.

Even when symptoms are present, however, a host of factors operate to enhance or minimize their self-relevance, which affect motivation and decisions for action. One such set of factors has emerged in our studies of the speed of seeking medical care by elderly in comparison to middle-aged persons. Our data showed (E. Leventhal et al., 1993) that elderly persons (over age 65), in comparison to middle-aged persons (ages 45 to 55), were motivated to minimize risk and avoid the depletion of resources when confronting symptoms seen as potentially serious threats to health. This risk aversion was apparent in the elderly subjects' swifter response to identify somatic symptoms as signs of illness and in their reduced avoidance of care seeking once they decided they were ill.

That older persons should adopt a conservation risk avoidance strategy should be no surprise. As people age, they become aware of and openly discuss changes in their resources, including reductions in energy level. Strategies to conserve and appropriately deploy available resources make good sense and can be observed at the biological, psychological and social level (Baltes & Baltes, 1990; Carstensen, 1992). Other motivational and coping effects are likely to emerge as we examine individual differences in responses at different stages of the illness episode.

Interpersonal Influence

Many people believe that private experience (e.g., symptoms, feelings of fatigue, moods, etc.) are the primary sources of information that people use for evaluating their health status. Social communication, however, exerts powerful effects on health behavior. In some respects, self-observation is limited; for example, we rely on others quite regularly for information on how we look. Comments such as "Do you feel okay?", "Were you up late?", can provide a strong impetus to self-observation, and more pointed remarks such as "You look tired," "Your color looks bad," or "It looks as if you have a rash on your face," can stimulate more active help seeking.

Stoller's review (chapter 2) makes clear that the interpretation and management of symptoms is embedded in a sociocultural context and that the self-regulation process might better be labeled "social self-regulation." All facets of the self-regulation system, that is, the representation or meaning assigned a symptom, the planning and performance of procedures for controlling it, and the appraisal of outcomes, are influenced by social communications as well as by the knowledge and temperamental characteristics of the actor. Social communication can be direct (e.g., sought and unsought advice from family, friends, and health professionals), indirect (e.g., observation of the nature and management of health problems in others), and culture-wide, (e.g., exposure to mass media and the institutions, values, and language of the culture) (see Cameron, Leventhal, & Leventhal, 1993).

The importance of the cultural context in defining the meaning of somatic symptoms and selecting procedures for management has been discussed at length by medical anthropologists (Chrisman, 1977). Kleinman (1980) has elaborated on the way in which Chinese culture and family values affect the interpretation of psychological symptoms and influence the choice of traditional or Western medicine. The impact of culture can be exceedingly selective. For example, the very same individuals may select traditional medicine on some occasions and Western medicine on others as a function of the perceived cause of the disorder, that is, whether it is caused by natural (choose Western) or spiritual agents (choose traditional).

The Self-Regulation Model and Our Understanding
of the Social Influence Process

Far too little is known about the way in which contextual factors influence the process of symptom self-regulation. Studies of individual differences have focused on factors such as hypochondriasis and illness behavior (Mechanic, 1986; Pilowsky, 1986) in order to identify individuals with strong proclivities to use health care and to attend to, report (Watson & Pennebaker, 1989), and remember illness symptomatology (Brownlee, Leventhal, & Balaban, 1992; Larsen, 1992). Other studies have examined the contribution of individual differences such as "health locus of control" (Wallston & Wallston, 1982) and self-efficacy (Bandura, 1977), factors that are expected to affect likelihood of engaging in active self-care procedures. Studies of self-efficacy have proliferated in several disease areas because of its ease of assessment. Virtually none of these studies, however, has examined how these individual difference factors work, that is, how they affect the self-regulation process and how they are affected in turn by other self-regulation factors.

Finally, as the relationship between the self-regulation system and the context is bidirectional, it is startling that virtually no studies have examined how and when symptom representations and coping procedures affect cultural values and the structure of the health care system. Personal experience with the wide array of symptoms and pain generated during the treatment of an uncontrollable, chronic disease can create local "cultures" of fear and despair with respect to a disease such as breast or colon cancer. These experiences can motivate individuals to enhance self-management by the creation of social arrangements ranging from self-help groups to political movements that demand new governmental organizations dedicated to the study and treatment of particular diseases. The most recent example is the impact of advocacy groups on research and treatment for HIV and breast cancer.

Prediction (Main Effects) May not Lead to Understanding

Many investigators enter factors such as gender and race in their statistical models in their efforts to predict behaviors that affect health. While these factors cannot be ignored, it is essential to recognize that they may enable us to improve our predictions of behavior while doing little to help us understand its determinants. Race and gender are complex variables, that is, they are internally heterogeneous and stand for a multifactor set of variables, of which any one or a combination may be responsible for observed differences among groups. As different factors within these sets may affect different outcomes, one must not assume that the same factors are responsible for differences among Blacks and Whites in disease rates, response to symptoms, and frequency of risk-taking behavior.

A major challenge facing the investigator, therefore, is to identify the factors mediating group differences. Meeting this challenge requires two steps: the development of models to account for specific outcomes (e.g., specific health and/or risk behaviors and specific diseases) within each group, and the identification of the factor(s) or pattern of factors responsible for particular group differences (see Dean, 1992). Each step requires multiple, cross-sectional and longitudinal investigations, and each will confront many complex problems. For example, if one finds contrasting disease outcomes in Hispanics versus Whites, or Blacks versus Whites, and wishes to see if self-care processes contribute to these differences, at the very minimum one must confront the following problems:

- The groups are not homogenous (e.g., Blacks may be African American or Caribbean; Hispanics may be Mexican, Puerto Rican, Cuban or of other South American origin).
- The groups differ on a host of factors associated with and in addition to race and/or ethnicity (e.g., education, income, religious identification, family size and structure, etc.), each of which may be respon-

sible for different outcomes and/or contribute differentially to the same outcome.

- The "same" variable or behavior may have a different meaning within each group (e.g., a college education may imply different degrees of learning, different social status, and/or different degrees of deviation from cultural norms for Hispanics from Cuba and Mexico).
- Individuals in a minority classification may be acculturated to different degrees to the values and behaviors of the majority (Hazuda, Stern, & Haffner, 1984). Assessment of both degree of acculturation and description of the values and behaviors of the minority and the majority culture will be needed.

In short, understanding group differences in the meaning and use of self-care requires a substantial research effort by multiple groups of investigators committed to a common analytic framework.

SELF-CARE AND THE HEALTH CARE SYSTEM

The final questions we wish to raise concern how the health care system, specifically the physician and nurse, can collaborate with, rather than ignore or work against, the self-care and self-regulation processes embedded in individual dispositions and group culture. In other words, how can the practitioner enlist the patient's active problem-solving processes to serve the needs of biologically sound self-care practices, whether these practices are focused on prevention, early diagnosis, treatment, and/or rehabilitation?

Most current intervention research is guided by one or another of the many existent cognitive-behavioral or social learning models, both of which focus heavily on behavioral skills. The cognitive-behavioral model emphasizes the individual's commitment to mental and overt rehearsal of behavioral skills while the social learning perspective emphasizes the development of a sense of self-efficacy. Although social learning models can accommodate both representational and appraisal processes, the models guiding research from that framework have paid relatively little attention to these factors (for exceptions see Goldfried & D'Zurilla, 1969, and Kanfer, 1977). The self-regulation framework proposed here argues that to be successful, interventions must attend to and integrate all components of the symptom self-regulation system.

What burden does a systems approach place on the practitioner? At the least, it suggests that the practitioner should identify the key features of patients' representations, that is, the somatic cues being monitored, their interpretation or labeling, their perceived cause, anticipated consequences, the anticipated timelines for both consequences and treatment, and the expectations regarding cure and control. Although monitoring requires that more time be allocated to physicians for each patient visit, a problem in today's managed care environment, a better understanding of the patient's representations would allow the physician to address competing representations and lead to improved self-care, which may ultimately decrease the number of needed visits. However, when an intervention focuses on only a part of the system, it can create the conditions for the individual to move away from biologically meaningful self-regulation. For example, providing self-efficacy training for the management of medication use while ignoring the way somatic sensations are attended to and interpreted, can lead a hypertensive patient to perfect use of medication in synchrony with symptoms such as face-flushing and headache that have little or no relationship to tonic blood pressure. Similarly, the physician who reassures a somatically vigilant individual that his visceral pains are benign but does not link it to a system, that is, define the elicitors of these pains and the procedures that can be used to regulate their intensity, leaves the individual with an unexplained and unregulated problem. When these pains recur, the individual will then try to control them without physician's counsel. The procedures used in this problem-solving effort may generate inaccurate reinterpretations of the identity, timeline, consequences (threat value), and controllability of the sensations.

CONCLUDING REMARKS

Self-care includes what we do at home and at work, by ourselves and in conjunction with friends and family to improve health and prevent, treat, and rehabilitate from both acute and chronic illness. It also includes how we decide to seek professional care, and what we do in adhering to or deviating from the treatment regimens provided by our expert advisors. Most importantly, self-care includes how people maintain function by the appropriate monitoring and execution of medical regimens that are to be performed as needed. Self-care is a vital part of health maintenance and disease avoidance across a full spectrum of diseases and treatments. It vanishes only when we are unconscious and are no longer participating in the treatment of our physical ills.

We have proposed a self-regulation framework for viewing and understanding the self-care process across these many different settings. Because the framework includes substantive constructs that are disease relevant, it directly addresses the self-care process. As it provides insight into the process, it provides clues for intervention; the constructs of the model are lodged in the database that people use to regulate health threats. The constructs are phrased, therefore, in language that can be used to address people about their risk perceptions and the relevance and value of behaviors that are effective for risk reduction.

There is a significant transition, however, from modeling the self-regulation process, that is, measuring the constructs that capture people's representations and procedures, to knowing how to address and/or intervene to change the self-regulation system. Knowing a construct by measurement is not the same as knowing it by manipulation. To address intervention in detail, we would have to explain how to uncover and communicate with the self-regulation process. For example, the model implies that health practitioners can best succeed in shaping the health protective and treatment behavior of the public if the two sides share a common representation of a disease risk and agree on the procedures best designed for prevention and treatment. Sharing, however, is a difficult task and can best occur in one-on-one relationships. If physicians were given adequate time and trained in techniques needed to elicit patients' views of their somatic conditions and in ways of shaping these views to better correspond with the psycho-biological factors controlling the patients' somatic experience, we could expect substantial improvement in adherence behaviors. And we could expect better use of treatments that are to be performed as needed.

Further, patients, practitioners, and investigators will benefit if the self-management of symptoms is placed in a larger self-regulation context. Investigators will benefit by having a model that identifies a broad set of factors affecting self-care and suggests hypotheses as to how they are interrelated. They will also be able to see how the representation and regulation of somatic experience may affect health-related behaviors, such as smoking and substance use, that are not typically considered within the framework of the self-management of symptoms. Finally, a self-regulation perspective on the processes of health and illness management will allow investigators to make a much needed contribution to behavioral science theory and to provide practitioners with a broader array of effective interventions to enhance health. The successful application of these principles will depend in large part on the structure and delivery of the health care system, which is undergoing unprecedented changes.

REFERENCES

Abramson, L. Y., Seligman, M. E. P., & Teasdale, J. (1978). Learned helplessness in humans: Critique and reformulation. *Journal of Abnormal Psychology, 87,* 49–74.

Alonzo, A. A. (1980). Acute illness behavior: A conceptual exploration and specification. *Social Science & Medicine, 14,* 515–526.

Ajzen, I. (1988). *Attitudes, personality, and behavior.* Homewood, IL: Dorsey.

Ajzen, I., & Fishbein, M. (1980). *Understanding attitudes and predicting social behavior.* Englewood Cliffs, NJ: Prentice Hall.

Baltes P. B., & Baltes, M. M. (1990). Psychological perspectives on successful aging: The model of selective optimization with compensation. In P. B. Baltes & M. M. Baltes (Eds.), *Successful aging: Perspectives from the behavioral sciences* (pp.1-34). Cambridge, MA: Cambridge University Press.

Bandura, A. (1969). *Principles of behavior modification.* New York: Holt, Rinehart & Winston.

Bandura, A. (1977). Self efficacy: Toward a unifying theory of behavioral change. *Psychological Review, 84,* 191–215.

Baron, R. S., & Logan, H. (1993). Desired control, felt control, and dental pain: Recent findings and remaining issues. *Motivation and Emotion, 17,* 181–204.

Becker, M. H., & Maiman, L. A. (1975). Sociobehavioral determinants of compliance with health and medical care recommendations. *Medical Care, 13,* 10–24.

Brownlee, S., Leventhal, H., & Balaban, M. (1992). Autonomic correlates of illness imagery. *Psychophysiology, 29,* 1–13.

Caccioppo, J. T., Andersen, B. L., Turnquist, D. C., & Petty, R. E. (1985). Psychophysiological comparison processes: Interpreting cancer symptoms. In B. L. Andersen (Ed.), *Women with cancer: Psychological perspectives* (pp. 141–171). New York: Springer-Verlag.

Cameron, L. C., Leventhal, E. A., & Leventhal, H. (1993). Symptom representations and affect as determinants of care seeking in a community dwelling adult sample population. *Health Psychology, 12,* 171–179.

Cameron, L. C., Leventhal E. A., & Leventhal, H. (1995). Seeking medical care in response to symptoms and life stress. *Psychosomatic Medicine, 57,* 34–47.

Carstensen, L. L. (1992). Social and emotional patterns in adulthood: Support for socioemotional selectivity theory. *Psychology and Aging, 7,* 331–338.

Chrisman, N. (1977). The health seeking process. *Culture, Medicine & Psychiatry, 1,* 351–378.

Croyle, R. T., & Jemmott, J. B. (1991). Psychological reactions to risk factor testing. In J. A. Skelton and R. T. Croyle (Eds.), *Mental representations in health and illness* (pp. 85–107). New York: Springer-Verlag.

Dean, K. (1992). Health-related behavior: Concepts and methods. In M. G. Ory, R. P. Abeles, & P. Darby Lipman (Eds.), *Aging, health, and behavior* (pp. 27–56). Newberry Park, CA: Sage.

DiClemente, C. C., Prochaska, J. O., Fairhurst, S. K., Velicer, W. F., Velasquez, M. M., & Rossi, J. S. (1991). The process of smoking cessation: An analysis of precontemplation, contemplation, and preparation stages of change. *Journal of Consulting and Clinical Psychology, 59,* 295–304.

DiClemente, C. C., Prochaska, J. O., & Gibertini, M. (1985). Self-efficacy and the stages of self-change of smoking. *Cognitive Therapy and Research, 9,* 181–200.

Easterling, D., & Leventhal, H. (1989). The contribution of concrete cognition to emotion: Neutral symptoms as elicitors of worry about cancer. *Journal of Applied Psychology, 74,* 787–796.

Goldfried, M. & D'Zurilla, T. (1969). A behavior-analytic model for assessing competence. In C. Spielberger (Ed.), *Current topics in clinical and community psychology* (pp. 151–196). New York: Academic.

Gregg, J., & Curry, R. H. (1994). Explanatory models for cancer among African-American women at two Atlanta neighborhood health centers: The implications for a cancer screening program. *Social Science & Medicine, 39,* 519–526.

Hazuda, H. P., Stern, M. P., & Haffner, S. M. (1984). Acculturation and assimilation among Mexican Americans: Scales and population-based data. *Social Science Quarterly, 69,* 687–706.

Johnston, M., & Wallace, L. (1990). *Stress and medical procedures.* New York: Oxford University Press.

Kanfer, F. H. (1977). The many faces of self-control, or behavior modification changes its focus. In R. B. Stuart (Ed.), *Behavioral self-management: Strategies, techniques, and outcomes* (pp. 1–48). New York: Brunner/Mazel.

Kleinman, A. (1980). *Patients and healers in the context of culture.* Berkeley, CA: University of California Press.

Larsen, R. (1992). Neuroticism and selective encoding and recall of symptoms: Evidence from a combined concurrent-retrospective study. *Journal of Personality and Social Psychology, 62,* 480–488.

Lau, R. R., & Hartmann, K. A. (1983). Common sense representations of common illnesses. *Health Psychology, 2,* 167–185.

Lerman, C., Rimer, B. K., & Engstrom, P. F. (1991). Cancer risk notification: Psychosocial and ethical implications. *Journal of Clinical Oncology, 9,* 1275–1282.

Leventhal, E. A., Easterling, D., Leventhal, H., & Cameron, L. (1995). Conservation of energy, uncertainty reduction and swift utilization of medical care among the elderly: Study II. *Medical Care, 33,* 988–1000.

Leventhal, E. A., Leventhal, H., Schaefer, P., & Easterling, D. (1993). Conservation of energy, uncertainty reduction, and swift utilization of medical care among the elderly. *Journal of Gerontology: Psychological Sciences, 48,* P78–P86.

Leventhal, H. (1970). Findings and theory in the study of fear communications. *Advances in Experimental Social Psychology, 5,* 119–186.

Leventhal, H., Baker, T., Brandon, T., & Flemming, R. (1989). Intervening and preventing cigarette smoking. In T. Ney & A. Gale (Eds.), *Smoking and human behavior* (pp. 313–336). New York: Wiley.

Leventhal, H., Diefenbach, M., & Leventhal, E.A. (1992). Illness cognition: Using common sense to understand treatment adherence and affect cognition interactions. *Cognitive Therapy and Research, 16,* 143–163.

Leventhal, H., & Leventhal, E. A. (1993). Affect, cognition and symptom reporting. In C. R. Chapman & K. M. Foley (Eds.), *Current and emerging issues in cancer pain: Research & practice* (pp. 153–173). New York: Raven.

Leventhal, H., Meyer, D., & Nerenz, D. (1980). The common sense representation of illness danger. In S. Rachman (Ed.), *Contributions to medical psychology* (Vol. II, pp. 7–30). New York: Pergamon.

Leventhal, H., & Watts, J. C. (1966). Sources of resistance to fear-arousing communications on smoking and lung cancer. *Journal of Personality, 34,* 155–175.

Leventhal, H., Watts, J. C., & Pagano, F. (1967). Effects of fear and instructions on how to cope with danger. *Journal of Personality and Social Psychology, 6,* 313–321.

Lorig, K., Chastain, R. L., Ung, E., Shoor, S., & Holman, H. (1989). Development and evaluation of a scale to measure perceived self-efficacy in people with arthritis. *Arthritis and Rheumtism, 32,* 37–44.

McAuley, E., Lox, C., & Duncan, T. E. (1993). Long-term maintenance of exercise, self-efficacy, and physiological change in older adults. *Journal of Gerontology, 48,* 218–224.

Mechanic, D. (1986). Illness behavior: An overview. In S. McHugh & M. Vallis (Eds.), *Illness behavior: A multidisciplinary model* (pp. 101–110). New York: Plenum.

Meichenbaum, D. (1977). *Cognitive-behavior modification: An integrative approach.* New York: Plenum.

Meyer, D., Leventhal, H., & Gutmann, M. (1985). Common-sense models of illness: The example of hypertension. *Health Psychology, 4,* 115–135.

Millar, M. G., & Millar, K. (1995). Negative affective consequences of thinking about disease detection behaviors. *Health Psychology, 14,* 141–146.

Misovich, S. J., Fisher, W. A., & Fisher, J. D. (in press). Social comparison as a factor in AIDS risk and AIDS preventive behavior. In B. Buunk & R. Gibbons (Eds.), *Health, coping and well-being.* (pp. 95–123). Hillsdale, NJ: Erlbaum.

Morrell, R. W., Park, D. C., Kidder, D. P., & Martin, M. (1997). Adherence to anti-hypertension medication across the lifespan. *The Gerontologist, 37,* 609–619.

Pilowsky, I. (1986). Abnormal illness behavior: A review of the concept and its implications. In S. McHugh & T. M. Vallis (Eds.), *Illness behavior: A multidisciplinary model* (pp. 391–395). New York: Plenum.

Prohaska, T. R., Keller, M. L., Leventhal, E. A., & Leventhal, H. (1987). Impact of symptoms and aging attribution on emotions and coping. *Health Psychology, 6,* 495–514.

Rosenstock, I. M. (1966). Why people use health services. *Milbank Memorial Fund Quarterly, 44,* 94ff.

Rosenstock, I. M., Stretcher, V., & Becker, M. (1988). Social learning theory and the health belief model. *Health Education Quarterly, 15,* 175–183.

Safer, M., Tharps, Q., Jackson, T., & Leventhal, H. (1979). Determinants of three stages of delay in seeking care at a medical clinic. *Medical Care, 17,* 11–29.

Skelton, J. A. & Croyle, R. T. (1991). *Mental representation in health and illness.* New York: Springer-Verlag.

Wallston, K. A. & Wallston, B. S. (1982). Who is responsible for your health? The construct of health locus of control. In G. S. Sanders & J. Suls (Eds.), *Social psychology of health and illness* (pp. 65–95). Hillsdale, NJ: Erlbaum.

Watson, D. & Pennebaker, J. (1989). Health complaints, stress and distress: Exploring the central role of negative affectivity. *Psychological Review, 96,* 234–254.

CHAPTER 6

The Role of Social Science Research in Understanding Technology Use Among Older Adults

Laura N. Gitlin

> *Technology is part of the answer, but that is not the question.*
> —Adapted from M. Scherer, *Living in the State of Stuck,* 1993

Technology is widely considered a cost-effective strategy to maximize an older person's independent performance in personal and instrumental activities of daily living. As a tool for living, the primary purpose of technology is to bridge the gap between an older person's declining capabilities and the unchanging environmental demands of home and community. The use of technology as a self-care practice may enable independent performance, increase safety, reduce risk of injury, improve balance and mobility, improve communication, limit complications of an illness, and make caring less burdensome (Childress, 1986; DeWitt, 1991; LaBuda, 1990, "Low Technology for Maximizing Independence," 1986).

Legislation such as the Technology-Related Assistance for Individuals with Disabilities Act of 1988 (Tech Act) and its reauthorization in 1994, the National Affordable Housing Act of 1990, and the Medicaid waiver program, represent important sources of funding for assistive technology services for the elderly (Brewer, 1996; Gavin, 1997). Although the use of such services and technology as a self-care practice has the potential to significantly improve the lives of older persons, its benefits can only be realized with the application of social science research. The purpose of this chapter is to articulate the major contributions of social science research in describing, explaining, and predicting the practice of technology use by older adults. The chapter first presents a definition of technology and then examines the existing research on its use. The principal findings from this research, the salient constructs, and their relationships form the foundation from which a model is proposed. This model is used as the basis for suggesting new research questions and approaches to inquiry involving a social science perspective to obtain a more comprehensive understanding of technology use. The potential contributions of social science research are explored and specific recommendations are made as to the next steps in research.

OVERVIEW OF TECHNOLOGY FOR SELF-CARE

There are many definitions and classifications of technology in the literature. Those technologies that extend human function and are most important from the perspective of self-care practices are referred to as either assistive devices, assistive technology, tools for living, equipment, or aids (Mann & Lane, 1991). According to Haber (1982, 1986), assistive devices can be classified as "ecological" technology, the purpose of which is to improve the quality of living and enable the performance of personal, instrumental, and leisure activities; mobility; communication; or participation in the workplace. In contrast, medical technologies or appliances (Vanderheiden, 1987) refer to those forms of technology that are life sustaining (e.g., drugs, pacemakers, ventilators). Assistive technologies have been designated in the Technology Assistance Act (Tech Act, §3:1, 1988) as: "Any item, piece of equipment, or product system, whether acquired commercially off the shelf, modified or customized, that is used to increase, maintain, or improve functional capabilities of individuals with disabilities."

Assistive devices have been categorized by degree of technological complexity as either low, medium, or high. Low technology refers to low cost objects that involve simple mechanical principles (e.g., walker, cane, grab bar, dressing stick, reacher, built-up utensil). Medium technology refers to devices and systems that involve more than simple mechanical manipulations (e.g., powered mobility aids, communication devices, telephones, TV, radio), whereas high technology involves electronic devices and more complex procedures which may be required for work or leisure (augmentative communication devices, alphabet boards, environmental control systems). Linking an assistive technology to a specific self-care need requires an appropriate match between the complexity of the device, demands of a task and the capabilities of the older person (Figure 6.1).

There are literally thousands of existing assistive technologies which can be used by older persons to assist in the performance of personal care, instrumental activities, or tasks outside the home (Enders & Hall, 1988; La Buda, 1988; Smith, Benge, & Hall, 1994).

For those elderly who enter the health care system, occupational therapy and physical therapy have a primary role in prescribing and training for use of assistive technologies (Mann, 1994; Mann & Lane, 1991; Schemm & Gitlin, in press; Smith et al., 1994). Older persons may also obtain assistive technologies on their own, through catalogues, or through participa-

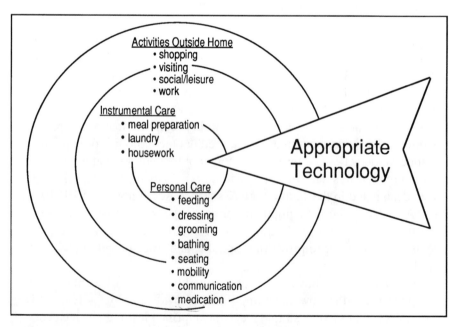

FIGURE 6.1   Appropriate technology for daily life activities.

tion in assistive technology programs sponsored by a number of states. Knowledge of and access to assistive technology however remains a major barrier to its widespread use (Gitlin, 1995; LaPlante, Hendershot, & Moss 1992; Mann, 1994).

RESEARCH ON TECHNOLOGY USE AND PRACTICES

Our understanding of an older person's use of assistive technology as a self-care practice is based on three streams of research: human factors research, descriptive survey research, and anthropological investigations. These bodies of literature are described by linking their primary constructs, pooling their results, and building a model from which to direct future research using a social science perspective. Figure 6.2 graphically displays the major constructs and their relationships as they have emerged in these bodies of literature.

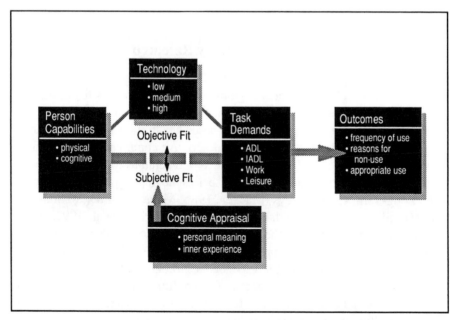

FIGURE 6.2   A model of major constructs from three streams of research.

Human Factors Perspective

Human factors methodologies have been used to successfully analyze the progressive problems encountered by older persons as they age in performing specific tasks of daily living. This approach characterizes person-environment transactions as a quantification of the physiological demands associated with a specific task such as meal preparation, lifting an object, or driving (Czaja & Barr, 1989; Czaja, Weber, & Nair, 1993; Faletti, 1985). The capabilities of older persons are assessed with regard to the biomechanical, sensory and cognitive demands imposed by a person-task transaction. The impact of age-related changes such as vision loss, a decline in reaction time, or musculoskeletal changes are examined as to their impact on the dynamics of task performance. Based on this information, specific interventions to reduce the demands of the task and improve individual performance are suggested. Intervention strategies may include the development of an assistive technology or the modification of a characteristic of the person (e.g., training to lift differently).

The human factors framework has significantly contributed to an understanding of the *objective fit* between an older person's capabilities, the demands of specific tasks, and the design of low, medium, and high technological systems.

Descriptive Survey Research

Human factors research has demonstrated that the use of assistive technology reduces the impact of physical or cognitive dysfunction on daily living. Recent research has focused on describing the rate of use of technology as a self-care behavior among the elderly. Population-based health surveys using probability sampling techniques and numerous descriptive community-based studies using convenience samples have produced rich detail as to the type of technology in use and differentials in use by sociodemographic profiles. Data from the Long-Term Care Surveys (Macken, 1986; Manton, Corder, & Stallard, 1993) and the National Health Interview Survey (LaPlante et al., 1992, 1997) have consistently shown that the elderly report the use of a wide range of assistive technologies, and not surprisingly, use aids for mobility and hearing proportionately more than younger respondents. Norburn and colleagues' (1995) national survey of self-care practices further confirms that the elderly use both environmental adjustments and low technological strategies to solve daily care issues resulting from physical and cognitive impairments.

The important analysis of the National Long-Term Care Surveys by Manton and colleagues (1993) shows a significant increase in the use of assistive devices and a concomitant decline in the use of personal assistance by older respondents with physical impairments. This finding has prompted much interest in the cost savings of assistive technology and the circumstances under which its use can replace the need for informal or formal care services.

Community-based surveys provide additional evidence of the use of assistive technology as a self-care strategy. Table 6.1 summarizes some of the initial key studies that examined device use among the elderly with different impairments and activity limitations. As shown, these studies differed vastly in sample size, sampling procedures, impairment groups, and consequently, in reported findings. These early studies found that the elderly reported an average of 8 to 14 devices at home, with use rates averaging from 44% to 80%. Reasons for abandoning devices have been reported to include lack of knowledge as to appropriate use, broken or lost devices, or preference for personal assistance (Gitlin, 1995, Spring).

The Consumer Assessments Study at the University at Buffalo represents a 10-year effort to examine issues related to older community dwellers' use of a range of low technology assistive devices. Approximately 500 older adults have participated in the first 5 years of the assessment study to date and an additional 500 are expected to be enrolled over the next 5 years. The multiple reports thus far generated from the ongoing survey have yielded a thick description of use rates for different impairment groups, types of devices found in homes of elders, and related technical difficulties (Mann, 1997; Mann, Hurren, & Tomita, 1993; Mann, Hurren, Tomita, & Charvat, 1994).

Little research exists on factors that explain technology use. Some research suggests that females tend to use devices more than males (Forbes, Hayward, & Agwani, 1993), that females with high disability who use equipment have lower well-being (Penning & Strain, 1994) and that the number of functional difficulties rather than impairment level may be associated with the use of specific types of devices (Zimmer & Chappel, 1994). In a study of older patients in rehabilitation, Gitlin, Schemm, Landsberg, and Burgh (1996) found that the expected need for device use while hospitalized and positive appraisals of devices were strong predictors of continued use upon return home.

Collectively, this growing body of research suggests that use rates may be determined in part by the type of device, time of onset of illness, type of impairment and level of functional difficulties that are experienced by

TABLE 6.1 Selected Research on Assistive Device Use

Author	N	Subject Characteristics	Study Design	Devices Studied	Major Findings
H. Bynum et al. (1987)	30	Discharged Homecare OT Patients AGE: 37-91 ($\bar{x} = 68$)	Descriptive Survey	Feeding, Dressing, & Bathing/ Toileting	1) 1.8 devices/person 2) 82% of devices used 3) 80% of devices for which no training occurred were used 4) Training occurred within 6 months of impairment or 1+ year after onset 5) Commode most frequently issued (n = 20) 6) 25% of commode recipients received training
C. Geiger (1990)	50	Rehab. OT Patients AGE: 19-85 ($\bar{x} = 60$)	Hospital Interview & Home Telephone Interview 4-6 Weeks Post-Discharge	Dressing, Bathing Aids	1) 54% non-use rate 2) Non-use reasons include no need & no device issued 3) Greater use among those living alone & those less than 69 years old
L. Gitlin et al. (1993)	13 Elderly 31 Home OT Therapists	Elderly Discharged from Rehab AGE: 61-84	Two Descriptive Pilot Studies: 1) Hospital	Bathroom, Eating, Dressing, Hygiene	PILOT 1 (Patients): 1) 5.5 devices issued/patient 2) Dressing & Bathing Devices most frequently issued

148

TABLE 6.1 Selected Research on Assistive Device Use *(continued)*

Author	N	Subject Characteristics	Study Design	Devices Studied	Major Findings
		($\bar{x} = 73$)	Interview & 3 Home Telephone Interviews 2) Mailed Survey to Therapists		3) In hospital, all reported devices helpful & expectations of use 4) Non-use reasons include: a) No need, b) Cumbersome, c) Available supports d) Device loss or failure 5) 45% of equipment seldom-never used one month post-discharge, 33% month two, and 42% month three PILOT 2 (OT): 1) 90% perceived mobility & bathing devices as most used 2) OT perception of reasons for non-use: a) Lack of knowledge & defective devices, b) Cost, c) Environmental fit, d) Time required, e) Family member 3) Suggestions for hospital personnel include: a) Develop innovative strategies, b) Empower clients thru education, c) Solicit needs & values, d) Involve caregivers, e) Understand complexity of home
L. Gitlin et al. (1996)	250	31 Lower Limb Amputation	Pre-Discharge Interview	Mobility, Bathing,	1) 1,885 devices issued 2) 8 devices/patient regardless of im-

TABLE 6.1 Selected Research on Assistive Device Use (*continued*)

Author	N	Subject Characteristics	Study Design	Devices Studied	Major Findings
		116 Orthopedic 103 Stroke		Dressing, Feeding, Seating, Grooming	pairment type (range 0–21) 3) Mobility, bathing, dressing most frequently issued 4) Functional measure inadequate index of type and number of issued devices except for stroke
W. Mann et al. (1993)	157	Elderly with Impairments AGE: 60-92 ($\bar{x}$ = 75.5)	2-Hour Home Interview	Physical, Hearing, Visual, Tactile, Cognitive and Other	1) Cognitive impairment greatest effect on function 2) 13.7 devices/person 3) 79% of devices used 4) 72% satisfied with devices 5) Device problems include: -Device not serving intended purpose -Inadequacy of device in meeting needs -Device creates attention
W. Mann et al. (1995)	30	Stroke patients AGE: 62-88 ($\bar{x}$ = 75.3)	2-Hour Home Interview	Physical, Hearing, Visual, Tactile, Cognitive and Other	1) 16 devices/person 2) 80% of devices used, 77% considered satisfactory 3) Patients express need for more devices

TABLE 6.1 Selected Research on Assistive Device Use *(continued)*

Author	N	Subject Characteristics	Study Design	Devices Studied	Major Findings
W. Mann, J. Karuza, D. Hurreur & M. Tomita (1992)	31	Cognitively impaired Age: 65–92 ($\bar{x} = 77.5$)	In-home interview primarily with caregivers	Broad range of physical disabilities: hearing, visual, tactile & cognitive devices	1) 5.8 devices/person (range 0–20) 2) 1.5 devices/person felt were needed, but did not have 3) 88% devices considered unsatisfactory 4) Less than 17% of used devices associated with cognitive impairment, 2/3 associated with physical disabilities 5) Degree of physical disability predictor of number of devices used
A. Neville-Jan et al. (1993)	80	Elderly caregivers & patients (primarily stroke, arthritis, & hip fx)	Mailed survey questionnaire 3 months post-discharge	Variety of technical aids	1) 78% survey return rate 2) 36% of devices never used or used temporarily 3) Reasons not used include: a) never needed (13%), b) temporal need (41%), c) device mechanics, lack of knowledge, installation, need assistance (46%)
M. Parker & M. Thorslund (1991)	57	Disabled Swedish elderly Age: 74+	Descriptive in-home survey	Variety of technical aids	1) 422 aids ($\bar{x} = 7.4$/person) 2) 75% of devices used 3) Hygiene & mobility were common ADL limitation

knowledge, installation, need

assistance (46%)

Author	N	Subject Characteristics	Study Design	Devices Studied	Major Findings
M. Parker & M. Thorslund (1991)	57	Disabled Swedish elderly Age: 74+	Descriptive in-home survey	Variety of technical aids	1) 422 aids (x = 7.4/person) 2) 75% of devices used 3) Hygiene & mobility were common ADL limitation 4) 29% of devices were mobility 5) 74% had 1+ aids granting autonomy 6) Bathroom adaptations most common
C. Simpson et al. (1991)	114	Elderly referred for physiother-apy Age: 45–97 ($\bar{x} = 75$)	Descriptive 3-month survey	Walking aids	1) 124 aids assessed 2) Patient falls primary reason for referral (29%) 3) 45% received instruction 4) Unacceptably high proportion of unsuitable use of aids (61.3%) 5) Physiotherapists most successful issuing walking aids
A. Van Der Heide et al. (1993)	197	2 Groups of RA patients: 1) Recently diagnosed ($n = 97$).	Cross-sectional	Auxilliary devices	Group 1 (Recent onset): 1) 66% did not use devices 2) Jar openers & raised toilet seats most frequently used Group 2 (Established disease):

TABLE 6.1 Selected Research on Assistive Device Use (continued)

152

the elderly. For example, Gitlin, Schemm, Lansberg and Burgh (1996) found that at home following hospitalization, older rehabilitation patients used 50% of the devices issued them. Mobility aids were used with the most frequency, with only 13% of those surveyed reporting abandoning their use (Gitlin, Schemm, and Shmuely, 1997). Furthermore, patients were issued an average of three mobility aids. The use of one aid replaced another (e.g., cane for walker) as function improved. Therefore, for the most part, the abandonment of an aid appeared to follow a therapeutic purpose. In a comparison of elders with different impairments, Mann and colleagues (1993) found that older adults with visual impairments reported very high use rates, while those with cognitive impairments used very few devices. In a comparison of use rates at different time points, Van Der Heide and colleagues (1993) reported that only 34% of subjects with recent onset of rheumatoid arthritis used devices compared to a 70% use rate for those who had had the disease for over one year.

Unfortunately, methodological differences continue to constrain the ability to derive cross-study comparisons and definitive conclusions from the research. Few studies provide the level of specificity required for interpreting the findings. Only a few authors report whether study participants were first-time or long-term users of technology or the time of onset of the illness or chronic condition, factors that may be important determinants of the pattern of use. Nevertheless, collectively, this research suggests five major points:

1. Older persons who have functional limitations are users of devices.
2. Older persons report the need for more devices than they have.
3. Age shows little association with the willingness to use an assistive device.
4. Frequency of use varies by device type, specific functional limitation, and time of onset of impairment.
5. There is wide intra- and interindividual variability in the acceptance and use of devices.

Anthropological Research

A small but growing body of research using qualitative methodologies has sought to understand the subjective or "personal experiences" of assistive technology use. These studies richly describe the personal context in which device use occurs and highlight the way in which cultural values shape adaptation to disability. Of importance is the consistent finding that device use has a dual outcome: At the same time that a device promotes independence, it appears to also raise concerns about social stigma, feelings of embarrassment, and issues related to personal identity and self-definition.

Studies of individuals with postpoliomyelitis (Kaufert, Kaufert, & Locker, 1987; Luborsky, 1993) and spinal cord injury (Scheer & Grace, 1988) suggest that personal interpretations of technology may have both positive and negative valences that require individuals to obtain other adaptive and coping strategies for the use of a device. In a study of adults with severe visual impairment and blindness, it was found that mobility aids (guide dogs and white canes) provided important opportunities for social engagement, work, and travel while also posing physical challenges and personal feelings of embarrassment (Gitlin, Mount, Lucas, Weirich, & Gamberg, 1997). Similarly, in a study of stroke patients, content analysis of their statements about devices suggested an underlying concern with social appraisals of their newly acquired mobility aids.

It's not like before. I used to feel sorry for people who had wheelchairs.

Glad to have gone outdoors and to have seen people's reactions before I went home.

I am the same person, I just can't walk.

Other types of devices issued in rehabilitation evoked similar concerns, although these aids were also perceived as facilitating independence, personal safety and well-being (Gitlin, Luborsky, & Schemm, in press). Research using life history and case study methods further suggests that, despite the liberating aspects of technology and even when necessary to sustain life, the use of devices may present dramatic compromises in social activities, role definition and self-identity (Kaufert et al., 1987; Gitlin, in press). Even taking medication may be governed by the degree to which an older person feels stigmatized or dependent by following the prescribed regimen (Zola, 1986).

This literature, as well as the broader field of inquiry on illness experiences, suggests that the meaning of disability is highly variable and that personal meanings reflect, in part, underlying cultural beliefs and social norms. Even though, as Frank (1994) indicates, the *self* in self-care characterizes the highly intimate nature of such daily practices, these practices occur within the context of sociocultural beliefs and values. The confluence of cultural beliefs, personal meanings and functional needs is clearly evident in the elder's appraisal of devices and the decision to use or not to use this strategy in daily life.

In summary, the qualitative, ethnographic framework highlights the importance of the *subjective fit* between an older person's changing capabilities, environmental demands and technology use (see Figure 6.2). Although a device may be an effective self-care strategy to enable independence, its use also may have considerable psychological and social consequences for an older person. Collectively, these studies suggest that the way in which older adults appraise and give meaning to the objective fit may influence the acceptance or rejection of the use of technology and its integration into self-care routines.

ROLE OF SOCIAL SCIENCE RESEARCH

The use of technology as a self-care practice occurs within an environmental context that is imbued with social, cultural, and personal meanings. It is the understanding of this complex context that social science research has much to offer to the study of technology use (Strain, Chappell, & Penning, 1993). The three streams of research described above have contributed in significant ways to examining assistive device use. However, the purposeful use of a social science perspective is important to further advance our knowledge of how technological strategies can best enhance the well-being of an older population that is characterized by its diversity in its needs, cultural preferences, and access to technology. Figure 6.3 displays a model that builds upon and extends current knowledge to inform future social science research on technology use and the elderly.

Five major contributions from the field of social science research to the study of technology use as a self-care practice among the elderly are proposed here. These include the expansion of the populations that are studied; the application of theories and models to describe, explain and predict technology use; the use of a multivariate approach; the development of multimethod or integrated research designs; and solutions to crucial measurement issues.

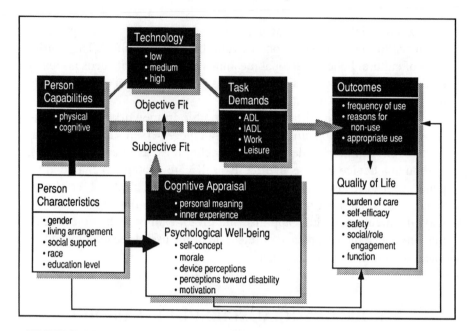

FIGURE 6.3   A model to guide social science research on technology use and the elderly. Constructs and their relationships that have been studied are displayed in black boxes and gray arrows. Those constructs that have not been studied and which would substantially contribute to a comprehensive understanding of technology use are denoted by the white boxes and black arrows.

Expansion of Study Populations

A major role for social science research is the careful identification of population groups who may benefit from the incorporation of assistive technologies into their self-care practices. Technology is not just an aid for those who are disabled or have functional limitations, although it is this group that has been the primary focus of previous research. As a tool for living (Wolff, 1980), technology can be conceptualized as of potential importance to five population groups. As shown in Table 6.2, these groups include

- individuals who are caring for a family member and for whom technology may decrease the burden of care
- individuals who are aging and who may benefit from using devices to promote safety and reduce the risk of injury
- individuals experiencing age-related changes or functional decline and

TABLE 6.2   Five Types of Potential Technology Users

Population	Technology experience	Reason for use
Caregivers	Potential new users	Self-care needs of elder own self-care needs assist elder in use of a device
Individuals who are aging	Potential new users	Increase safety reduce injury risk
Individuals experiencing age-related changes and/or functional decline	First-time users	Increase safety maintain independence compensate for functional limitation
Individuals with first-time disability and/or multiple chronic conditions	First-time or previous users	Compensate for functional limitation task performance
Individuals aging with a disability	Long-term users	Task performance life sustaining

who may benefit from technologies that enable independent performance and prevent disability
- those who have a first-time disability or multiple chronic conditions and may require numerous assistive devices to perform personal care activities
- individuals who are aging with a disability and who may be long-term users of assistive technologies to sustain a range of daily and instrumental activities.

Although maintaining independence may be the primary goal for issuing an assistive device to those with a functional limitation, there are many other potential purposes and outcomes of device use and these may differ for each group listed in Table 6.2. For example, the use of assistive technology may have a buffering effect (Verbrugge & Jette, 1994). That is, it may moderate the transition from impairment to disability as older adults move in and out of environments that offer different levels of support or present higher or lower demands, or *press,* on performance. On the other hand, an assistive device such as a grab bar may protect against injury and serve as a health-promoting self-care strategy.

Each population suggested in Table 6.2 may vary in its preference for, adaptation to, and use of technology. Comparisons across these five groups as well as within each one would provide a basis from which to identify the conditions under which older persons become technology users and the differential benefits that are derived.

Theories and Models

Another major contribution of social science research is the application of theories and models to describe, explain, and predict assistive technology use by different groups of older persons. While the extant research remains largely descriptive, the use of theory would advance our understanding of the circumstances or life contexts in which an assistive technology solution is sought and adapted by older adults. Models to predict technology use by different populations and a framework from which to derive testable hypotheses and intervention strategies to improve appropriate technology use remain largely undeveloped.

The application of theories and models that have been used to explain other forms of health behaviors may be of value for understanding assistive device use. Theories of health-protective behaviors have been applied to a wide range of self-care behaviors, such as participation in cancer screening programs (DeVellis, Blalock, & Sandler, 1990) and mammography (Montano & Taplin, 1991), and behaviors associated with cardiovascular risk reduction (Fleury, 1992). As discussed elsewhere in this volume (see chapters by Stoller, Prohaska, and Leventhal), the health belief model and the theory of reasoned action offer similar perspectives on the relationship between the intention to perform a behavior and actual behavior (Weinstein, 1993). These theories suggest that the intention to participate in a specific health behavior may be determined in part by sociocultural norms as well as the person's attitude toward the behavior. In a study of assistive device use by older rehabilitation patients, two factors during hospitalization strongly predicted actual home use following discharge: personal perceptions that the devices were beneficial and the expectation that a device would be used posthospitalization. The personal expectation of device use was significantly associated with psychological well-being in inverse proportion to negativity toward devices. However, personal expectation of device use, was not associated with functional status or age (Gitlin et al., 1996).

The application of personal control theory to disablement may be useful to explain the personal benefits of device use (Williamson & Schulz, 1992; Schulz, Heckhausen, & O'Brien, 1994). This approach suggests that as an adaptive strategy, device use may potentially enhance perceived self-control and self-efficacy (Schulz, Heckhausen, & O'Brien, 1994), and minimize depression associated with functional loss (Gitlin, Mann, and Tomita, 1997).

Theories of motivation that examine the costs and expected utility associated with technology use may also provide a basis from which to explain why some older persons are successful device users and others choose a different strategy to perform the same task (Kemp, 1988, 1993). Also, motivation theories may provide the basis for developing a risk model to identify those in greatest need for a device, but who are least likely to continue with its use.

The disability literature also offers a number of constructs that should be examined and applied to an understanding of the motivations to use technology by the five aging groups in Table 6.2. In particular, the concept of social stigma suggests that the normative context of assistive device use and the expectation of negative social judgments may influence the conditions under which a device becomes an acceptable alternative self-care strategy (Fine & Asch, 1988). Alternately, the potency of the meaning of a device may be related to its purpose and the circumstances under which it is used. Mobility aids, for example, are more public and visible; for certain individuals, they may raise concerns about social judgments. Aids for grooming or dressing, on the other hand, are more frequently used in a person's private life space and their use may be less costly to a person's self-evaluation. The public/private parameter raises empirical questions in need of investigation through the application of appropriate theory and methodologies.

Multivariate Approach

The complex interactions among biological, functional, social, cultural, environmental, behavioral, and psychological factors associated with technology use need to be reflected in the development of appropriate theoretical frameworks, methodologies, and analytic approaches. As we examine the characteristics, capacities, and limitations of older persons in relation to new technologies, the challenge will be to employ a multivariate approach to examine technology's complex role and use. With the availability of multivariate statistical models, it is feasible to examine the independent and combined effects of individual characteristics (functional status, psychological profile, gender, race, social support), situational characteristics (social support, physical dimensions of the home and community), and device capabilities, (aesthetic properties, durability and purposes) on the intention to use a device and on its integration into daily life (Figure 6.3). Also, such an approach would facilitate comparative designs by which to contrast the five groups of potential technology users (Table 6.2) as to the: (a) specific factors that predict device use for each group, (b) particular factors that present barriers to device use, (c) circumstances under which personal assistance or an assistive device is preferred over the other, or used in combination and (d) positive and/or negative outcomes that may be associated with device use.

Assistive technology use, as well as other self-care practices, may be mediated by certain person-based characteristics. Gender, race, living arrangement, social support, impairment type, and functional level may contribute to use or disuse in distinct ways for different populations (Figure 6.3). Furthermore, the role of social supports in facilitating and encouraging technology use as well as the environmental factors that make its use more or less likely, remain unknown areas of investigation that must be guided by theory and a concern for multivariate explanations.

The Use of Multimethod Designs

Another important contribution of social science research is the introduction of innovative methodologies to examine the interrelationship of the objective and subjective components of assistive device use. In the study of technology use among the elderly, as in many areas of aging research and health care practice, more attention has been given to an objective measure of what a person can do. The subjective component—how a person appraises his or her situation and the concomitant emotive responses and outcomes—remains largely unexplored. Nevertheless, the introduction of assistive technology and its integration into daily life to reestablish old routines is essentially a personal and lifestyle issue. Understanding a person's interpretations of and search for meaning in an illness, disability, change in ability, or need for family assistance may be as critical, if not more, than the objective determination of technology need.

Clearly, the context of assistive device use must be examined and understood from both its objective and subjective components: the reality of the older person's condition and need for a device as well as the person's interpretation or inner experience of that condition. The use of multiple methods to examine the interaction of objective and subjective factors is an important direction for future research. The intent of a "multi-method" or "integrated" approach is to strengthen a study by selecting and combining designs and methods from experimental and qualitative paradigms so that one complements the other to benefit or contribute to an understanding of the whole (DePoy & Gitlin, 1994). The attempt to integrate diverse research paradigms has only recently become a focus in health and human service research, but one which would greatly advance the study of technology use by older persons. Furthermore, research suggests the context-rich nature of device use. The circumstances of each person's life, cultural and social orientation and relationships with the environment are unique, dynamic, and change over time. The aggregation of individuals and the search for generalizability must be combined with systematic case designs to fully explicate the context of device use for older persons with diverse cultural values, personal routines, and self-care practices.

Issues Related to Measurement

There are several related issues concerning the measurement of technology use that need careful consideration. These issues include (a) the need to develop and test reliable methods for identifying the devices which are used by older persons and determining the frequency of their use, (b) the need to include assessments of appropriate use of devices, (c) and the need to expand the outcome measures included in assistive device studies.

The first issue concerns how we assess frequency of assistive technology use. Most surveys of older adults, as described in Table 6.1, use either a dichotomous response set ("yes" or "no") or a 5- or 7-point Likert-type scale ("always, frequently, occasionally, sometimes or never") to assess frequency of use of a device. However, there has been no evaluation as to the reliability of broad frequency categories and the ability of older persons to accurately recall device use over a day, week, or month. Furthermore, our understanding of these frequencies remains rather imprecise. For example, a response of "sometimes" may indicate that the respondent conducts the activity with infrequency and therefore only uses the device sometimes. On the other hand, such a response can be interpreted to mean that the activity is performed frequently but the device is only used occasionally.

As Stoller points out in chapter 2, the use of health diaries to examine specific self-care practices such as medication taking, adherence to exercise regimens, or illness behaviors has been an effective methodology for varied population groups among the elderly (Stoller, Forster, & Portugal, 1993). This approach may be appropriate in the study of technology use as well. Daily recording of performance of specific activities and the use of strategies such as a device, personal assistance, or both would greatly enhance our understanding of the patterns of use and the integration of multiple self-care strategies into a daily routine.

Another related issue concerns the need to evaluate the reliability of methods for identifying devices in the homes of older persons. The practice of relying on self-report as to the type of device in the home may not yield consistent information. For example, in the Gitlin et al. (1996) study of assistive device use, patients often confused a raised toilet seat with a commode and reported owning one and not the other although the opposite was found to be true. Investigators also found that older persons developed their own vocabulary and special names for the devices they were issued that differed from their technical designate. Using checklists, pictures or showing the actual devices may enhance the ability of older persons to report accurately as to whether they own a device and use it. Observations of the devices and where they are stored in the home may also enhance reliable reporting.

The second major measurement issue involves evaluating whether an assistive device is used appropriately by an older person. Some devices may be used in an unconventional manner or for a purpose different from its intention. Simpson and Pirrie (1991), in a study of elderly patients referred for physical therapy, found that 61% of mobility devices were used inappropriately. A study of the use of environmental modifications by family caregivers of dementia patients learned that caregivers often developed their own creative solutions to daily care difficulties. However, many solutions posed new safety hazards or needed refinement by a health professional to be effective (Gitlin & Corcoran, 1993; Gitlin, Schemm, & Shmuely, 1997).

The third major measurement issue involves expanding the outcomes of technology use to include quality-of-life concerns. Although the primary role of an assistive technology may be to decrease dependency and enhance function, there may be other derived benefits as well as consequences. A range of outcomes and their measurement need careful consideration. For example, assistive technologies that enable participation in social activities (e.g., adapted game boards, communication devices, mobility aids) may promote engagement and lessen depression and social isolation, factors that are associated with mortality risk. The use of technology to enable a caregiver to provide care to another may decrease physical burden (Gitlin, Corcoran, & Shmuely, 1997). Furthermore, personal goals, and not functional status, may influence the type of assistive device that is needed and used. Older adults may choose to use assistive devices to facilitate those activities that they identify as personally meaningful and satisfying. They may have generally anticipated goals such as independent dressing or safe stair climbing, or "smaller," but important, goals such as picking up objects (e.g., mail) from the floor. These "small" gains (Ory & Williams, 1989) may not be detected by our broad measures of functional status, but may, in fact, reflect the improvements in daily life that older persons value and seek in assistive technology use.

Furthermore, assistive technology use may also reflect an individuals effort to maintain control over a changing context. It may enable older persons to gain a greater sense of self-efficacy in their daily self-care practices. Self-efficacy and other quality-of-life constructs need to be identified along with the diligent development of instrumentation that is sensitive enough to measure the small gains that may be achieved through technology use.

Implications of Social Science Research for Health Policy and Health Care Practices

Ultimately, the full potential of an assistive device intervention, its acceptability to fiscal reimbursement mechanisms, and its recognition by legislative efforts and in health policy (Figure 6.3), depend on our understanding the relationship between technology use and its outcomes. Recent legislation has begun to establish a service structure for the provision of assistive technology. However, a social science perspective is required to broaden an understanding of the role of assistive technology as a self-care strategy and its outcome on function and general well-being. Broadening the context of the study of technology use to include a social science perspective will have profound implications for the development of appropriate reimbursement policies, the training of health professionals in effective methods of instructing older persons in the use of technology, and the development of new assistive technologies and their marketing.

An effective delivery system remains one of the most important barriers to optimizing the use of assistive technologies by older adults. Research is needed to guide the development of effective strategies, service delivery programs, and policies that are relevant to the specific and changing needs of older persons. Actions must reflect the heterogeneity of this population and promote the multiple purposes of assistive devices.

Research in aging has demonstrated that older persons are receptive to technologies if they perceive them as useful, if they are provided with adequate training, and if the technical system or device is relatively easy to use (Czaja et al., 1993). Furthermore, the manipulation of external variables such as pacing instruction, offering adequate practice time, and providing instruction within the context in which a device will be used has been shown to reduce age differences in learning ability. Applying adult learning principles and knowledge of age-related changes to the development of technology intervention strategies for older persons is an important mission for social science. These learning principles need to be adapted to assistive technology instruction and systematically tested for their effectiveness for older persons.

In conclusion, technology may enable older adults to maintain independence in those personal and instrumental activities that are valued. However, there are many unanswered questions and research challenges that must be met through a social science perspective. The proposed model shown in Figure 6.3 can be used as a starting point to guide future research endeavors. It raises the following questions for systematic inquiry.

1. What factors contribute to the acceptance or rejection of a device type by diverse groups of older persons?
2. What are the pscyhosocial correlates of assistive device use? What is the role of motivation and device/disability perceptions in shaping assistive device use?
3. What is the role of gender, race, functional level, type of impairment, social support and environmental factors in promoting or hindering assistive device use?
4. Are there particular tasks for which older persons prefer technological aids over personal assistance?
5. How do family members use assistive devices to support their caregiving activities?
6. What is the most effective technology service delivery system for older persons and their caregivers? What are the best methods of instruction in technology use for older persons?
7. How does assistive technology as one self-care practice interface with other care strategies for different population groups among the elderly?

8. What are the outcomes of technology use for role enactment, sense of efficacy, personal goal accomplishment, safety in the home, burden of care or level of personal assistance required?
9. What are the interrelationships between the objective need for assistive technology, subjective interpretation of change in function, and the adaptation to and use of assistive devices as a self-care practice?

REFERENCES

Brewer, J. (1996). Introduction to Tech Act. *Technology and Disability, 5*, 237–238.

Childress, D. S. (1986). Technology for functional ability and independent living. In S. J. Brody & G. E. Ruff (Eds.), *Aging and rehabilitation: Advances in the state of the art* (pp. 303–313). New York: Springer Publishing.

Czaja, S. J., & Barr, R. A. (1989). Technology and the everyday life of older adults. *Annals, 503,* 127–137.

Czaja, S. J., Weber, R. A., & Nair, S. N. (1993). A human factors analysis of ADL activities: A capability-demand approach. *Journal of Gerontology, 48* (Special Issue), 44–48.

DePoy, E., & Gitlin, L. N. (1994). *An introduction to research: Multiple strategies for health and human services.* St. Louis: Mosby.

DeVellis, B. M., Blalock S. J., & Sandler, R. S. (1990). Predicting participation in cancer screening: The role of perceived behavioral control. *Journal of Applied Social Psychology, 20*, 639–660.

DeWitt, J. C. (1991). The role of technology in removing barriers. *Milbank Quarterly, 69*(Supplements 1/2), 313–332.

Enders, A., & Hall, M. (Eds.). (1988). *Assistive technology sourcebook.* Washington, DC: The Rehabilitation Engineering and Assistive Technology Society of North America.

Faletti, M. V. (1985). From can openers to computers, technology can enhance functional ability and independence for the aged. *Caring, 4*(1), 56–58.

Fine, M., & Asch, A. (1988). Disability beyond stigma: Social interaction, discrimination, and activism. *Journal of Social Issues, 44*(1), 3–21.

Fleury, J. (1992). The application of motivational theory to cardiovascular risk reduction. *Image: Journal of Nursing Scholarship, 24*(3), 229–239.

Forbes, W. F., Hayward, L. M., & Agwani, N. (1993). Factors associated with self-reported use and non-use of assistive devices among impaired elderly residing in the community. *Canadian Journal of Public Health, 84*(1), 53–57.

Frank, G. (1994). The personal meaning of self-care occupations. In C. Christiansen (Ed.), *Ways of living: Self-care strategies for special needs* (pp. 27–49). Rockville, MD: American Occupational Therapy Association.

Gavin, J. (1997). Assistive Technology: Federal policy and practice since 1982. *Technology and Disability, 6*(1,2) 3–16.

Geiger, C. M. (1990). The utilization of assistive devices by patients discharged from an acute rehabilitation setting. *Physical & Occupational Therapy Geriatrics, 9*(1), 3–25.

Gitlin, L. N. (1995). Using mobility devices to maximize human potential: The unknown experience. *Maximizing Human Potential, 3*(2), 4–5.

Gitlin, L. N. (1995, Spring). Why older people accept or reject assistive technology. *Generations,* 41–45.

Gitlin, L. N. (in press). From hospital to home: Individual variation in the experience with assistive devices among the elderly. In D. Gray & L. Quadrano (Eds.), *Designing and using assistive technology: The human perspective.* Brookes.

Gitlin, L. N., & Corcoran, M. (1993). Expanding caregiver ability to use environmental solutions for problems of bathing and incontinence in the elderly with dementia. *Technology and Disability, 2*(1), 12–21.

Gitlin, L. N., Corcoran, M. C., & Shmuely, Y. (1997). Managing the dementia patient at home with environmental adjustments: What do families do and what are the benefits? Manuscript submitted for publication.

Gitlin, L. N., Levine, R., & Geiger, C. (1993). Adaptive device use in the home by older adults with mixed disabilities. *Archives of Physical Medicine and Rehabilitation, 74,* 149–152.

Gitlin, L. N., Luborsky M., & Schemm, R. L. (1997). Emerging concerns of assistive device use by older stroke patients in rehabilitation. Manuscript submitted for publication.

Gitlin, L. N., Mann, W. C., & Tomita, M. (in press). Relationship of depression to use of home environmental strategies in physically frail older adults. *The Gerontologist.*

Gitlin, L. N., Mount, J., Lucas, W., Weirich, L., & Gamberg, L. (1997). The physical costs and the psychosocial benefits of travel aids for persons who are visually impaired. *Journal of Visual Impairment and Blindness, 91*(4), 347–359.

Gitlin, L. N., Schemm, R. L., Landsberg, L., & Burgh, D. Y. (1996). Factors predicting assistive device use in the home by older persons following rehabilitation. *Journal of Aging and Health, 8*(4), 554–575.

Gitlin, L. N., Schemm, R. L., & Shmuely, Y. (1997). Mobility aid use at home by older adults discharged from rehabilitation. Manuscript submitted for publication.

Haber, P. A. L. (1982). The role of technology in the long-term care for the aged. *Medical Instrumentation, 16*(1), 7–8.

Haber, P. A. L. (1986). Technology in aging. *The Gerontologist, 26,* 350–357.

Kaufert, J. M., Kaufert, P. A., & Locker, D. (1987). After the epidemic: The long-term impact of poliomyelitis. In D. Coburn et al. (Eds.). *Health and Canadian society* (pp. 345–362). Toronto: Fitzhenry.

Kemp, B. J. (1988). Motivation, rehabilitation, and aging: A conceptual model. *Topics in Geriatric Rehabilitation, 3*(3), 41–51.

Kemp, B. J. (1993). Motivational issues in the use of technology by older persons. *Technology and Disability, 2*(1), 65–70.

LaBuda, D. R. (1990). The impact of technology on geriatric rehabilitation. In B. Kemp, K. Brummel-Smith & J. W. Ramsdell (Eds.), *Geriatric rehabilitation* (pp. 209–222). Boston: College Hill Press.

LaPlante, M. P., Hendershot, G. E., & Moss, A. J. (1992). *Assistive technology devices and home accessibility features: prevalence, payment, need and trends.* (Advance data from vital and health statistics; No. 217). Hyattsvile, Maryland: National Center for Health Statistics. (DHHS Publication No. PHS-92-1250).

LaPlante, M.P., Hendershot, G.E., & Moss, A.J. (1997). The prevalence of need for assistive technology, devices and home accessibility features. *Technology and Disability, 6*(1/2), Feb., p 17-28.

Low technology for maximizing independence. (1986, Fall). *Generations.*

Luborsky, M. (1994). Adaptive device appraisals by lifelong users facing new losses: Cultural, identity, and life history factors. In S. Hey & G. Kiger (Eds.), *Studies in disabilities.* Salem, OR: Willamette University Press.

Luborsky, M. R. (1993). Sociocultural factors shaping technology usage: Fulfilling the promise. *Technology and Disability, 2*(1), 71–78.

Macken, C. L. (1986). A profile of functionally impaired elderly persons living in the community. *Health Care Financing Review, 7*(4), 33–49.

Mann, W. C. (1994). Technology. In B. R. Bonder & M. B. Wagner (Eds.), *Functional performance in older adults* (pp. 323–338). Philadelphia: Davis.

Mann, W. C. (1997). Aging and assistive technology use. *Technology and Disability, 6*(1/2), 63–75.

Mann, W. C., Hurren, D., & Tomita, M. (1993). Comparison of assistive device use and needs of home-based older persons with different impairments. *American Journal of Occupational Therapy, 47*(11), 980–987.

Mann, W. C., Hurren, D., Tomita, M., & Charvat, B. (1995). Assistive devices for home-based older stroke survivors. *Topics in Geriatric Rehabilitation, 10*(3), pp. 75–86.

Mann, W. C., Karuza, J., Hurren, D., & Tomita, M. (1992). Assistive devices for home-based elderly persons with cognitive impairments. *Topics in Geriatric Rehabilitation, 8*(2), 35–52.

Mann, W. C., & Lane, J. (1991). *Assistive technology for persons with disabilities: The role of occupational therapy.* Rockville, MD: American Occupational Therapy Association.

Manton, K. G., Corder, L., & Stallard, E. (1993). Changes in the use of personal assistance and special equipment from 1982 to 1989: Results from the 1982 and 1989 NLTCS. *The Gerontologist, 33*(2), 168–176.

Montano, D. E., & Taplin, S. H. (1991). A test of an expanded theory of reasoned action to predict mammography participation. *Social Science Medical, 32*, 733–741.

Neville-Jan, A., Pierson, C. V., Kielhofner, G. & Davis, K. (1993). Adaptive equipment: A study of utilization after hospital discharge. *Occupational Therapy in Health Care, 8*, 3–18.

Norburn, J. E., Bernard, S. L., Konrad, T. R., Woomert, A., DeFriese, G. H., Koch, G. G., Ory, M. G., Kalsbeek, W. D. et al. (1995). Self-care and assistance from others in coping with functional status limitations among a national sample of older adults. *Journal of Gerontology, 50*B, S101–S109.

Ory, M. G., & Williams, T. F. (1989). Rehabilitation: Small goals, sustained interventions. *Annals, 503*, 61–76.

Parker, M. G., & Thorslund, M. (1991). The use of technical aids among community-based elderly. *American Journal of Occupational Therapy, 45*, 712–718.

Penning, M. J., & Strain, L. A. (1994). Gender differences in disability, assistance, and subjective well-being in later life. *Journal of Gerontology: Social Sciences, 49*, S202–S208.

Scheer, J., & Groce, N. (1988). Impairment as a human contrast. *Journal of Social Issues, 44*(1), 23–37.

Schemm, R. L., & Gitlin, L. N. (in press). How occupational therapists teach older patients to use bathing and dressing devices in rehabilitation. *American Journal of Occupational Therapy.*

Scherer, M. J. (1993). *Living in the state of stuck: How assistive technologies affect the lives of people with disabilities.* Cambridge, MA: Brookline.

Schulz, R., Heckhausen, J., & O'Brien, A. T. (1994). Control and the disablement process in the elderly. In D. S. Dunn, (Ed.), Psychosocial perspectives on disability (Special Issue). *Journal of Social Behavior and Personality, 9*(5), 139–152.

Simpson, C., & Pirrie, L. (1991). Walking aids: A survey of suitability and supply. *Physiotherapy, 77*(3), 231–234.

Smith, R., Benge, M., & Hall, M. (1994). Technology for self-care. In C. Christiansen (Ed.), *Ways of living: Self-care strategies for special needs* (pp. 379-422). Rockville, MD: American Occupational Therapy Association.

Stoller, E., Forster, L., & Portgual, D. (1993). Self-care responses to symptoms by older people: A health diary study of illness behavior. *Medical Care, 31*, 24–41.

Strain, L. A., Chappell, N. L., & Penning, M. J. (1993). The need for social science research on technology and aging. *Technology and Disability, 2*(1), 56–64.

U.S. Congress, Office of Technology Assessment. (1982). *Technology and handicapped people.* Washington, DC: US Government Printing Office.

Vanderheiden, G. C. (1987). Service delivery mechanisms in rehabilitation technology. *American Journal of Occupational Therapy, 41*(11), 703–710.

Van Der Heide, A., Jacobs, J. W. G., Van Albada-Kuipers, G. A., Kraaimaat, F. W., Geenen, R., & Bijlsma, J. W. J. (1993). Self report functional disability scores and the use of devices: Two distinct aspects of physical function in rheumatoid arthritis. *Annals of the Rheumatic Diseases, 52,* 497–502.

Verbrugge, L., & Jette, A. (1994). The disablement process. *Social Science and Medicine, 38*(1), 1–14.

Weinstein, N. D. (1993). Testing four competing theories of health-protective behavior. *Health Psychology, 12,* 324–333.

Williamson, G. M., & Schulz, R. (1992). Physical illness and symptoms of depression among elderly outpatients. *Psychology and Aging, 7,* 343–351.

Wolff, H. S. (1980). Tools for living: A blueprint for a major new industry. In J. Bray & S. Wright (Eds.), *The use of technology in the care of the elderly and the disabled.* CT: Greenwood.

Zimmer, Z., & Chappell, N. L. (1994). Mobility restriction and the use of devices among seniors. *Journal of Aging and Health, 6*(2), 185–208.

Zola, I. K. (1986). Thoughts on improving compliance in elderly arthritics. *Geriatrics, 41*(8), 81–83.

CHAPTER 7

Self-Care in Minority and Ethnic Populations: The Experience of Older Black Americans

Lucille Davis and May L. Wykle

T he increase in longevity has produced a rapidly growing group of older people in this country. With the dramatic growth in numbers of elders 65 and older, and especially 85 and older, comes an awareness of the health care needs of elders. Older persons have at least one chronic condition and some experience a number of diseases that limit their function (American Association of Retired Persons [AARP], 1995; Hobbs & Damon, 1996). With health problems, there is concern about the health care needs of older adults and their ability to meet them. Thus, self-care becomes an important issue for older people, particularly the Black aged, who often do not seek formal health care services for symptoms of illness. Because Blacks have had limited access to the health care system, they have routinely used self-care, mostly in the form of various home remedies. Self-care, however, as a regular practice among Black elders, has received little attention until recently. Many older adults are quick to share home remedies that they believe work for various illness symptoms. It is not known, however, how many of these remedies actually are harmful or delay the person's seeking needed and appropriate medical attention. Much research is needed to determine the extent of self-care used by Black elders for illness symptoms and associated outcomes.

There is a dearth of knowledge about self-care in minority/ethnic low-income populations, particularly among elders. While self-care beliefs and practices are applicable to other minority/ethnic groups, this chapter will focus on health beliefs and self-care practices among Black elders. Although there are a variety of self-care studies on older people (DeFriese, Konrad, Woomert, Norburn, & Bernard, 1994; Kart & Dunkle, 1989; Norburn et al., 1995; Stoller, 1993a), few of them have included representative samples of Black elders.

MINORITY/ETHNIC DIFFERENCES IN SELF-CARE

As a result of sampling bias, it is unclear how Black and White elders differ in their self-care practices. Differences could include the range of self-care responses, such as home remedies, lay consultations, and other lay strategies (Davis & McGadney, 1993). Black elders are a heterogeneous group in this country, and as such it is difficult to make a collective statement about their health beliefs and practices (Gibson, 1994; Giger, Davidheizer, & Turner, 1992). Nevertheless, it is important to consider those self-care practices that are associated with Black elders who have low incomes, and who may encounter barriers that prevent access to formal health care.

As Wykle and Haug (1993) point out, there have been very few studies that have examined differences between cultural groups taking into account ethnicity, economic variation, and class differences. In their study on multicultural and social-class aspects of self-care (1993), they found more likenesses than differences between Whites and Blacks relevant to their most frequently occurring health symptoms. However, they identified differences in treatment modalities between Blacks and Whites with Whites seeking professional advice more than Blacks. It is interesting to note that Blacks were judged by evaluators to be less healthy than other populations, but were more likely to evaluate their health as "good." This is consistent with Stoller's observation (1994b) that elders who believe their health is good are less likely to interpret their symptoms as threatening and have more confidence in their own resilience. Therefore, it makes sense that Blacks would be more likely to engage in self-care practices.

CULTURAL ORIGINS OF SELF-CARE BEHAVIORS IN MINORITY POPULATIONS

The uniqueness of many health beliefs and practices of ethnic minorities, including self-care behaviors of Black elders, can be traced to their cultural history and to the continuing social and economic inequalities that still exist today. From a historical perspective, Blacks have generally been responsible for providing for their own health needs, beginning with slavery and often persisting today because of economic inadequacy and institutional racism. Because of these barriers Black elders are often reluctant to utilize formal health care until their symptoms become acute or when self-care practices no longer provide symptom relief.

On the other hand, Black elders' beliefs about health are consistent with those that underlie the current health promotion movement; that is, the belief that good health is an individual responsibility. Blacks' beliefs about health maintenance emphasize harmony, balance, and moderation. "Some of these practices are very specific, such as always wearing an undershirt in the winter, not washing one's hair during menstruation, or never going to bed on a full stomach" (Davis & McGadney, 1993).

The importance of self-care in maintaining health or treating illnesses is illustrated in a Black newspaper editorial:

> In general, African Americans traditionally have had a high regard for the value of health and life. The fact is easily realized when one considers the countless herbs, ointments, toddies and other home remedies that our fore-fathers used to fight illnesses and to improve the quality of their lives during and after 1619 (when the first slave ship landed on American shores). (*Chicago Defender,* April 2, 1990, p. 11).

Many Black elders have southern roots, and subsequently their health beliefs and self-care practices are often a blend of African and Southern traditions. In many cases, health practices learned in the South have been maintained and further blended with mainstream medicine. These health care practices, which may be an amalgam of African, American southern, and modern medicine, can vary according to cultural orientation, experience, and income. In some cases the same practices are found in both "well-to-do" and low-income homes (White, 1977).

The literature on health practices of Blacks, particularly Black elders, refers to such practices as "folk medicine." However, folk medicine is not unique to Blacks and the concept is germane to many cultural and ethnic groups (Giger et al., 1992). In fact, many groups may use folk medicine in combination with mainstream medicine. The significance and the extent to which folk medicine is used varies among ethnic and cultural groups, including Blacks, depending on education and socioeconomic status (Bullough & Bullough, 1982).

Although many health care beliefs and practices have their origin in West Africa, Black American folk medicine has also been influenced by beliefs that developed in countries such as Haiti, Jamaica, and Trinidad (Smith, 1976). Slavery resulted in the combination or blending of African cultures with those of French, Creoles, and American Indians, resulting in health beliefs and practices that are unique and have been handed down from generation to generation.

Black folk medicine is based on the belief that disease or illness arises from either natural or unnatural causes. Natural diseases or illnesses are seen as arising from physical causes, such as a cold wind that might cause pneumonia or an illness that could occur when dangerous elements commonly found in the environment enter the bloodstream through various impurities found in food, water, and air. What is interesting about these beliefs is that they sound very much like health professionals' and others' rationales for environmentally induced illnesses, such as linking cancer to smoking and pollution. Natural illnesses may also be spiritual in nature and seen as "divine punishment," suggesting that the fear of illness may function as an instrument of social control (Watson, 1984).

Unnatural illnesses are believed to be the work of evil spirits and conflict in the social network (Snow, 1974; Watson, 1984). The cultural underpinnings of folk medicine continue to influence health beliefs and practices of Black elders; even in this age of information, some Black elders equate good health with luck or success. An illness or disease is often associated with bad luck, fate, or family conflict. This perspective, too, is very similar to professionals' understanding and discussion of the relationship between family stress and disease. In these cases, elders may consult a health professional only after attempts with home remedies have failed. Therefore, it is often safe to assume that all known and available cultural home remedies have been tried before a physician is seen.

Snow's (1974) research on lower-class southern Blacks illustrates the significance of beliefs about illnesses. It also illustrates how scientific terms are shaped by cultural understanding (Kleinman, 1978; Stoller, 1993b). For example, Snow discusses hypertension, called "high blood" by this group of Blacks. This idea of high blood was based on the belief that blood has an antiregulatory function and that high pressure opens the skin pores and allows excess blood to be sweated out. Treatment consisted of the use of astringent substances such as vinegar, lemon juice, pickles, and epsom salt; all of the latter were thought to cause the "blood to go down." Yet practices such as eating pickles, which are often salty, might not be healthy for a Black older person with hypertension. These treatments are still practiced today and in some cases seen by Black elders as more legitimate than the medicines prescribed by doctors. Thus, sometimes, family self-care measures are considered more effective than professional medical intervention. A case in point is an elderly Black woman who said, "I know when my pressure is up and I take my garlic water and lemon juice along with my pills."

Historically, some Black elders use folk medicine out of tradition, while others use it because of previous discriminatory practices in the health care system. As Bullough and Bullough (1982) suggest, folk medicine became the mainstay for many Blacks because of economic necessity or "disenchantment" with the segregated, inferior medical care system available to them (Giger et al., 1992). Presently, although low-income Blacks have access through mainstream medicine, they may continue to refuse to use the system, citing reasons such as insensitive treatment, high cost and lack of trust in doctors. In some cases, they will see a doctor only to get access to otherwise unavailable prescription medications.

Moreover, beliefs about illness will determine if the older person consults a doctor at all. Black folk practitioners may be consulted first, such as a person who is generally knowledgeable about various types of home remedies that can be made from herbs, spices, and roots. Alternatively a "spiritualist" may be consulted who combines rituals, spiritual beliefs, and herbal medicines to treat illnesses and other psychosocial conditions.

Even today, Black elders who live in isolated areas, such as the rural South, or in isolated public housing in the North, where economic resources and medical resources are both limited, will rely more on informal sources. In these cases folk beliefs and practices that have Southern origins will be dominant. In ethnographic interviews, Black elders who had migrated from the South as young adults discussed how they had limited access to doctors when they were raising their families and often had to send their children "back home" because "they know how to take care of you"—referring to self-care practices such as "feeding you good food and allowing you to get fresh air."

In a pilot project conducted by one of the authors among a group of low-income Black elders, several main reasons were identified by black elders for engaging in self-care: (a) fragmentation in the health care system, (b) preference for lay consultation, (c) beliefs about efficacy of treatment, and (d) perceived cause of illness. Some reasons identified by Blacks for engaging in self-care behaviors are illustrated in the following vignettes (Davis & McGadney, 1993, pp. 77–78).

Fragmentation in the health care system is illustrated by the case of a 70-year-old Black female who was recently diagnosed with glaucoma and hypertension. On her clinic day, she had an appointment in the glaucoma clinic and the doctor told her that her pressure was fine. In the afternoon, when visiting the high blood pressure clinic, she was told that her pressure was "up" Not recognizing the distinction between pressure in the eye and in the vascular system, she decided not to come back to me clinic. She stated: "The doctors don't know anything—one says my pressure is up and the other one that it is OK—I think I will be better off taking care of myself."

The use of the lay consultation system is demonstrated by a 72-year-old Black man who had a persistent cough for several weeks and consulted with his neighbors in the senior building where he lived. His neighbor suggested a toddie of "lemon, honey and a shot of whiskey." When he did not experience any relief from these remedies, he then consulted his pharmacist, and finally went to the doctor after the cough increased to the point where he could not sleep at night.

Beliefs about the efficacy of treatment can be heard in the statement of a 65-year-old woman who explained that she only used her high blood pressure medicine when she really needed it. "I know when my pressure is up," she said. "I get spots in front of my eyes and a heavy feeling in my chest, and when that happens I take my garlic water and then my pills if I still have some left."

Finally, perceived cause of illness is illustrated by a 74-year-old Black female who stated, "I can put up with all the pain because arthritis runs in my family and all of us get it when we get old."

POSITIVE BENEFITS OF SELF-CARE
FOR OLDER BLACK AMERICANS

From a historical perspective, self-care can be seen as positive because it allowed Blacks to act proactively and use informal support systems when they were isolated from the formalized health system. These informal support systems resulted in strong family bonds, neighborhood self-help groups and practitioners of folk medicine (Watson, 1984); and are still highly significant resources for Black elders today.

Regardless of the reasons why Black elders engage in self-care, as Watson (1984) correctly argues, self-care has been valuable and positive for Blacks. These practices have allowed Blacks to survive, act proactively and develop and use strong information support systems when isolated from the formalized health care system. As DeFriese et al. (1994) suggest, the proactive mobilization of personal and social resources by individuals and groups can enhance the quality of their lives and prolong life.

Family and church are two primary systems, which still significantly influence health beliefs and self-care practices among Blacks. The importance of these systems in relation to health are well documented (Burton et al., 1995; Wood & Parham, 1990). The church can be thought of as an extended family and remains a significant provider of emotional and social support for Black elders. Many churches have health ministries, and are viewed as important sites where health information and health promotion programs can be conducted (Smith, 1976). Ministers and members of the church frequently provide instrumental and expressive assistance during an illness; they are sources of consultation and are involved in defining symptoms and negotiating treatment strategies, including self-care measures such as prayer and faith in God. In this case, God is perceived "in a very personal way and is considered as much a part of the informal support system as family, friends, or neighbors" (Wood & Wan, 1993, p. 49).

Another cultural coping response is "accommodating oneself to the situation" (Segall & Wykle, 1988–1989), which is similar to the concept of "overcoming." This response or feeling can be captured in some of the Negro spirituals, such as "I've Come This Far By Faith" or the more contemporary song, "We Shall Overcome." You may hear Black elders say, "I'm just glad that I've lived this long." This response can be viewed as logical when placed in a cultural and life course perspective.

Unfortunately, mainstream medicine and many health professionals label elders, especially Black elders, as noncompliant when they use self-care measures, particularly if they do not fit the conventional scientific paradigm. Yet, in many cases, self-care measures are beneficial or neutral. It has been pointed out that the boundaries between folk medicine and scientific medicine is fluid; many self-care practices are derived from scientific medicine, and scientific medicine practices are based on home remedies. If self-care practice is not harmful, then Black elders should not be discouraged from their beliefs. Hautman (1987, p. 234) suggests that "one way of minimizing ethnocentric tendencies is to reconceptualize what has been traditionally termed 'folk practices' to the less culturally biased term, 'self-care practices.' "

RESEARCH QUESTIONS AND DIRECTIONS

Giger, Davidheizer, and Turner (1992) also argue that professionals should differentiate between cultural practices that are efficacious, neutral, or dysfunctional. In developing self-care manuals for Black elders, Davis and McGadney (1992) found that it was important to include cultural vignettes that capture Black elders' self-care measures and provide information about them in relation to their effectiveness or their potential harm. This information was made available only after gaining trust from and spending time talking with the Black elders. Presently, Black elders do practice self-care, and use a variety of self-treatments that include home remedies, folk medicine, advice from family and church affiliations, and sometimes refraining from treatment. It is yet to be determined how health beliefs and self-care practices will change in future cohorts of blacks. If economic or social changes are not made in our society and in health care, future older cohorts may be more similar than different.

From a policy perspective, more research is needed to:

1. determine how self-care practices differ between and among different ethnic/cultural groups, including Black elders
2. develop better measures of self-care practices, taking into account how cultural and social class influences shape these practices and behaviors
3. identify the role of informal systems, such as the extended family and the church, in the decision-making process in relation to self-care
4. examine health beliefs and self-care practices from a life course perspective
5. determine the types of self-care practices associated with physical and mental symptoms.

REFERENCES

American Association of Retired Persons [AARP] (1995). *A portrait of older minorities.* Washington, DC: Author.

Bullough, V. L., & Bullough, B. (1982). *Health care for other Americans.* New York: Appleton-Century-Crofts.

Burton, L., Kasper, J. D., Shore, A., Cagney, K. A., LaViest, T. A., Cubbine, C., & German, P. S. (1995). The structure of informal care: Are there differences by race? *The Gerontologist, 35,* 744–752.

Davis, L., & McGadney, B. (1993). *Social factors in the health of black urban elders. Final report* (NIA IR2/GD7). Chicago: Chicago Northwestern University.

Davis, L., McGadney, B., Perri, P. (1992). Learning to live with hypertension: a self care manual for Black elders. Lisle, IL: Tucker Publishing Co.

DeFriese, G. H., Konrad, T. R., Woomert, A., Norburn, J. E., & Bernard, S. (1994). Self-care and quality of life in old age. Chapter in R. P. Abeles, H. Gift, and M. G. Ory, (Eds.) *Aging and quality of life* (pp. 99–117). New York: Springer Publishing.

Gibson, R. C. (1994). The age-by-race gap in health and mortality in the elderly population: A social science research agenda. *The Gerontologist, 34*(4).

Giger, J. M., Davidheizer, R. E., & Turner, G. (1992). Black American folk medicine health care beliefs. *Association of Black Nursing Faculty, 2,* 42–46.

Hautman, M. A. (1987). Self-care responses to respiratory illness among Vietnamese. *Western Journal of Nursing Research, 9,* 223–236.

Hobbs, F. B., & Damon, B. L. (1996). 65+ in the United States. In U.S. Bureau of the Census, *Current population reports* (Special Studies, p. 23–190). U.S. Government Printing Office, Washington, DC.

Kart, C. S., & Dunkle, R. (1989). Assessing capacity for self-care among the aged. *Journal of Aging and Health, 1,* 430–450.

Kleinman, A. (1978). Concepts and a model for the comparison of medical systems and cultural systems. *Social Science and Medicine, 12,* 85–93.

Norburn, J. K., Bernard, S., Konrad, T. R., Woomert, A., DeFriese, G., Kalsbeek, W., Koch, G., & Ory, M. (1995). Self-care and assistance from others in coping with functional status limitations among a national sample of older adults. *Journal of Gerontology: Social Sciences, 50B,* S101–109.

Segall, L. M., & Wykle, M. (1988–1989). The Black family's experience with dementia. *Journal of Applied Social Sciences, 13,* 170–191.

Smith, J. A. (1976). The role of the black clergy as applied health care professionals in working with black patients. In Luckcraft (Ed.), *Black Americans: Implications for black care,* (pp. 12–15). New York: American Journal of Nursing.

Snow, L. E. (1974). Folk medical beliefs and their implications for care of patients.

Review based on studies among black Americans. *Annals of Internal Medicine, 81,* 82–96.

Stoller, E. L. (1993a). Gender and the organization of lay health care: A socialist-feminist perspective. *Journal of Aging Studies, 7,* 151–170.

Stoller, E. L. (1993b). Interpretation of symptoms by older people: A health diary study of illness behavior. *Journal of Aging and Health, 5,* 58–81.

Watson, W. (Ed.). (1984). *Black folk medicine: The therapeutic significance of faith and trust.* New Brunswick, NJ: Transaction.

White, E. H. (1977). Giving health care to minority patients. *Nursing Clinics of North America, 12,* 27–40.

Wood, J. B., & Parham, I. A. (1990). Coping with perceived burden: Ethnic and cultural issues in Alzheimer's family caregiving. *Journal of Applied Gerontology, 9,* 325–339.

Wood, & Wan. (1993). Ethnicity and minority issues in family caregiving to rural Black elders. In C. M. Baress & D. E. Stull (Eds.), *Ethnic elderly and long-term care,* (pp. 39–57). New York: Springer Publishing.

Wykle, M., & Haug, M. (1993). Multicultural and social class aspects of self-care. *Generations, 3,* 25–28.

CHAPTER 8

International Perspectives on Self-Care Research

Kathryn Dean

C ommonalities and differences in international perspectives on self-care research are found across North America and European countries. Academic disciplines which cut across international boundaries have exerted strong influence on research on health-related behavior in different countries (Dean, 1992). The dominant values and social structures in different countries influence academic as well as lay thinking in a subject area, and thus determine the acceptability of a subject and its priority funding.

HISTORICAL APPROACHES TO RESEARCH ON HEALTH-RELATED BEHAVIOR

When the subject of self-care emerged and received a great deal of attention two decades ago, it had long been known that the bulk of all illness care in any country is provided in lay networks (Dean, 1981; Levin, Katz, & Holst, 1976). Since that time, the fundamental influence of personal behavior on health protection, early detection of disease, and control of chronic health problems has become widely recognized in industrialized societies (Hamburg, Elliott, & Parran, 1982; Ory, Abeles, & Lipman, 1992; U.S. Department of Health, Education, & Welfare [USDHEW], 1979). The concept of self-care reflects changes in concepts and approaches to population health. Conceptualizing health-related behavior as self-care rather than professional care seeking challenged dominant attitudes about sources of health protection and health care, and about approaches to population health promotion (Dean & Kickbusch, 1995).

The manner in which the term *self-care* appeared and exerted influence in the health sector illustrates how social systems interact with academic traditions to influence research and practice. Extensive research on health-related behavior was conducted in both North America and Europe prior to the emergence of the concept of self-care in the 1970s. When self-care became conceptualized as a subject distinct from prior work on "health-related behavior," it did not have the same appeal in all countries and the acceptance factor influenced both the type and the amount of self-care research conducted.

For many years behavioral research focused on health was rather clearly divided into epidemiological and social science approaches (Dean, 1992). (See also chapter 1, by Konrad, for a discussion of different research perspectives.) The dominant influence determining the way health research on behavior was conducted was the academic discipline in which the researcher was trained.

In most social science research, behavior was studied as the outcome variable of interest. The purpose of the research was to identify factors related to what was generally differentiated as health behavior and illness behavior. The early period of social science research on these topics was characterized by the entry of sociologists into population health research, mostly in departments of medical sociology or as sociological researchers attached to departments of administrative medicine or social medicine. This era was a manifestation of the rapid development and expansion of modern medical care systems. As reflected in the name *medical sociology,* the field was concerned with social studies of medical care. Medical anthropology and health economics also developed rapidly during this period. Utilization of medical services was the topic most often studied during the early period of social science research on health-related behavior.

The other major behavioral tradition in population health research derives from behavioral epidemiology. In the epidemiological tradition, either specific diseases or mortality, have generally been the outcome variables, with behaviors studied as the determinants of disease. Other causal influences are examined as "confounders" affecting the statistical influence of the behavioral "risk." Behavioral epidemiology is based on the risk factor model of research on disease and mortality, the dominant paradigm in contemporary epidemiology (Dean, 1993). Heavily influenced by studies finding relationships between habits of daily living and subsequent morbidity and mortality in the United States in the early 1970s (Belloc & Breslow, 1972; Berkman & Breslow, 1983), risk factor research looking for associations between individual behavioral habits and a wide range of diseases mushroomed in both the United States and Europe. The narrow range of behavioral habits examined in early research exerted fundamental influence on this body of work. Alcohol and tobacco consumption, exercise, and fat content in the diet became popular subjects of behavioral epidemiology.

BEYOND PROFESSIONAL CARE: EMERGENCE OF THE CONCEPT OF SELF-CARE

The notion that people consciously and actively intervene in their own health interest was only vaguely and implicitly a part of the research on health-related behavior prior to the emergence in the 1970s of the subject of self-care. Self-medication, home remedies, and decisions to monitor symptoms before taking action, behaviors that account for the bulk of all health-related behavior, were treated as "fringe," rather than "mainstream," practices. Even though the findings from the multitude of studies conducted on utilization of medical services had documented repeatedly that self-care and family care accounted for the bulk of all illness care, the focus remained on utilization of professional services.

Thus, in spite of the extensive documentation of the extent of self-care, the emergence of the concept was not associated with the traditional empirical research on health-related behavior. Consultation in lay networks became a variable of interest after the appearance of overwhelming documentation of the extent of illness cared for without professional help. However, it was studied from the standpoint of its effects on professional care seeking rather than as a resource in its own right. Except for work in the women's health movement and of innovators in rural health care, predominantly in developing countries (Werner, 1977), self-care as the fundamental health care resource and determinant of both the use of professional services and treatment outcomes was not seriously considered.

The concept of self-care arose from sources quite far removed from the research documenting the volume of personal health care performed without consulting professional caregivers. The major causes leading to new thinking with regard to health-related behavior were the growing evidence and awareness of the limits of medical care for improving the health of populations and the skyrocketing costs of health care. The needs of many who could be helped by professional services remained unmet in the face of ever-increasing costs for health care systems that were widely criticized (Fuchs, 1974; Illich, 1976; McKeown, 1979). Highly educated populations expected better information and greater participation in decision making in matters concerning their health. The consequences of unnecessary and often dangerous treatment and screening services focused attention on patients' rights and the need to reduce iatrogenic disease and disability.

One of the earliest publications directly taking up the subject of self-care clearly shows the lack of continuity with the traditional research literature on health-related behavior. Following the International Symposium on the Role of the Individual in Primary Health Care, held in Copenhagen in 1975, Levin and his colleagues (1976) named the demystification of professional services, better educated populations with greater expectations, and the limits of high-technology medicine as among the more important reasons for the growth of interest in self-care. The complementary nature of self-care and professional care was stressed as a reason to make better use of lay care resources.

INTERNATIONAL POLICY PERSPECTIVES AND SOCIAL VALUES: WHO HAS RESPONSIBILITY FOR HEALTH?

With the introduction of the self-care concept, national differences in thinking and research emerged. In some countries the term was vigorously debated. Major issues revolved around the possibility that the concept of self-care could be used to individualize responsibility for health (Dean & Kickbusch, 1995). The dangers of using self-care arguments to reduce health care expenditures by pushing more responsibility onto individuals and families were debated widely. A related concern has been the victim-blaming potential of emphasizing self-care and self-help (Crawford, 1977). These concerns are somewhat similar to the arguments heard today against the victim-blaming aspects of proposals which would tie treatment services or insurance for treatment services to health-related behaviors such as smoking and alcohol consumption.

Acceptance of the concept of self-care in different countries has been related to different systems of organizing, financing, and delivering professional services. In the Scandinavian countries, where publicly financed and managed health services are the norm, major concerns revolve around fears of misuse of the self-care concept in attempts to dismantle the social welfare system (Tibblin, 1979). In countries with less structured approaches to organizing and funding health services, most particularly the United States, the concept of self-care has been more favorably received, even though parallel concerns have been raised about the danger that the self-care concept would be used politically to withhold health care from those who could not pay or from people with diseases statistically associated with behavioral practices (DeFriese, Woomert, Guild, Steckler, & Konrad, 1989).

The self-care acceptance factor can be said to have divided along lines of policy perspectives and social values regarding individual and collective responsibility for health. The relationship between the type of health service system and interest in the concept of self-care is not, however, a simple factor of the degree of public/private organization and funding. For example, the research and policy interest in the subject of self-care has taken quite different forms in the Scandinavian countries, Israel, and Canada, all of which have publicly financed health systems.

A series of studies documented the extent of self-care in Denmark, along with the influence of social and situational influences on the types and amount of self-care practiced (Dean, 1989b, 1992; Dean, Holst, & Wagner, 1983). It was found that self-care decisions were generally safe and appropriate (Petersen, 1976). Similar findings were also reported in England (Williamson & Danaher, 1980). Still, the same controversy surrounded the subject of self-care in Denmark as in the other Scandinavian countries and the concept essentially disappeared from research and practice after the initial period of recognition and interest.

In Israel, attention to the concept of self-care was shaped by professional perspectives. Research on attitudes toward self-care and lay autonomy found that physicians and allied health professionals had negative attitudes toward self-care (Shuval, Javetz, & Shye, 1989; Shye, Javetz, & Shuval, 1990). Israeli lay people, expressing strong medically dependent views toward health care, reported corresponding reservations about the concept of self-care (Shye, Javetz, & Shuval, 1991). Physician utilization was positively related to dependent attitudes toward physicians and inversely related to confidence in one's own ability to care for symptoms. Consistent with other studies, a positive relationship was found between education and favorable attitudes toward self-care. Views in support of lay independence were more often found among persons who tended to question physician directives. While Israeli citizens apparently did not experience the type of open controversy that surrounded the subject in Scandinavia, the dominant picture was one of negative attitudes toward active self-care behavior both among professional and lay people in a medically dependent population.

Quite different developments occurred in Canada, where self-care became a core component of the policy framework for national health promotion efforts (Milio, 1986; World Health Organization [WHO], 1986). Research—including a nationally funded research initiative on the subject—was both encouraged and supported. In contrast to the other examples, the concept of self-care was favorably received in Canada and interest in the subject has been sustained (Chappell, 1987; Dean, 1996a; Penning & Chappell, 1990; Segall & Goldstein, 1989).

Even though the acceptance factor differs from country to country, the emergence of the concept of self-care is a sign of the forces challenging medical dominance in health care systems and in professional–patient interactions. Conceptualizing health-related behavior as self-care, rather than professional care-seeking, represents a change in attitudes about sources of health protection and health care. International differences in accepting and building on the self-care concept reflect opposing interests and concerns that grow out of organizational structures, professional control, and the values underlying different systems.

Due to the quite divergent sources of interest in self-care, it has been viewed at one and the same time as a conservative trend in some circles and a progressive trend in others (Dean & Kichbusch, 1995). Professional resistance to the term arose, regardless of the type of service system (DeFriese et al., 1989; Shye et al., 1993; Tibblin, 1979). When political and professional resistance to self-care came together, acceptance of the concept was especially low. In many countries, as illustrated above, the concept was simply ignored after an initial flurry of attention and/or controversy.

CROSS-NATIONAL DIFFERENCES IN DEFINING SELF-CARE AND HEALTH PROMOTION CONCEPTS

The concepts of self-care and health promotion have common origins (Dean & Kickbusch, 1995). Both represent new thinking about the roles of the professional and lay sectors in health protection. The two concepts did not, however, attain the same level of stability and legitimacy. DeFriese and his colleagues (1989) found that after a period of intense focus on self-care in research and policy in the United States, the subject of self-care as an independent topic dropped from public prominence. At the same time, they documented the emergence of self-care in disease management and functional health status maintenance programs as well as in the research of the clinical health professions. Self-care, pulled into the wellness movement, had, by the start of the nineties, been integrated into a diverse array of professional health promotion programs. In Europe, while the term self-care was less often used, activating patient behavior also became an important component of professional fitness and rehabilitation programs.

In contrast to self-care, the health promotion concept attained greater legitimacy. The meaning attached to the concept of health promotion and the role given self-care in relation to health promotion developed in different ways in the United States and Europe. In the United States, *health promotion* generally refers to policies and programs focused on the behavioral practices of individuals. Self-care and health promotion could, to a certain degree, be considered synonymous terms. While the *self-care* term is also used to refer to the self-management of chronic conditions and acute symptoms, both forms of health-promoting actions taken during illness, both concepts refer to the health-related behavior of individuals.

In Europe the concept of health promotion assumed a strong health policy perspective. It became contrasted with *disease prevention,* which focused on the health education of individuals. The Canadian perspective on health promotion and self-care was similar to the European, and indeed influenced the development of the field in Europe (Raeburn & Rootman, 1989). The policy perspective that characterizes the European and Canadian concepts of health promotion and self-care is reflected in the WHO European Targets for Health for All (1985) and the Ottawa Charter on Health Promotion (WHO, 1986). These two documents influenced health policies and programs in Europe, including perspectives on how the behavior of individuals should be approached in health policy and practice.

The WHO policy document accepted by the member states of Europe places emphasis for promoting the health of populations on health policy, lifestyles conducive to health, healthy environments, health development support, and appropriate care. An underlying theme is that the health of populations cannot be improved without addressing inequalities in health, both within and between nations. Individual behavior is addressed within the context of lifestyles, recognizing that health-related behavior is shaped within social, cultural, and economic environments.

In this contextual framework, health-enhancing behaviors are not simple choices based on information, but grow out of options and skills for making healthy choices. This perspective is underscored by the European emphasis on multisectoral approaches to policy development in the interest of national health. In the words of the European WHO document, improving health-related behavior requires "legislative, administrative and economic mechanisms providing broad intersectoral support and resources." Appropriate care is conceptualized as including the entire range of both lay and professional care.

The majority of care is self-care or care provided by family members and friends. Unfortunately, there is too little recognition of this fact by health professionals, planners, and politicians. As a consequence, individuals and families are often not given sufficient information to make informed choices or to participate on an equal basis with health professionals in decision making concerning their own health (WHO, 1985).

Community participation in the development of health policy and individual participation in all levels of personal health care are the fundamental self-care perspectives defined in the European policy document. These perspectives were carried forward in the Ottawa Charter for Health Promotion adopted at the first international conference on health promotion sponsored by WHO, Health and Welfare Canada, and the Canadian Public Health Association.

Promoting the health of populations requires building "healthy" public policies that cross sectors of public action. The approach to personal behavior in the Ottawa Charter is the development of personal skills enabling individuals to make choices conducive to health and interact effectively in the environments affecting health. The reorientation of health services, community action, and supportive environments for health development are the means to achieve health promotion. These perspectives have stimulated broader approaches to health action in Canada (Pederson, O'Neill, & Rootman, 1994) and some European countries, including research and programs concerned with health-related behavior. The arenas for influencing behavior were expanded beyond health services and traditional health education to policy development and environmental contexts, as reflected in the WHO-sponsored Healthy Cities and Health Promoting Schools projects.

EFFECTS OF THE SELF-CARE CONCEPT
ON HEALTH RESEARCH IN EUROPE:
BROADENING RESEARCH AGENDAS

The impact of conceptualizing health-related behavior as self-care was to make explicit the fact that lay persons determine the content and amount of their own health-protective behavior. Previous emphasis on identifying group characteristics that determined how medical services were used, delays in seeking medical care, or compliance with medical directives, gave way to the study of lay health behavior in its own right.

Inherent in the concept of self-care is the recognition that whatever factors and processes shape behavior, and whether or not self-care is effective and interfaces appropriately with professional care, it is the individual person that acts, or does not act, to preserve health and respond to symptoms (Dean, 1992). The shift in perspective opened the way to study both individual behavior and health service systems and their use in new ways.

The total spectrum of health-related behavior became important (Calnan, 1989; Dean, 1989b; Dean, Colomer, & Perez-Hoyos, 1995). Rather than assess the medical utilization bias of subjects, such as delay in seeking care, researchers studied decisions to take no action in response to symptoms from a neutral perspective, recognizing that doing nothing about self-limiting symptoms may sometimes be the most appropriate and safest response to illness (Bentzen, Christiansen, & Pedersen, 1989; Dean, 1983, 1986). Understanding constraints on self-care behavior and ways to facilitate it became acceptable subjects of inquiry (Segall & Goldstein, 1989). Professional and lay attitudes towards self-care were equally relevant to study (Shuval et al., 1989; Shye et al., 1990, 1991); discrepancies between professional and lay views were documented (van Agthoven & Plomp, 1989). Recent research recognizes and values lay knowledge (Dean & Hunter, 1996; Milburn, 1996; Popay & Williams, 1996).

Along with the conceptual changes in research on health behavior, a broader range of methodological approaches has been used to study lay behavior (Dean, 1989a, 1992), including clinical trial approaches to evaluating the effectiveness of self-care initiatives (Ramussen, 1989; Winkler, Underwood, Fatovich, James, & Gray, 1989). Another new development is the integration of qualitative and quantitative methods to study interactions between personal health behavior and other factors that influence health (Blane, 1996). Theoretical and methodological challenges impart great potential for using the concept of self-care to expand knowledge about health and behavior (Dean, 1989a, 1989b; 1996b; Dean & Hunter, 1996; Dean, Kreiner, & McQueen, 1993; Dean & McQueen, 1996).

THE MERGING OF INDIVIDUAL AND SOCIAL PERSPECTIVES: FORGING NEW INTERNATIONAL ALLIANCES

The self-care movement in the United States and the richness and diversity of the U.S. fitness programs and wellness movement stimulated new thinking in Europe about the role of the individual in health protection. The limits of health services for improving the health of populations are now well recognized. The social perspectives built into the field of health promotion in Europe are, in turn, influencing developments in the United States. Healthy Cities and Health Promoting Schools projects building on the principles of health promotion outlined in the Ottawa Charter now operate in the U.S. as well.

Self-care, including the active participation of lay people in professional–patient interactions is no longer considered fringe behavior. The apparent contradiction in self-care's identification with conservatism in some circles and progressivism in others reveals a merging of the individual and social perspectives and mirrors the new alliances based on changes in attitudes toward social development in the wider community (Dean & Kichbusch, 1995).

CONCLUSION

The accumulation of evidence about the limits of curative care and of health education focused predominantly on changing the behavior of individuals provided the foundation for new thinking in the health sector. It is not surprising that the acceptance of the concept of self-care was affected by the structure and organization of health care delivery systems and by national differences in attitudes toward individual and social responsibility for health. With the merging of individual and social perspectives, self-care can be both recognized and placed in a contextual framework. The fundamental importance of the appropriate range of lay and professional care for health protection and the effective functioning of health care systems is now widely recognized.

It is possible that self-care will reemerge in research and practice as the basic form of care, determining health and well-being as well as the types and amount of professional services used. It is important to gain more knowledge about the determinants of appropriate self-care and the forces that create self-care deficiencies. A self-care research agenda must utilize research methods that can provide valid knowledge about the complex causal processes shaping both behavior and health; scientific quality will ultimately determine the usefulness of self-care research. Nevertheless, the use of research results in policy and practice may well remain country specific.

REFERENCES

Belloc N., & Breslow L. (1972). Relationship of health practices and mortality. *Preventive Medicine, 2*, 67–81.

Bentzen N., Christiansen T., & Pedersen K. M. (1989). Self-care within a model for demand for medical care. *Social Science and Medicine, 29*, 185–193.

Berkman L., & Breslow L. (1983). *Health and ways of living: The Alameda County study*. New York: Oxford University Press.

Blane, D. (1996). Collecting retrospective data: Development of a reliable method and a pilot study of its use. *Social Science and Medicine, 42*, 751–758.

Calnan, M. (1989). Control over health and patterns of health-related behavior. *Social Science and Medicine, 29*, 131–136.

Chappell, N. (1987). The interface between three systems of care: Self, informal, and formal. In R. Ward & S. Tobin (Eds.), *Health in aging: Sociological issues and policy directions* (pp. 159–179). New York: Springer Publishing.

Crawford, R. (1977). You are dangerous to your health: The ideology and politics of victim blaming. *International Journal of Health Services, 7*, 663.

Dean, K. (1981). Self-care responses to illness: A selected review. *Social Science and Medicine, 15A*, 673–687.

Dean, K. (1986). Self care: Implications for aging. In K. Dean, B. Holstein, & T. Hickey (Eds.), *Self care and health in old age* (pp. 58–93). London: Croom Helm.

Dean, K. (1989a). Conceptual, theoretical and methodological issues in self-care research. *Social Science and Medicine, 29*, 117–123.

Dean, K. (1989b). Self-care components of lifestyle: The importance of gender, attitudes and the social situation. *Social Science and Medicine, 29*, 137–152.

Dean, K. (1992). Health related behavior: Concepts and methods. In M. Ory, R. Abeles and P. D. Lipman (Eds.), *Aging, health, and behavior* (pp. 27–56). Newbury Park, CA: Sage.

Dean, K. (1993). Integrating theory and methods in population health research. In K. Dean (Ed.), *Population health research: Linking theory and methods* (pp. 9–36). London: Sage.

Dean, K. (1996a). *Self care: The most effective means to preserving and promoting health* (Community Paper Series, No. 5). Victoria, BC: University of Victoria Center on Aging.

Dean, K. (1996b). Using theory to guide policy relevant health promotion research. *Health Promotion International, 11,* 19–26.

Dean, K., Colomer, C., & Perez-Hoyos, S. (1995). Research on lifestyles and health: Searching for meaning. *Social Science and Medicine, 41,* 845–855.

Dean, K., Holst, E., & Wagner, M. (1983). Self-care of common illnesses in Denmark. *Medical Care, 25,* 965.

Dean, K., & Hunter, D. (1996). New directions for health: Towards a knowledge base for public health action. *Social Science and Medicine, 42,* 745–750.

Dean, K., & Kickbusch, I. (1995). Health related behavior in health promotion: Utilizing the concept of self care. *Health Promotion International, 10,* 35–40.

Dean, K., Kreiner, S., & McQueen, D. (1993). Researching population health: New directions. In K. Dean (Ed.), *Population health research: Linking theory and methods* (pp. 227–237). London: Sage.

Dean, K., & McQueen, D. (1996). Theory in health promotion. *Health Promotion International, 11,* 7–9.

DeFriese, G., Woomert, A., Guild, P., Steckler, A., & Konrad, T. (1989). From activated patient to pacified activist: A study of the self-care movement in the United States. *Social Science and Medicine, 29,* 195–204.

Fuchs, V. (1974). *Who shall live?* New York: Basic Books. New York: Pantheon.

Hamburg, D., Elliott, G., & Parran, D. (Eds.). (1982). *Health and behavior : Frontiers of research in the biobehavioral sciences.* Washington, DC: National Academic Press.

Illich, I. (1976). *Medical nemesis: The expropriation of health.* New York: Pantheon.

Levin, L., Katz, A., & Holst, E. (1976). *Self-Care.* New York: Prodist.

McKeown, T. (1979). *The role of medicine: Dream, mirage or nemesis.* Oxford: Basil Blackwell.

Milburn, K. (1996). The importance of lay theorizing for health promotion research and practice. *Health Promotion International, 11,* 27–33.

Milio, N. (1986). *Promoting health through public policy.* Ottawa: Canadian Public Health Association.

Ory, M., Abeles, R., & Lipman, P. D. (Eds.). (1992). *Aging, health and behavior.* Newbury Park, CA: Sage.

Pederson, A., O'Neill, M., & Rootman, I. (1994). *Health promotion in Canada: Provincial, national and international perspectives.* Toronto: Saunders.

Penning, M., & Chapell, N. (1990). Self-care in relation to informal and formal care. *Ageing and Society, 10,* 41–59.

Petersen, P. (1976). Patienters selvbehandling inden henvendelse til praktiserende lÏge. [Patients' self-treatment prior to consultation with a general practitioner.] *Ugeskrift für Loeger,* 138.

Popay, J., & Williams, G. (1996). Public health research and lay knowledge. *Social Science and Medicine, 42,* 759–768.

Raeburn, J., & Rootman, I. (1989). Towards an expanded health field concept: Conceptual and research issues in a new age of health promotion. *Health Promotion International, 3,* 383–392.

Rasmussen, F. (1989). Mothers' benefit of a self-care booklet and a self-care educational session at child health centres. *Social Science and Medicine, 29,* 205–212.

Segall, A., & Goldstein, J. (1989). Exploring the correlates of self-provided health behavior. *Social Science and Medicine, 29,* 153.

Shye, D., Javetz, R., & Shuval, J. (1990). Patient initiatives and physician-challenging behaviors: The views of Israeli health professionals. *Social Science and Medicine, 31,* 719–727.

Shye, D., Javetz, R., & Shuval, J. (1991). Lay self-care in health: The views and perspectives of Israeli laypeople. *Social Science and Medicine, 33,* 297–308.

Shuval, J., Javetz, R., & Shye, D. (1989). Self-care in Israel: Physicians' views and perspectives. *Social Science and Medicine, 29,* 233–244.

Tibblin, G. (1979). EgenvŒrd manniskosyn och polik [Self care, view of people and politics]. *Lakaretidningen, 76,* 2765.

U.S. Department of Health, Education, and Welfare. (1979). *Healthy people: The Surgeon General's report on health promotion and disease prevention.* Washington, DC: Government Printing Office.

van Agthoven, W., & Plomp, H. (1989). The interpretation of self-care: A difference in outlook between client and home-nurses. *Social Science and Medicine, 29,* 245–252.

Werner, D. (1977). *Where there is no doctor.* Palo Alto, CA: Hesparian Foundation.

Williamson, J., & Danaher, K. (1980). *Self-care in health.* London: Croom Helm.

Winkler, R., Underwood, P., Fatovich, B., James, R., & Gray, D. (1989). A clinical trial approach to the management of chronic headache in general practice. *Social Science and Medicine, 24,* 213–220.

World Health Organization. (1985). *Targets for health for all: Targets in support of the European regional strategy for health for all.* WHO Regional Office for Europe, Copenhagen.

World Health Organization. (1986). *The Ottawa charter on health promotion.* Ottawa: Canadian Public Health Association.

Afterword: Toward a Research Agenda for Addressing the Potential of Self-Care in Later Life

Gordon H. DeFriese, Marcia G. Ory, and Donald M. Vickery

SELF-CARE AND AGING:
RESEARCH NEEDS AND PRIORITIES

While there has been a resurgence of self-care research in the past decade, there is still a dearth of systematic studies on the nature, extent, and modifiability of self-care behaviors across the life course. We need to know much more about the readiness for and acceptance of self-care and health promotion behaviors among older adult populations. Our concern must include a consideration of the variability among special populations (e.g., minorities, low-income populations) in response to these ideas and practices. In this connection, we need to know more about the way in which notions of prospective health are incorporated within the life course and world view of the older adult.

Additional information is needed about the way in which patterns of self-care cluster with other aspects of health behavior and attitudes. Are those

Ideas in this synthesis paper are drawn from the 1994 National Invitational Conference on Research Issues Related to Self-Care and Aging, particularly the reports from working groups on self-care processes, interventions, clinical practice and social policy.

who practice medical self-care for minor illnesses or health conditions also likely to cope with functional limitations through self-care, or use positive behavioral approaches to health promotion and enhancement? Do some types of self-care practices essentially duplicate the effects of other types of self-care behavior?

We need to know if the individual lay person's decision to engage in self-care for a given symptom or condition is automatic and reactive, or whether there is an elaborate decision-making process through which information is sifted and sorted while actions are planned accordingly. In order to consider the way in which self-care by lay persons interrelates with formal (often primary) care from physicians, nurses, or other health care professionals, we need to develop strategies that involve health care providers in the process of designing educational programs to impart these skills and this knowledge to lay persons.

In view of the variability in self-care practice among older adult populations, we need to devote significantly more research attention to understanding the availability of opportunities for self-care and other less professionally dependent responses to symptoms. This would include increased information about the levels of self-care knowledge and capabilities among older adults in diverse social situations.

Also with an eye to variability, there is a need for increased knowledge about the appropriateness of lay self-care response to illness symptoms or functional limitations. We also need to know the extent to which self-care skills and information need periodic renewal, as in the sense of continuing education. In this connection, it is important to clarify the most relevant outcomes of each of the three domains of self-care (e.g., health promotion/disease prevention, chronic disease/assistive care, and medical self-care).

We also know that self-care may be practiced for quite different reasons at different periods in one's life (early, in response to acute illness conditions; later, in response to more chronic conditions). We need better understanding of the so-called trajectories of self-care as a basis for better targeting the interventions for different age cohorts. Here again, the impact of social and cultural factors may prove to be important mediating influences on the effect of self-care.

Throughout this volume, authors have reiterated a need for encouraging diversity in intervention research. Variations in self-care may occur among:

- settings: health care programs and facilities, senior centers, retirement communities

- geographic areas: rural, small town, urban areas
- population subgroups: African Americans, Hispanics, Asian Americans
- delivery mechanisms: different types of health care organizations and providers.

Too few self-care studies have been conducted among underserved populations. It is very important that such research take place through effective and genuine community/practitioner and researcher partnerships, that anticipation of these partnerships be built into research solicitations. It is important to discover whether interventions "proven" to work in certain contexts also are effective with underserved populations.

THE READINESS FOR RESEARCH

The chapters contained in this volume address the readiness of the research community to address key-aging and self-care issues. It is time to move toward a more systematic and integrated program of study, rather than relying on post hoc analyses. Several observations can be made which together suggest the present capacity and commitment to carry out the kinds of studies thought necessary in this area. First of all, intervention research is iterative science. In intervention research, one of the principal objectives is to constantly extend the boundaries of current knowledge and experience with respect to particular interventions among different target groups. It is important to discover whether what works for middle class White older adults also works for African American older adults. This is a developmental process that moves in at least two directions. Building process and cost analyses into a study can provide not only information about whether or not an intervention worked, but also insight into why it did or did not work, and can identify useful parameters (for example, the cost of a successful smoking cessation program among older adults).

There are now many previously unrecognized opportunities to "piggyback" investigations of self-care on existing studies and existing databases to answer questions about interventions (e.g., the cost-effectiveness of interventions or the impact of interventions on health outcomes). Piggybacking is more than secondary data analysis and reviewing existing information. It emphasizes collaboration, for example, where one researcher may be an interventionist and another may be a process evaluator. Collaborating on existing studies may provide added insights. Piggyback collaboration also may provide an efficient mechanism for collecting sets of items of interest to different researchers or developing larger databases with multiple uses.

Given the importance of process to implementation success for self-care interventions, researchers should be encouraged to document and study the process and implementation of intervention research in this field in order to find out not only what works, but what did not work, for whom does it work or not, and under what conditions. Not only is process evaluation helpful to the next study, but process analysis also is important to practice and informs practitioners about how to implement the basic intervention under conditions of practice.

Research is now under way, involving investigators with requisite expertise, addressing each of the three domains of self-care—engaging in healthy lifestyles, self-care in response to symptoms and illnesses, and compensation for functional limitations and disabilities. Knowledge and implementation experience in each of these domains are at quite different stages in terms of scientific development, and different theoretical models may apply to each. Yet, research in all three is important and needs attention.

The need at present is for a progression of research at several levels—from developmental and theory-based research, to pilot and observational studies, to more controlled studies and randomized control trials (RCTs). We need to be able to conduct subgroup and cost analyses related to a wide variety of interventions conducted in a diverse range of settings. We need efficacy studies, and then effectiveness and cost-effectiveness studies. This sequence of research not only advances science, but also helps to assure that resources are not ineffectively allocated to RCTs before there is a solid foundation of research at an earlier phase.

PRINCIPLES FOR FUTURE INVESTMENT IN SELF-CARE AND AGING RESEARCH

The following principles are offered as guides to further investment. Research in this area should

- carefully differentiate self-care practices in each of the three principal domains (health promotion and disease prevention, medical self-care and disability care).

- specify the structural context within which proposed interventions will be launched and look for opportunities to study the differential effectiveness of these interventions across a number of venues
- carefully define the various subcomponents of interventions and make special efforts to measure and assess the relative contributions of each to the overall impact
- employ common and standardized core measures of key variables (symptoms, symptom response, health outcomes, quality of life, etc.) and encourage future research to contribute to the cumulative science of the area by recommending adherence to conventional definitions and measures wherever possible
- specify pathways linking changes in self-care behavior to particular outcomes of interest
- seek to extend the relevance and understandings of self-care impact among diverse populations, particularly among minorities and low-income groups

THE CLINICAL AND PUBLIC POLICY IMPLICATIONS OF SELF-CARE PRACTICE AMONG OLDER ADULTS

One of our more dramatic observations is the simplicity of some of the most effective self-care interventions. It appears that informational and instructional self-care materials, even when disseminated to target audiences of older adults by mail, have been effective in improving functional outcomes or lowering costs of health care utilization. Yet, individuals vary considerably in their personal levels of responsiveness to self-care or other health educational messages. Health care providers wishing to incorporate a self-care dimension into their conventional approach to patient care will do well to understand some of the findings of the growing behavioral literature on individual behavioral response to illness symptoms.

From a public policy viewpoint, there are obvious decision points with respect to self-care intervention policies. The loci of interventions are a major aspect of disagreement within the field. In the life course approach to the topic of health and illness, there is a growing but still developing literature on the individual, lay decision-making context within which self-care strategies are considered. Strong voices are emerging, urging the incorporation of self-care within organizational and societal efforts to restructure health care systems. In this latter respect, self-care is seen as a major dimension by which the forces creating the demand for expensive formal health care may be more effectively managed.

There is a general feeling that some of the new knowledge now needed in this area might be gained by fusing an interest in self-care with already operational large-scale studies of health care utilization behavior. Another potential source of information might be secondary analyses of the program outcomes of projects involving older adults and their families, (e.g., those designed to increase the frequency of end-of-life decisions via "living wills" and "advance directives").

From a policy point of view, one of the most troubling aspects of this whole field is the question of the most appropriate setting or context for self-care education or practice. If a clinical care setting is used, then concrete efforts must be made to make health care providers more aware of the potential of self-care and to train them in more effective methods for promoting self-care skills among their older adult clients and patients. The general movement toward managed care now encompasses large numbers of older persons. While there is much speculation about the impact of managed care arrangements on doctor–patient interactions, the full impact of evolving care arrangements on professional encouragement of different self-care practices for patients with varying health statuses is still unknown.

Finally, there is the policy implication of the presumed substitutability of self-care for other forms and types of health care and personal assistance among older adults of differing ages. We need more information about the extent to which lay caregivers or those providing social support tend to maintain their availability when lay persons assume greater levels of self-care.

CONCLUSION

As our nation moves to deal with the challenge of defining the most appropriate and effective strategies, programs, and policies for assuring the availability of adequate health and social services for our rapidly increasing older adult population, self-care and programs to increase the readiness of older adults to practice it should gain greater attention. The chapters in this volume clearly indicate the depth and speed with which the literature of this field has grown over the space of two decades. Self-care, while once an ideological threat to some providers of formal health care services, has now been fully integrated with the care offered to patients who suffer from chronic disabling conditions. We have yet to realize the full potential of self-care strategies for general health maintenance and the enhancement of functional independence of older adults in the United States. These chapters have outlined a wide spectrum of new research opportunities and challenges for the decade ahead, ones we hope our readers will accept with enthusiasm and new levels of commitment.

Appendix: Self-Care in Later Life—An Annotated Bibliography of Research Findings and Policy Issues

Alison Woomert

Although the term is relatively new to the health field, self-care is the oldest and most widespread form of individual health-related behavior. Growing numbers and proportions of the aging population in their increasing diversity are bringing renewed interest in self-care strategies as promising approaches for reorganizing health care delivery and achieving healthy aging. Yet, self-care research and programs for older adults have been limited. Furthermore, self-care conceptualizations are amorphous and multifaceted, thus, determinants and outcomes differ according to the definition employed. Because separate bodies of research literature have developed around various conceptualizations, making comparisons of findings is cumbersome.

The purpose of this bibliography is to illustrate the breadth of current literature on self-care in late life as well as to provide selected background and historical works of interest to health care policy makers, practitioners,

This work was supported by the National Institute on Aging. I thank Dr. Marcia G. Ory for her careful reviews and thoughtful comments on conceptualization and content. I am grateful to Dr. Gordon H. DeFriese for his helpful comments and permission to use the extensive literature files housed at the Cecil G. Sheps Center for Health Services Research at the University of North Carolina at Chapel Hill. Ms. Carol A. Borack provided excellent editorial assistance and categorized publications by keywords.

and researchers. The collection includes research, intervention, and policy literature covering the wide range of self-care definitions and theoretical models representing lay and professional perspectives.

Discussions of research and policy on self-care in late life may be useful to a variety of social, health, and health-related professions and service organizations that assist elderly persons to continue living at home for the maximum possible time through effective and cost-effective services and programs. Research findings may have a number of clinical applications. For example, they may be useful to medical and home health nursing practices in estimating and facilitating the capacity for independent living. Educators working with older adults may use research findings to help them modify or reinforce health behaviors. Findings also may help policy makers and planners refine predictive models to estimate long-term care needs and other clinical and social outcomes.

Substantive focus of the bibliography is on three broad areas of self-care contained in the WHO 1983 World Health Organization definition. First is the growing body of literature on *health promotion and disease prevention (HPDP) activity* and related healthy lifestyle and risk avoidance behaviors among older adults. This literature is becoming more diverse and sophisticated. Lifestyle behaviors have been linked to health outcomes and, more recently, have become integral parts of interventions for older adults. A second key area is *medical self-care,* which incorporates self-care for acute illness, self-medication, and symptom response among older adult populations. Despite the small body of literature pertinent to older adults, programs and manuals have been developed for this population. The third area is *self-care for functional disability and self-management of chronic illness* for specific conditions common in older adulthood. A sizable literature exists for the general population, and a growing trend emphasizes such programs and research for older adults. This bibliography presents illustrative publications representing disease-specific programs and studies, for example, arthritis, hypertension, and heart disease management by older adults.

The diversity of the aging population must be integrated into future research and policy on health, aging and self-care. Despite its importance, not much research addresses self-care in terms of the differences represented by *special population subgroups.* Examples are provided of self-care research with oldest-old and frail populations, rural elder populations, and minority and ethnic populations. Whether or not informal care is included in the definition of self-care, it is critical to understand the various and dynamic informal and formal health care contexts in which self-care operates, so the bibliography also illustrates this literature. While this collection concentrates on literature specific to elderly adults, some publications summarize general self-care issues or broad population studies incorporating older populations.

ORGANIZATION OF THE BIBLIOGRAPHY

Citations with abstracts are arranged alphabetically under three topics. Section I, "Background, Conceptualization and Social Context of Self-Care and Aging," describes the historical and conceptual background of the self-care movement and reviews general conceptualizations and definitions of self-care and its distinctions from related concepts such as self-help and health education. Section II, "Prevalence, Correlates and Dynamics of Self-Care Among Older Adults," illustrates epidemiologic work related to the extent and prevalence of self-care practices. Publications review the links of behavior and health, and the relationship of self-care and health promotion practices to health outcomes. They also illustrate a wide range of studies on the nature, correlates, antecedents and predictors of self-care behaviors, skills and technology. Section III, "Design, Implementation and Evaluation of Self-Care Programs for Older Adults," concentrates on design and content of self-care programs and materials, and summarizes results of program evaluations.

Substantive areas and discussions about methodology, policy issues, and population subgroups of older adults are dispersed among the sections. Because mutually exclusive categorization of the multifaceted literature was impossible, keywords after each abstract provide further content distinctions. The appendix lists and explains the keywords.

EXCLUSIONS FROM THE BIBLIOGRAPHY

Although not feasible to encompass the entire scope of self-care literature here, omitted self-care components deserve careful attention in their own right. This collection excludes self-help and mutual aid groups, general patient and health education interventions, caregiving, and spiritual self-care. Only an illustrative bibliography and policy discussion of non–Western or alternative sources of care (Sakala, 1989a, 1989b) is included. Although citing illustrative publications, the collection largely excludes definitions of self-care from medical professional perspectives (e.g., self-care defined as use of medical services, compliance with medical regimes or prescribed medications, and screening by medical professionals for various acute and chronic diseases). Self-screening or self-monitoring tests and procedures (such as self-tests to detect colorectal cancer) often are considered to be self-care strategies. Since they are frequently incorporated within general self-care programs or interventions or included among self-management strategies for chronic conditions, they are represented in self-care program and self-management literature in this bibliography.

SECTION I. BACKGROUND AND CONCEPTUALIZATION OF SELF-CARE AND AGING

Abeles, R. P., Gift, H. C., & Ory, M. G. (Eds., with assistance of D. M. Cox). (1994). *Aging and quality of life: Charting new territories in behavioral sciences research.* New York: Springer Publishing.

The contributors discuss advances in behavioral sciences research that can inform policy about ways to improve the quality of life of an increasingly diverse and aging population. Based on a multidisciplinary conference, this volume links what is known about aging and quality of life to interventions that enhance healthy aging. Quality of life refers to "an individual's overall life satisfaction and total well-being" (p. 4) and incorporates physical, mental, and social well-being. Introductory chapters underscore the need for research differentiating aging processes from declines in health and functioning, highlight research priorities for enhancing quality of life, and present a conceptual framework for research and practice. The first section describes linkages among health, disease, and disability from an epidemiologic perspective on the aging population. It includes a review of predictors of healthy aging by Kaplan and Strawbridge, and discussion of self-care for coping with declining capacities (see DeFriese, Konrad, Woomert, Norburn, & Bernard, 1994, in this section). Other sections explore physical health, focusing on quality-of-life measures and on general frailty versus specific conditions prevalent in old age; relationships of social and physical environments to health and functioning of older adults (see Barr, 1994, section II); and diversity of the aging population, the implications of changing social structures, and ethnic factors. The final section discusses research implications for public policy and interventions, framing agendas in the context of the changing health care environment. A crucial conclusion is that adapting the social environment to the needs of the diverse and aging population is a "major health promotion and disease prevention strategy for adding years to life, as well as life to years" (p. 14).

Keywords: aged, chronic self-management, conceptual, functional status, HPDP, policy, psychosocial factors, quality of life, review.

Chappell, N. L. (1987). The interface among three systems of care: Self, informal, and formal. In R. A. Ward & S. S. Tobin (Eds.), *Health in aging: Sociological issues and policy directions* (Chapter 6). New York: Springer Publishing, pp. 159–179.

The paucity of research on self-care, the predominant form of primary health care, is particularly evident for older populations. Based on pilot results of in-person interviews with older adults in Winnipeg, this chapter examines relationships among self-care, informal care, and formal care within the context of social networks and health beliefs. Self-care measures included healthy habits and self-care responses to 10 common symptoms. Findings support the distinctiveness and complementarity of the three systems of care, which seem to coexist but not substitute for each other, and which may fill different functions.

Keywords: aged, conceptual, functional status, HPDP, informal vs. formal care, medical self-care, psychosocial factors.

Dean, K. (1989). Conceptual, theoretical and methodological issues in self-care research. *Social Science and Medicine, 29*(2), 117–123.

Dean's introduction to this issue on "Health Self-Care" reviews conceptual and methodological issues. Self-care is the oldest and most widespread form of individual health-related behavior. Consensus points to a broad definition of self-care as "range of behavior undertaken by individuals to promote or restore their health" (p. 117). While often comprising the majority of care for chronic conditions, usually such self-care is practiced in conjunction with professional care. Even then, self-care denotes active cooperation between lay and professional providers. Much is known about self-care. Most illness care is self-care; also, functioning, morbidity, and mortality are influenced by individual health behavior. Much evidence doc-

uments influences of socioeconomic, demographic, cultural, and social variables on use of medical services and medicine, as well as the influences of lay networks and illness attribution in seeking medical care. Some evidence suggests illness self-care is appropriate and effective. Nevertheless, components of self-care have received little research attention. Dean recommends studies focusing on behavior and interaction patterns, and on effects of psychosocial distress and social situational variables on attitudes and health.
Keywords: conceptual, methods, policy, prevalence, psychosocial factors, self-care (general).

Dean, K. (1992). Health-related behavior: Concepts and methods. Chapter 2 in: M. G. Ory, R. P. Abeles, & P. D. Lipman (Eds.), *Aging, health and behavior* (p.27–56). Newbury Park: Sage.

While researchers now view aging as a mutable process involving biological, behavioral, psychological, and social factors, the mechanisms by which these interact are not yet understood. Models must now explore multiple health behaviors. Dean summarizes the current state of the art of self-care research. Self-care is part of the continuum of health-related behavior in which the individual decides "to do nothing, to actively promote health, to self-treat, or to seek care from another, and to follow advice" (p. 34; see also WHO, 1983, this section). For the older population, self-care for chronic illness may be most pertinent. At this point, consistent relationships have not been established between health maintenance behaviors and age. Dean finds few studies of age and symptom response. Most self-care studies focus on specific health practices. For example, extensive self-medication with previously prescribed drugs has been found with old age. While only limited clinical research exists, it generally appears that self-care practiced before professional consultation is appropriate and safe. Research is needed to understand the development, maintenance, and clustering of self-care practices over the life course, and the multiple determinants of these behavior patterns. To illustrate current work toward building a cumulative base, Dean summarizes coordinated Danish self-care studies with older adults. She identifies distinct age-related self-care patterns, such as greater medication use, more frequent consultation with professionals, and less preventive behavior with older age.
Keywords: aged, behavior change, conceptual, HPDP, international, medical self-care, methods, policy, review.

Dean, K., & Kickbusch, I. (1995). Health related behavior in health promotion: Utilizing the concept of self-care. *Health Promotion International 10*(1), 35–40.

Health promotion constitutes a major development for improving population health; however, controversy surrounds self-care. The authors discuss self-care's close connection to health promotion and its importance in optimizing health-related behavior. Defined by WHO (1983), self-care also is "social behavior that is learned in cultural contexts" and an "integral part of the wider social context" (p. 39). The authors trace the concept's history from evidence about limits of medical care, growing health care costs, and the need to reduce iatrogenic illness. The concept exerted a broadening influence on health-related behavior research, for example, by focusing on the neglected roles of the lay person and lay networks as the basic form of health care. Concerns about self-care included its potential use in policy arguments about individual responsibility for health to justify blaming the victim or cutting needed services. Some feared, while others cheered, that self-care was challenging medical dominance. Narrowly focusing on changing discrete behaviors can waste resources on useless or dangerous interventions. In contrast, self-care offers understanding of general patterns of daily lifestyles that promote health. Although self-care has been integrated into many professional services, an important question is whether the programs provide optimal care that is woven into daily patterns of living. Research priorities range from studying appropriate self-care to barriers to care. The authors argue that sufficient evidence exists to indicate that effective self-care is necessary for effective professional care. Thus, policies should legitimize the basic role of lay persons in health promotion and integrate lay persons into decision making about health care.

Keywords: behavior change, conceptual, history, HPDP, informal vs. formal care, international, policy, review, self-care (general).

Dean, K., Hickey, T., & Holstein, B. E. (Eds.). (1986). *Self-care and health in old age.* London: Croom Helm.

This classic monograph focuses on self-care and its relationship to health and quality of life of elderly populations from an international perspective. Overall issues remain and this volume still offers insight into their conceptualization and potential solutions. Illsley's preface reviews the history and conceptualization of self-care as a complement, rather than an "anti-professional" substitute for formal health care. Hickey defines self-care as an "individual's immediate and continuing behavioral reactions to illness, his [or her] basic coping strategies, as well as the steps taken to preserve and maintain personal health" (pp. 3–4). Self-care includes basic daily health maintenance, recognition and interpretation of symptoms, interactions with social support and formal health care systems, assertive roles in making decisions, self-treatment, health education skills, and compliance or noncompliance with prescribed routines. The collection includes excellent discussions of self-care's salience for older populations, including implications of ageist stereotypes, summaries of research, and comparisons of programs and medications among countries. It also addresses the social context of self-care, including the relationship between doctor and older patient. Finally, it integrates the major themes in a discussion of policy, practice, education, and research.

Keywords: aged, conceptual, history, international, interventions, medical self-care, policy, quality of life.

DeFriese, G. H., & Konrad, T. R. (1993). The self-care movement and the gerontological healthcare professional. *Generations, 17*(3), 37–40.

The authors review policy implications of the self-care movement for gerontological professionals and the aging population in terms of that population's increasing chronic health problems, functional impairments, and demand for health services. Self-care may increase quality of life, and may be an adjunct to professional care. The authors address self-care in response to acute illness symptoms and to manage chronic illness and functional impairment. Health care professionals may encourage patients to learn these skills, offer instruction, or provide educational programs. The article discusses the potential of self-care within the organization, structure, and financing of the health care system, and the transformation of the doctor–older patient relationship, especially in light of health care reform. Health maintenance organizations (HMOs) are targeting older adults and offering services specifically for older adult needs. Their financing mechanisms may encourage more preventive care. Such systems also may facilitate multidisciplinary care necessary for geriatric care. Particularly in large retirement communities, competition among HMOs for Medicare clients, together with efforts of informal and formal organizations, may increase the knowledge and "empowerment" of older adults.

Keywords: aged, chronic self-management, conceptual, informal vs. formal care, medical self-care, policy.

DeFriese, G. H., Konrad, T. R., Woomert, A., Norburn, J. E. K., and Bernard, S. (1994). Self-care and quality of life in old age. In R. P. Abeles, H. C. Gift, & M. G. Ory (Eds., with assistance of D. M. Cox), *Aging and quality of life* (pp. 99–117). New York: Springer Publishing.

This chapter reviews history and conceptualizations of self-care, and discusses the importance of self-care in national policy that emphasizes social and behavioral aspects of healthy aging. While many medical professionals in the 1970s feared self-care carried a countermedical message, the legitimacy of self-care now is evidenced by its integration into clinical medicine. The authors present three domains of self-care employed in the national "Self-Care Assessment of Community-Based Elderly" study: (a) healthy lifestyle practices to enhance health, reduce risk factors, or prevent disease; (b) medical self-care to diagnose and treat common acute conditions; and (c) self-care related to basic (BADL), mobility (MADL), and instrumental (IADL) activities of daily living, often in response to chronic conditions. The chapter focuses on dimensions of IADL: use of special equipment, environmental modifications, and behavioral adjustments in everyday activities. It considers the dynamic informal social and formal health care contexts of self-care, highlights research on self-care education and practice in health care, and presents preliminary findings from the national study. It suggests potential benefits of increased self-care research and practice in conjunction with policies aimed at higher quality of life for the aging population.
Keywords: aged, chronic self-management, conceptual, functional status, history, HPDP, medical self-care, policy, psychosocial factors, quality of life, review.

DeFriese, G. H., & Woomert, A. (1992). Informal and formal health care systems serving older persons. In M. G. Ory, R. P. Abeles, & P. D. Lipman (Eds.), *Aging, health and behavior* (pp. 57–82). Newbury Park, CA: Sage.

The authors summarize conceptual frameworks and research integrating self-care within the context of the informal and formal health care system. They subsume self-care within a definition of informal care proposed as the personal care provided by one's primary care group (such as relatives, friends, and neighbors). There has been controversy concerning the extent to which self-care (or informal care) is an addition or substitute to formal health care. The authors review evidence in terms of two questions. First, is self-care or informal care a supplement to or substitute for formal care? Evidence indicates people tend to depend on lay knowledge first, before turning to formal medical care, and use their self-care skills appropriately. Nevertheless, clear evidence does not exist to determine whether or to what extent self-care practices substitute for formal services in either general or aging populations. Second, they ask whether formal care is a supplement to or substitute for informal care. While evidence has tended to see informal and formal care as alternatives, a complementary model may be more appropriate than a substitution model. For example, informal care is of value throughout the illness and formal care experience; also, there is little evidence that self-care necessarily reduces formal service use or is an effective strategy for cost savings. The authors discuss the potential for integrating informal and formal care to address needs of the aging population. *Keywords:* aged, conceptual, history, informal vs. formal care, interventions.

DeFriese, G. H., & Woomert, A. (1983). Self-care among U.S. elderly. *Research on Aging, 5*(1), 3–23.

The authors discuss the self-care movement, emphasizing programs for senior citizens in the United States. Issues facing the movement include commercialism, professional dominance, potential of self-care groups as political interest groups, and program impact evaluation issues. Based on self-care programs for older adults from a national inventory (DeFriese, Woomert, Guild, Steckler, & Konrad, 1989, below), the authors characterize the range of sponsorship and settings, targets, staffing, implementation methods, and goals and activities.
Keywords: aged, chronic self-management, conceptual, HPDP, interventions, medical self-care, review.

DeFriese, G. H., Woomert, A., Guild, P.A., Steckler, A. B., & Konrad, T. R. (1989). From activated patient to pacified activist: A study of the self-care movement in the United States. *Social Science and Medicine, 29*(2), 195–204.

A national survey identified 2,000 self-care programs covering diverse content and sociodemographic groups including older adults. The article describes program content, organizational sponsorship, staffing, and principal prevention emphases. Over 75% offered instruction or activities to increase health through lifestyle changes, reduce risk factors, and/or prevent illness or injury. Relatively few lay persons functioned as instructors. The article describes absorption of self-care into mainstream health care.
Keywords: chronic self-management, conceptual, HPDP, interventions, medical self-care, prevalence, review.

Hattinga Verschure, J. C. M. (Ed.). (1980). *Changes in caring for health.*
    Aylesbury, Buckinghamshire: HM and M.

This classic monograph offers a helpful perspective on the conceptualization of self-care and its connection to informal social and formal health care systems. Based on an international conference, it introduces the history and prospects of self-care in Europe and the United States. Emphasizing "caring" aspects of self-care, it distinguishes three forms of care delivery: professional, cover (mutual small groups), and self-care. Self-care refers to all kinds of care by an individual to meet his or her own health maintenance or restoration needs.
Keywords: conceptual, informal vs. formal care, international, psychosocial factors, self-care (general).

Hickey, T., Dean, K., & Holstein, B. (1986). Emerging trends in gerontology and geriatrics: Implications for the self-care of the elderly. *Social Science and Medicine, 23*(12), 1363–1369.

This article reviews studies funded by the Kellogg International Scholarship Program on Health and Aging examining international diversity and similarities in self-care among elderly populations. It finds support for an interactive process between lay and professional health care systems. While finding that international differences in patterns of self-care are based on the differences in social context and ideological distinctions of societies and their health care systems, several independent factors had a larger impact. These include demographic and economic imperatives, cohort changes, biomedical models of professional care, and professional and geriatric policy initiatives. Policies should encourage elderly persons' participation in decision making about their care. Self-care and other informal care systems must be balanced with formal systems.
Keywords: aged, conceptual, demographics, informal vs. formal care, international, policy, self-care (general), review.

Levin, L. S. (1976, November 3–4). *Self care.* Proceedings of a session convened in Atlanta by the Bureau of Health Education. Available from: Community Program Development Division, Bureau of Health Education, Centers for Disease Control, Department of Health and Human Services, Atlanta, GA 30333.

This classic monograph distinguishes self-care education from health education and self-help, noting a risk of professional cooptation of a popular movement. Other discussion topics include educational methods, tactics of implementing self-care curricula, and content and age appropriateness of self-care education. Discussants recommended several policy and program options for facilitating self-care education. Traditional health education is evaluated in terms of client conformity to professionally valued benefits. Self-care education seeks outcomes defined in terms of lay persons' abilities to gain competence as the primary determinant of their health. Self-help or homogeneous disease/disability groups differ most from self-care in their mutual support character rather than individuals serving their own needs.

Keywords: conceptual, interventions, methods, policy, self-care (general).

Levin, L. S., & Idler, E. L. (1981). *The hidden health care system: Mediating structure and medicine.* Cambridge, MA: Ballinger.

This pioneering work examines the hidden health care system to facilitate a shift from seeing lay persons as consumers to seeing them as primary providers. It draws extensively on epidemiological and sociological research. Individuals provide most care through mediating structures—formal and informal groups that mediate between individuals and the larger societal institutions. Mediating structures include family, religious groups, and ethnic communities. Professional care is supplementary. The authors present ethnographic studies of three mediating structures: home birth movement, charismatic healing activities, and development of community and mutual aid groups.

Keywords: conceptual, history, informal vs. formal care, policy, psychosocial factors, self-care (general).

McBride, S. H. (1991). Comparative analysis of three instruments designed to measure self-care agency. *Nursing Research, 40*(1), 12–16.

Orem's self-care deficit nursing theory views the individual as a self-care agent (i.e., person taking action). *Self-care agency* is the capability that a person possesses for performing self-care actions. Demands for care require deliberate self-care actions. When the self-care agency is insufficient in meeting the demand, the deficit indicates a need for nursing. This study explores latent traits associated with three instruments measuring self-care agency. Four common elements emerged from factor analyses—knowledge, attention to health, self-concept, and skill/action. Knowledge and attention to health are common to all instruments. Both factor analyses and canonical analyses supported the common trait skill/action in Deynes and Hanson-Bickel instruments. Factor analyses, but not canonical analyses, supported the commonality of the self-concept trait in Deynes and Kearney-Fleischer instruments. Unique components identified in factor analyses were "feelings and values" (Deynes), "motivation" (Kearney and Fleischer), and "reasoning and decision making" (Hanson and Bickel). Employing just one instrument fails to incorporate the multidimensional character of self-care agency.

Keywords: behavior change, conceptual, methods.

McEwan, P. J. M. (Ed.), & Dean, K. (Guest Ed.) Health self-care. [Special Issue]. *Social Science and Medicine, 29*(2), 1989.

This international issue covers conceptual and methodological issues and findings related to self-care. Topics range from self-care for acute to chronic disease, from medical self-care to health promotion, covering lay and professional perspectives, health service use, and interventions. For articles focusing on self-care related to older adults and long-term care, see discussions by Dean (1989) on theory and methodology, DeFriese et al. (1989) on self-care programs in this section, Haug, Wykle, and Namazi (1989; section II) on self-care responses to symptoms among older adults, and Lorig and Holman on long-term care implications of arthritis self-management.

Keywords: aged, chronic self-management, conceptual, HPDP, interventions, long-term care, medical self-care, methods, utilization.

Ory, M. G., Abeles, R. P., & Lipman, P. D. (Eds.). (1992). *Aging, health and behavior.* Newbury Park, CA: Sage.

This book highlights recent developments in conceptual and research work that recognize the dynamic nature of the life course process of aging and its interactions with health and behavior change. Conceptual frameworks and research from social, behavioral, and biopsychological perspectives represent the dynamic nature of health and behavior change in the life course process. An introduction presents guidelines for aging research that incorporate the multifaceted process of aging, its social context, and its mutability, making it a candidate for a wide range of interventions. Much emphasis has shifted to chronic illness and disability. The first section addresses conceptualization of self-care and informal and formal health care behaviors, for example, in the chapters by Dean and by DeFriese and Woomert, which are reviewed above. The second section discusses biophysical mechanisms linking health and behavior, such as active coping to reduce health risks and stress, sense of control, and coping with chronic disease and disability. A third section addresses social and behavioral interventions, as illustrated by chapters on preventive and health promotion

behavior (Rakowski, reviewed in section II, below) and macro social structural interventions. Finally, public policy implications are addressed.
Keywords: aged, conceptual, behavior change, chronic self-management, functional status, health status, HPDP, informal vs. formal care, interventions, methods, policy, psychosocial factors.

Sakala, C. (1989a, October). *Alternative health in the United States and other industrial nations: Selected bibliography, with an emphasis on documentary, evaluative, policy, and reference resources.* Prepared for and supported by the Henry J. Kaiser Family Foundation. Available from: Carol Sakala, Boston University Health Policy Institute, 53 Bay State Rd, Boston, MA 02215.

This extensive bibliography supplements Sakala's (1989b, see below) research and policy synthesis on alternative healing. It cites a broad range of topics, beginning with overviews of alternative healing traditions in the U.S., Canada, and Europe. Chinese traditions, chiropractic systems, faith healing, homeopathy, naturopathy, therapeutic touch, and behavior medicine modalities are included. Specific conditions include AIDS, cancer, cardiovascular disease, rheumatic disorders, and pregnancy. Also covered are specific populations; empirical studies of alternative healing systems; typologies, research, and iatrogenic effects of alternative therapies; critiques of biomedicine and alternative healing; clinical perspectives; alternative healing and the worksite; policy issues; and publications.
Keywords: alternative healing, conceptual, international, policy, psychosocial factors, review, utilization.

Sakala, C. (1989b, October). *Alternative health in the contemporary United States: A research and policy synthesis.* Prepared for and supported by the Henry J. Kaiser Family Foundation. Available from: Carol Sakala, Boston University Health Policy Institute, 53 Bay State Rd, Boston, MA 02215.

This paper reviews the state of knowledge about nonbiomedical healing and discusses future research and policy issues. Sakala sees the growth of interest in alternative healing activities as part of broader social trends, including recent political and health empowerment movements. Characteristics of an alternative healing tradition are that it "generally is not taught in biomedical education, is not practiced by biomedical providers, or is not reimbursed by major insurers" (p. 5). Contrary to popular notions, the participants are well educated, middle class, financially secure, and are not vulnerable to severe illness. Evidence suggests alternative approaches effectively meet subjective needs, but there is little research to address objective efficacy. Findings are inconsistent about relative benefits and dangers, and methodologies have been weak. Nevertheless, evidence indicates alternative approaches are very safe and less harmful than many biomedical approaches. Further evidence indicates that most alternative practitioners do not exploit clients and fees tend to be modest or nonexistent. Alternative approaches emphasize values such as encouraging health promotion and prevention, minimizing harmful side effects, finding low-technology solutions, treating the whole person, encouraging informed choice, and minimizing costs. Although most policy makers currently would not support funding, a carefully planned research program could be useful in finding positive contributions of alternative approaches to meet scarce health care resources.

Keywords: alternative healing, conceptual, costs, HPDP, international, policy, review, utilization.

U.S. Department of Health and Human Services, Public Health Service. (1990). *Healthy people 2000: National health promotion and disease prevention objectives* (DHHS Publ. No. PHS 91-50213). Washington, DC: Author.

This volume describes a national strategy for achieving specific health promotion and disease prevention objectives to improve the health of the nation by the year 2000. These are opportunities to cut health care costs, prevent disease and disability, and achieve healthier lives. Personal responsibility plays a key role. The document presents detailed objectives covering health promotion, health protection, preventive services, special populations and age-related objectives. It also recommends surveillance data systems for monitoring progress toward specific objectives. Objectives related to older adults are presented throughout the priority areas, and one chapter focuses on this age group. Preventing major causes of death among older people (health disease, cancer, stroke, chronic obstructive pulmonary disease, pneumonia, and influenza) is a major concern. Preventing disability and maintaining function are of equal importance. Managing chronic problems such as arthritis, osteoporosis, incontinence, visual and hearing impairments, and dementia are particularly important because of their impact on daily activities. The report reviews research showing that older adults can benefit from quitting smoking and improving nutrition and exercise habits. Primary care and preventive services most crucial for older adults include controlling high blood pressure, screening for cancer, immunization against pneumonia and influenza, counseling to promote health behaviors, and therapies to help manage chronic conditions. Addressing issues such as social isolation and depression also are crucial for enhancing functioning and quality of life among older adults.

Keywords: aged, chronic self-management, conceptual, demographics, HPDP, policy, prevalence, review.

U.S. Department of Health and Human Services, Public Health Service. (1991). *Healthy people 2000: National health promotion and disease prevention objectives.* Washington, DC: U. S. Government Printing Office.

This is the full report of detailed health promotion and disease prevention objectives for the year 2000. It presents the national objectives within the context of extensive supporting literature reviews and consideration of policy issues pertaining to our nation's health. Introductory chapters discuss research findings and policy issues in terms of age groups and special populations, overall goals for the nation, priorities for health promotion and disease prevention, and shared responsibilities at federal, state, and community levels. Health promotion objectives cover physical activity and fitness, nutrition, tobacco, alcohol and other drugs, family planning, mental health and mental disorders, violent and abusive behavior, and educational and community-based programs. Health protection objectives cover unintentional injuries, occupational safety and health, environmental health, food and drug safety, and oral health. Preventive services objectives cover maternal and infant health, heart disease and stroke, cancer, diabetes and chronic disabling conditions, HIV infection, sexually transmitted diseases, immunization and infectious diseases, and clinical preventive services. Separate age-related objectives are presented for children, adolescents and young adults, adults and older adults. Special population objectives address people with low incomes, particular minority groups, and people with disabilities. The report also discusses surveillance and data systems.

Keywords: aged, chronic self-management, conceptual, demographics, history, HPDP, methods, minority groups, policy, prevalence, review, self-care (general).

World Health Organization. (1983). *Health education in self-care: Possibilities and limitations. Report of a scientific consultation.* Geneva: Author.

This working conference convened in 1983 to advise WHO on the role of self-care education as part of a global strategy for health. While findings are dated, this report remains an excellent background reference on conceptual and policy issues. Its classic definition of self-care has guided much subsequent research:

Self-care in health refers to the activities individuals, families and communities undertake with the intention of enhancing health, preventing disease, limiting illness, and restoring health. These activities are derived from knowledge and skills from the pool of both professional and lay experience. They are undertaken by lay people on their own behalf, either separately or in participative collaboration with professionals. (p. 2)

Keywords: conceptual, history, international, policy, self-care (general).

SECTION II. PREVALENCE, CORRELATES AND DYNAMICS OF SELF-CARE AMONG OLDER ADULTS

Abdellah, F. G., & Moore, S. R. (Eds.). (1988). *Surgeon General's workshop: Health promotion and aging* (Proceedings of workshop held in Washington, DC, March 20-23, 1988.) Washington, DC: Public Health Service, U.S. Department of Health and Human Services.

This document contains the proceedings from the 1988 "Surgeon General's Workshop on Health Promotion and Aging." Sessions described activities related to aging Americans, year 2000 objectives for the nation, legislative interests in geriatric health promotion, Healthy Older People program to educate older Americans about healthy practices, Project Age Well (University of Arizona) for coordinated preventive geriatric care, and international (World Health Organization) activities in geriatric health promotion. The report presents detailed recommendations on unmet health promotion needs for older adults in the areas of alcohol abuse, dental (oral) health, physical fitness and exercise, injury prevention, medications, mental health, nutrition, preventive health services, and smoking cessation. Each set of recommendations covers education and training (for providers and the public), service, research, and policy.

Keywords: aged, behavior change, HPDP, interventions, policy.

Barr, R. A. (1994). Human factors and aging: The operator-task dynamic. In R. P. Abeles, H. C. Gift, & M. G. Ory (Eds., with the assistance of D. M. Cox), *Aging and quality of life* (pp. 202–215). New York: Springer Publishing.

By finding ways to better match individuals' abilities with the demands of the physical environment, the human factors framework offers great potential to improve performance of everyday activities by older adults and to avert costs of care. Yet, few studies pertain to older adults. Barr reviews new directions and illustrates recent findings relevant to the aging population concerning instrumental activities of daily living (IADLs), medication adherence, driving, and work. The human factors approach modifies the "operator-task environment" by training the "operator" or changing tasks, technology, and other environmental aspects. For example, IADLs such as meal preparation have been broken into general actions such as lifting objects. This information, then, can suggest interventions to reduce demands and improve performance, either by modifying the characteristics of the person (e.g., by training to increase stamina) or of the tasks (e.g., with equipment). Following similar procedures, a computer voice mail system was designed to counteract memory difficulties in taking medicines, and intersection crashes were decreased by matching perceptual and attention skills with the design of highways and road signs. Human factors research also offers insights into strategies for minimizing potential declines in work skills, facilitating adaptation of older workers to new technologies, and capitalizing on experience of older workers in making transitions.

Keywords: aged, behavior change, chronic self-management, conceptual, environment, functional status, medical self-care, psychosocial factors, review.

Berg, R. L., & Cassells, J. S. (Eds.). (1990). *The second fifty years: Promoting health and preventing disability.* Washington, DC: National Academy Press.

This report from the Institute of Medicine's (IOM) Division of Health Promotion and Disease Prevention expands IOM's interest in disease-focused cure and prevention to incorporate disability prevention and coping strategies. A major goal is to foster the belief among health professionals that growing old need not entail frailty or disability. The study analyzed 13 diseases, injury causes, and risk factors that contribute to disability, affect large numbers of elders, and have available interventions and adequate data to draw conclusions beneficial to the aging population. Chapters cover medication misuse, social isolation, physical inactivity, osteoporosis, falls, sensory loss, depression, oral health, cancer screening, nutrition, smoking, high blood pressure, and infectious diseases. Each discussion defines associated health risks; describes incidence, prevalence, costs, and "remediability"; and offers recommendations for research, education, and service. Suggestions for self-care practices and interventions are included. Illustrative conclusions follow: Older adults can and do benefit from smoking cessation, physical activity, oral and dental self-care, cancer screening and education about appropriate medication use. Furthermore, they can engage effective self-care practices (e.g., appropriate exercise) to prevent osteoporosis, decrease risk of falls, and help manage depression.

Keywords: aged, behavior change, chronic self-management, demographics, functional status, HPDP, policy, psychosocial factors, predictor, prevalence.

Bernard, S. L., Kincade, J. E., Konrad, T. R., Arcury, T. A., Rabiner, D. J., Woomert, A., DeFriese, G. H., & Ory, M. G. (1997). Predicting mortality from community surveys of older adults: The importance of self-rated functional ability. *Journal of Gerontology: Social Sciences, 52B*(3): S155–S163.

This paper reports findings from the National Survey of Self-Care and Aging (NSSCA) (see Norburn et al., 1995, in this section) and follow-up mortality data from Medicare beneficiary records, the National Death Index, and other sources. The authors introduce the use of a global measure of perceived functional ability with a national sample of older adults from Medicare beneficiary files. In-person interviews were conducted with 3,485 older adults selected in a stratified random sample with equal numbers by gender and by three age groups. The global self-rated functional ability item measured autonomy in the ability to care for oneself. Analyses indicate that the global measure of perceived functional ability had an independent contribution to the risk of death among older adults. Based on multivariate models that accounted for self-rated health, age, gender, medical conditions, functional status, and assistance from others, poor self-ratings on the global functional ability item nearly doubled the risk of death during the 2 and 1/2-year follow-up period. The potential prognostic importance of self-ratings of both health and functional ability among older adults may be useful both to researchers and clinicians.

Keywords: aged, functional status, health status, methods, predictor, psychosocial factors.

Buchner, D., & Wagner, E. Preventing frail health. (1992). *Clinics in Geriatric Medicine, 8*(1), 1–17.

In an overview of frailty prevention, Buchner and Wagner highlight the importance of health habits and the multiple benefits to older adults of exercise and changing sedentary lifestyles. They present conceptual models, and review evidence about the pathogenesis and prevention of frailty.

Preventing frailty is important to older adults for maintaining independence and may reduce future long-term care costs. The authors follow
recent trends by linking frailty to losses in independence and vulnerability to functional limitations. They define frailty as reduced physiological
reserves that increase risks of disability. Its primary physiologic components are deficits in neurologic control, mechanical (musculoskeletal) performance, and energy metabolism. Disease is an important cause of frailty,
but recent epidemiologic and experimental evidence shows that disuse also
induces frailty. Disuse includes bed rest that accompanies illness and
sedentary lifestyles. Obstacles to recovery include the myth that rest necessarily aids recovery, lack of knowledge about exercise for older adults,
and barriers to activity including "falls, medications, stressful life events,
and depressive illness" (p.8). Preventive strategies include (a) monitoring
physiologic indicators, (b) promoting regular exercise to prevent low-grade
physiologic loss, (c) treating illness such as depression, giving flu vaccinations, reducing risks of falls, counseling about stressful life events to
prevent acute episodes of loss, (d) anticipating episodes of functional loss
by boosting physiologic reserves prior to threatening events, and (e) removing obstacles to recovery, for example, through geriatric evaluation
and management.
Keywords: aged, behavior change, functional status, frail, HPDP, review.

Camacho, T., Strawbridge, W., Cohen, R., & Kaplan, G. (1993). Functional
    ability in the oldest old: Cumulative impact of risk factors from the pre-
    ceding two decades. *Journal of Aging and Health, 5,* 439–454.
There are few studies of the oldest old, yet understanding the factors
contributing to their functional ability is becoming ever more important
for this fastest growing age group. Using a sample of oldest-old adults
from the longitudinal Alameda County community studies, the investigators examine functional ability and its relationships with cumulative measures of behavioral and psychosocial risk factors. They analyzed data from
baseline and follow-ups on all of the surviving 91 subjects who were 80
years or older. Sleep patterns and smoking history were dropped from
analyses since no consistent relationships were found with final functional
status scores. About 20% of these oldest-old subjects experienced no more
than one difficulty with daily activities, almost half functioned at least rea-
sonably well, and only 12% had severe impairment in daily activities. Better functional status was associated with consistent physical activity,
absence of depression, being other than African American, higher educa-

tional level, and being married or never married. There was much inconsistent practice of health behaviors over the 19 years. Nevertheless, for each health practice and the overall index, more reports of positive health practices were associated with increased functional ability scores. The strongest of these relationships were for physical activity and the overall Index of Health Practices. When controlling for chronic conditions, strong significant associations with functioning remained for ethnicity, education, depression, and the overall Index of Health Practices (although the effects were reduced). With this control, the association of functioning with physical activity became nonsignificant, while associations with social contacts and marital status increased but generally were not significant. The investigators conclude that poor functioning can be a serious problem, but it is not a necessary concomitant of aging. Disadvantages of socioeconomic status on functioning persist into old age. Consistency of positive health behaviors over previous years is related to higher functional abilities of the oldest-old adults.

Keywords: aged, behavior change, frail/oldest-old, HPDP.

Cameron, L., Leventhal, E. A., & Leventhal, H. (1993). Symptom representations and affect as determinants of care seeking in a Community-dwelling, adult sample population. *Health Psychology ,12*(3), 171–179.

The investigators conducted a field study with 366 middle-aged and older adults to explore cognitive and emotional determinants in the process of making decisions to seek medical care. They describe a self-regulatory model in which responses to symptoms initiate the decision process (see also in this section Leventhal, Leventhal, & Schaefer 1992; Prohaska, Keller, Leventhal, & Leventhal, 1987). The model assumes that individuals use symptoms to create and elaborate illness representations and coping procedures. The investigators conclude that symptoms are a necessary but not sufficient stimuli for seeking medical care. Care seekers developed more elaborate symptom representations concerning seriousness, disruption of activity and consequences than did the asymptomatic controls. Care seekers also reported more elaborate coping strategies, and were more likely to communicate about their symptoms with others. Decisions to seek care were predicted by the representations that there was a serious health threat, belief in inability to cope with a threat, advice from significant others to seek care, and stress. Differences were not found by age.

Keywords: aged, behavior change, medical self-care, utilization.

Clark, N. M., Becker, M. H., Janz, N. K., Lorig, K., Rakowski, W., & Anderson, L. (1991). Self-management of chronic disease by older adults: A review and questions for research. *Journal of Aging and Health, 3*(1), 3–27.

This article reviews the large body of literature on self-management among the general population and older adults for five chronic diseases: arthritis, asthma, chronic obstructive pulmonary disease, diabetes, and heart disease. It also reviews studies on psychological coping skills for managing chronic disease. Self-management generally refers to the daily tasks performed by an individual "to control or reduce the impact of disease on physical health status" (p. 5), usually in collaboration with a health care provider. The review identified 12 essential types of self-management tasks common across the five conditions: recognizing symptoms, responding to symptoms, self-medication, managing acute episodes, maintaining nutrition, taking adequate exercise, quitting smoking, using relaxation techniques, interacting with health care providers, adapting to work, managing interpersonal relations, and managing psychological responses to illness. There were insufficient studies dealing with older adults to compare these basic types of self-management tasks to other populations or age groups. Nevertheless, differences in the context in which older adults operate, such as experiencing more comorbidity and differing social and economic circumstances, probably affect their chronic disease management.

Keywords: aged, behavior change, chronic self-management, conceptual, review.

Community-based initiatives to reduce social isolation and to improve health of the elderly. (1988). *Danish Medical Bulletin* [Special Supplement Series No. 6].

Empowerment is a key component of self-care definitions. This supplement explores the relationship of psychosocial factors to self-care and community-based initiatives from an international perspective, based on a work group representing 11 industrial and developing countries. The contents focus on elderly populations and cover social isolation and other psychosocial factors in relation to empowerment and health of older adults, and community-initiated programs and interventions.

Keywords: aged, behavior change, conceptual, health status, international, interventions, psychosocial factors, self-care (general).

De Jong, F. J., Atchison, K., Lubben, J.E., Schweitzer, S.O., Mayer-Oakes, S. A., & Matthias, R. E. (no date, circa 1993). *The empirical dimensions of protective health behaviors among a well elderly population.* Paper prepared for a project funded by the Health Care Financing Administration. Available from: Fred J. De Jong, PhD, School of Social Work, MRF Rm. 214, USC, University Park, Los Angeles, CA 90089.

This paper examines the multidimensionality and stability over time of potentially beneficial health behaviors in a well elderly population. The study is part of the UCLA Medicare Screening and Health Promotion Trial. Factor analyses examined relationships among 10 categories of health behaviors: not smoking, moderate alcohol use, sleep, eating breakfast, receiving recommended immunizations, seeking health information, exercise, receiving recommended professional health examinations, using risk avoidance measures, and maintaining appropriate weight for height. The modest correlation levels are consistent with previous research, and analyses failed to find support for a unidimensional health behavior construct. Analyses identified five dimensions of protective health behaviors: information seeking, screening examinations, alcohol use, health routines, and immunizations. With the exception of dental examinations, factor analyses showed the dimensions generally appeared to be stable over the 3-year period. The authors call for further testing with a variety of older population groups, and for clearer conceptualization of the structural relationships among health behaviors.

Keywords: aged, behavior change, conceptual, HPDP, methods.

Elward, K., & Larson, E. B. (1992). Benefits of exercise for older adults: A review of existing evidence and current recommendations for the general population. *Clinics in Geriatric Medicine, 8*(1), 35–50.

While exercise is a standard component of health promotion and preventive programs for young and middle-aged adults, current medical practice still does not widely recommend incorporating exercise into preventive regimes for most older adults. This thorough review examines evidence on whether exercise is beneficial for older adults. It presents state-of-the-art research describing the physiology of aging and exercise capacity, and the effects of exercise on glucose metabolism and diabetes, functional ability, neuropsychological function, and osteoporosis, and discusses their implications for the elderly population. Evidence varies in rigor, but supports certain beneficial effects. Benefits of moderate exercise to older adults seem to be numerous and complementary, such as improving cardiovascular sta-

tus and functional ability and reducing risk of osteoporosis, falls and fractures. Exercise seems to be safe and create few complications for older adults. Interventions need to be tailored to individual and special subgroup needs of older adults. Nevertheless, "vigorous weight-bearing exercises" (e.g., walking) offer safe, cheap, and effective benefits to the general elderly population.
Keywords: aged, behavior change, health status, HPDP, policy, predictor, review.

Haug, M. R., Akiyama, H., Tryban, G., Sonoda, K., & Wykle, M. (1991). Self care: Japan and the U.S. compared. *Social Science and Medicine, 33*(9), 1011–1022.

This research, one of few cross-cultural studies of self care, identifies differences between American and Japanese middle-aged and older adults in decisions to use self-care. It defines self-care as the "response behavior to a perceived symptom without the involvement of physicians" (p. 1011). Symptom responses include doing nothing, using over-the-counter medicine, and self-treatment and care from others (informal care) without advice from medical personnel. The health belief model frames the research (see below, Haug, Wykle, & Namazi 1989). The investigators postulate that self-care is facilitated by "positive health" and "negative views of physician care." They explore responses to 29 symptoms experienced in the 3 months preceding the study for adults 45–59, 60–74, and 75 and older. Among the Japanese, 47% reported experiencing no symptoms, compared to only 10% of the Americans. Among those experiencing symptoms, more Japanese (50%) used self-care only than Americans (27%). Some older adults in Japan were more likely than older Americans to feel they had a right to autonomous relationships with physicians or to obtain information. More Americans reported experiencing physician error. Japanese older adults seemed to experience less psychological distress than their American counterparts. Self-perceived health was about the same, but about two thirds of Americans reported one or more chronic conditions compared with only one third of the Japanese. On the other hand, Americans seemed more oriented to maintaining good health in terms of sleep, diet, alcohol consumption, smoking, and exercise. More Americans (32%) reported good health habits (as defined by the researchers) than the Japanese (only 17%). Multivariate analyses found better self-reported health and fewer good health habits were related to use of self-care in both countries, while other factors varied.

Keywords: aged, behavior change, conceptual, health status, HPDP, informal vs. formal care, international, medical self-care, predictor, psychosocial factors, utilization.

Haug, M. R., Wykle, M. L., & Namazi, K. H. (1989). Self-care among older
   adults. *Social Science and Medicine, 29*(2), 171–183.
   The article analyzes determinants of self-care among older adults, where self-care is defined as a decision to respond to a perceived illness symptom (see Haug et al., 1991, reviewed above). In-person interviews conducted with a random sample of noninstitutionalized adults aged 45–94 ascertained health belief predictors and behavioral responses to 32 illness symptoms in the 4 months preceding. Rates of self-care reflected the proportion of behavioral responses in which respondents did not seek any professional assistance. Self-care rates differed according to perceptions of a symptom's severity, with self-care more likely for symptoms perceived to be less severe. Contrary to assumptions, age did not significantly affect propensity to engage in self-care. Findings did not show any pattern in type of self-care which varied consistently across symptoms. Predictors of self-care rates differed depending on the perceived severity. Better health status was significantly associated with decisions to engage in self-care when symptoms were not perceived as serious and to a lesser but still significant degree, when symptoms were perceived as serious. For symptoms perceived as serious, lack of faith in doctors was a significant predictor of self-care. Nevertheless, regression analyses of rates of self-care for moderate versus serious symptoms on independent and control variables accounted for only a small fraction (less than 10%) of total variance.
   Keywords: aged, behavior change, conceptual, medical self-care, predictor, prevalence, psychosocial factors.

Jensen, J., Counte, M. A., & Glandon, L. (1992). Elderly health beliefs,
   attitudes, and maintenance. *Preventive Medicine, 21,* 483–497.
   With policy concerns about the ability of the health care system to meet needs of the growing older population comes interest in delaying health problems or maintaining or improving functional status and life quality for older adults. This study uses the health belief model to guide analyses of complex predictors of health maintenance of adults 62 years and older. Health maintenance behaviors considered included use of preventive medical and dental services, smoking and drinking abstinence, health practices, safety practices, and "environmental hazard avoidance" practices. Health

beliefs included general health motivation, medical care satisfaction, health locus of control, perceived vulnerability to disease, perceived efficacy of personal health practices and activities, medical skepticism, and a health information inventory. Generally, regression analyses showed different sets of predictors for each of the health maintenance behavior variables. Health beliefs contributed significantly to predicting health maintenance outcomes, but insurance coverage and other sociodemographic variables also showed significant contributions. Thus, interventions must be developed specific to health beliefs and sociodemographic differences.

Keywords: aged, behavior change, conceptual, HPDP, psychosocial factors.

Kaplan, G. A., & Strawbridge, W. J. (1994). Behavioral and social factors in healthy aging. In R. P. Abeles, H. C. Gift, & M. G. Ory (Eds., with the assistance of D. M. Cox), *Aging and quality of life*. New York: Springer Publishing.

Healthy aging refers not only to "optimal" levels of health and functioning, but emphasizes heterogeneity and potential for improvement. The authors summarize evidence from Alameda County, Longitudinal Study of Aging (LSOA), National Health and Nutrition Examination Survey II (NHANES II), Established Populations for Epidemiological Studies of the Elderly (EPESE) and other longitudinal studies that support the critical role of behavioral and social predictors of healthy aging, defined in terms of longevity, physical function, and environment. The strongest evidence in the abundant literature linking behaviors to mortality or longevity comes from studies of smoking and physical activity. Both smoking and low levels of physical activity are strongly associated with increased risk of death among older adults, and are modifiable behaviors. Social factors shown to be related to increased mortality risks among older adults include low social network and social activities participation, and low socioeconomic and educational levels (although this association is not consistently found). Preventing and delaying chronic illness and acute incidents such as falls offers great potential for preventing declines in physical function. Nevertheless, the mechanisms need further study. Preliminary evidence suggests smoking and physical activity may predict difficulties with physical functioning, although temporal order is not clear. A small body of literature suggests socioeconomic status, marital status, social network participation, and social support may predict or modify physical functioning. Predicting healthy aging with physical environment modifications remains relatively unstudied. Despite meager evidence about effects of health care delivery

on functional status, studies show potential benefits of rehabilitative services and exercise interventions may postpone frailty. Evidence also exists that modifying the social environment through interventions affecting social support and autonomy may have beneficial physical function outcomes.
Keywords: aged, behavior change, chronic self-management, environment, functional status, health status, HPDP, predictor, psychosocial factors, quality of life, review.

Kincade, J. E., Rabiner, D. J., Bernard, S. L., Woomert, A., Konrad, T.R., DeFriese, G. H., & Ory, M. G. (1996). Older adults as a community resource: Results from the National Survey of Self-Care and Aging. *The Gerontologist, 36*(4): 474–482.

Analyses employ the first wave of the longitudinal National Survey of Self-Care and Aging (NSSCA), collected in 1990–1991 (Norburn et al., 1995; Rabiner et al., 1997; both reviewed in this section). The authors examine the extent and type of assistance older adults provide to others as well as the characteristics of both the providers and recipients of that assistance. They define four types of assistance: personal care or 15 specific activities of daily living, child care, volunteer work, and listening or offering advice. Approximately one-third (8.5 million) of the community-dwelling older adults provided assistance with personal care, almost 16% (4.4 million) provided child care, almost 17% (5.5 million) performed volunteer work, and 40% (11 million) listened or offered advice to others. Age, gender, and perceived health status were the most consistent predictors of assistance. Help with instrumental activities of daily living, either alone or in combination with other activities of daily living, was the most common type of personal care provided. The authors conclude that older adults serve as a tremendous resource to their communities.
Keywords: aged, behavior change, chronic self-management, conceptual, demographics, environment, functional status, predictor, prevalence, psychosocial factors.

Leventhal, H., Leventhal, E. A., & Schaefer, P. M. (1992). Vigilant coping and health behavior. In M. G. Ory, R. P. Abeles, & P. D. Lipman (Eds.), *Aging, health and behavior* (pp. 109–140). Newbury Park, CA: Sage.

The authors describe a systems framework of "commonsense models of illness" that reflects subjects' views of reality and rules for decision making rather than imposing external conceptual frameworks (pp. 111–113). The commonsense model focuses on underlying cognitive mechanisms that form health and illness behavior, including cognitive and emotional aspects

of representing and reacting to illness, and strategies for coping and appraising illness outcomes. The ongoing processes are shaped by the social context, biological characteristics of diseases, and characteristics of individuals such as age. (See also Cameron, Leventhal, & Leventhal et al., 1993; Prohaska et al., 1987; both in this section). The authors present evidence from studies of well and ill adults indicating that older adults have higher levels of preventive behavior and treatment compliance than younger persons, and hypothesize that "older persons are more vigilant and responsive to health threats than middle-aged or younger persons" (p. 124). To detect model components involved in the "vigilance effect," they examine the data for connections between age differences and differences in cognitive representations and emotional responses to illness for older and middle-aged adults. They found no differences among age cohorts in terms of their representations of disease, interpretations of symptoms, or stereotypes of chronic diseases as part of the aging process. Contrary to expectations, they found older adults showed lower levels of emotional distress about illness threats. Further study suggested that older adults differ in their coping and appraisal procedures; by seeking care more quickly and thereby reducing both objective health threats and uncertainty with its concomitant emotional distress, they may be more risk averse and energy conserving. There was evidence that attributing symptoms to aging did slow the typically vigilant coping process of older persons. While many questions remain to be answered, such research exploring these mechanisms and processes should be particularly helpful in developing educational programs for changing health knowledge, attitudes and behavior for older adults, and all ages.
Keywords: aged, behavior change, conceptual, HPDP, medical self-care, psychosocial factors.

Manton, K. G., Corder, L., & Stallard, E. (1993). Changes in the use of personal assistance and special equipment from 1982 to 1989: Results from the 1982 and 1989 NLTCS. *The Gerontologist, 33*(2), 168–176.
　　Analyzing nationally representative longitudinal data from the National Long Term Care Surveys of the chronically disabled, elderly community-based population, the authors describe changes in use of personal assistance and equipment for coping with disability by specific chronic impairments, age, and gender. Functional impairment was measured by ADL and IADL (basic and instrumental daily activities) questions. Tables show distributions of chronic disability for community and institutionalized populations, estimates of disabled community residents for specific ADLs and

IADLs, and estimates of disabled community residents for type of assistance by gender and age and disability level. From 1982 to 1989, equipment use increased both for mildly disabled elders overall, and for severely disabled elders as a supplement to personal assistance. Also, dependence on personal assistance declined as a sole strategy for coping with chronic disability. Solely relying on either equipment or personal assistance seemed to be insufficient for elders coping with higher disability levels. Women and younger ages were more likely to depend on equipment. These changing need patterns carry important implications for long-term care policy and overall costs, because personal assistance service involves recurrent costs while equipment involves nonrecurrent costs. Thus, when equipment use substitutes appropriately for personal assistance, long-term care costs could decline.

Keywords: aged, behavior change, chronic self-management, costs, environment, functional status, policy, utilization.

McPherson, M. L. (1993). Self-care and medication management: Pharmacists and older adults. *Generations, 17*(3), 45–48.

McPherson reviews special needs of the older adult population in terms of medication management, one of the more important areas of their self-care. Significant issues include comorbidities and chronic conditions, multiple medications and potential drug interactions, multiple physicians, changing physiological processes, and compliance to drug regimens. The author discusses the responsibilities of pharmacists and older adults in forming an alliance to improve medication therapy outcomes. She outlines the functions of pharmacists in designing a therapeutic plan with the doctor and client and in counseling and monitoring. Pharmacists also may help patients manage medications by keeping a patient profile. Patients' responsibilities include providing personal demographics, medical history, and functional limitations, as well as implementing the drug regimen. Being informed about a drug is a joint responsibility. Appended to the article are a pharmacy patient's "bill of rights," questions all patients should ask their pharmacists, and a list of elder-health booklets on medications and their management.

Keywords: aged, behavior change, interventions, medical self-care.

Mockenhaupt, R. (1993). (Ed.). Self-care and older adults [Special issue]. *Generations, 17*(3).

Emphasizing self-care for older adults is a relatively recent phenomenon, and this special issue illustrates research and program work being conducted in this expanding field. Definitions of self-care applied to the older population focus on preventing disease and improving or maintaining health, and self-care as a coping strategy for chronic illness. Articles represent various definitions and cover these topics: self-care as a strategy for increasing the relevance of the health care system for older adults (Mettler & Kemper); self-care management for chronic illness (Lorig & Holman, 1993), cost-effective self-care strategies for retirees (Senior Healthtrac mail program), self-care in institutional settings, multicultural and social class aspects of self-care (Wykle & Haug, 1993 [reviewed below]), self-care as a rural health care strategy (Muchow, 1993 [above]), spiritual self-care, self-care movement and gerontological professional (DeFriese & Konrad, 1993 [see section I]) partnership between physicians and older adults; medication management (McPherson, 1993 [above]), complementary (non–Western) self-care strategies, limits of self-care (Vickery & Levinson), self-care responsibility, and modification of a longitudinal research study into a primary care program (Health Watch).

Keywords: aged, alternative healing, behavior change, conceptual, chronic self-management, costs, HPDP, informal vs. formal care, interventions, medical self-care, minorities, psychosocial factors, rural.

Moore, E. J. (1990). Using self-efficacy in teaching self-care to the elderly. *Holistic Nursing Practice, 4*(2), 22–29. 1990.

Moore reviews the principles of Albert Bandura's self-efficacy theory of behavioral change as a framework for teaching self-care to older adults and helping them become partners in care. The author argues that teaching self-care by increasing self-efficacy can help older adults promote their health and prevent disease and its complications, while empowering them to control their own health. Self-care incorporates not only carrying out daily living activities but also personal growth and nurturing activities, and minimizing personal health risks. While self-efficacy research has seldom examined elderly populations, a review found much support for the ability of self-efficacy to explain or predict health and addictive behavior change and maintenance, as well as to predict participation in programs and enhance program effects. Furthermore, self-efficacy has been found to mediate effects of stress on health and to predict depression (including among older adults), mental distress, and recovery. Moore discusses potential applications of self-efficacy to self-care education of older adults, noting the importance of integrating specific characteristics of the developmental process of aging.

Keywords: aged, behavior change, conceptual, interventions, predictors, psychosocial factors.

Mor, V., & Rakowski, W. (Eds.). (1993). Disease prevention strategies in the elderly [Special issue]. *Rhode Island Medicine, 76*(1). 1993.

This special edition gathers discussions on issues pertaining to prevention and health promotion for older adults. Articles address primary prevention of functional decline, prevention of functional decline among hospitalized elders, specific healthy lifestyle behaviors such as alcohol use and exercise, and screening of older adults. Other topics are the status of health behavior indicators among high risk older adults, health promotion among older African Americans, and participation in a health promotion and disease prevention program for Medicare beneficiaries.

Keywords: aged, functional status, frail/oldest-old, HPDP, interventions, minorities, review.

Muchow, J. A. (1993). Self-care as a rural healthcare strategy. *Generations, 17*(3), 29–32.

Muchow discusses traditional and modern concepts of self-care for meeting distinctive needs of the rural older adult population. She identifies features of rural communities (e.g., remoteness, sparse settlement) and the accompanying health care system barriers that self-care strategies can appropriately address. In comparison to urban residents, rural (and rural aged) residents tend to have higher poverty rates, poorer health, higher rates of chronic disabling conditions, higher rates of fatal injuries, and lower rates of health services use. They are less likely to have private health insurance. Evidence also shows, however, that rural elders are receptive to health promotion and preventive education and programs. Self-care can meet their needs, for example, through low-cost and appropriate management of chronic conditions and education to prevent injuries. Muchow cautions that the population's diversity must be taken into account, and illustrates ways in which needs and self-care may differ for minority and other subgroups. Self-care strategies also may reduce the health impact of access and availability barriers to services by offering relief from symptoms and reducing unnecessary trips for care. Difficulties faced by rural hospitals and shortages of health professionals in many rural areas are discussed. Encouraging modern self-care strategies in rural areas can build on traditional self-reliance and home remedies, and adapt health educational interventions to the resource, cost, and transportation circumstances. The "Healthwise for Life" program, which used an interactive video to train 15,000 rural residents, is described as an illustration.

Keywords: aged, behavior change, chronic self-management, conceptual, HPDP, minorities, rural.

Norburn, J.E.K., Bernard, S. L., Konrad, T. R., Woomert, A., DeFriese, G. H., Kalsbeek, W. D., Koch, G. G., and Ory, M. G. (1995). Self-care and assistance from others in coping with functional status limitations among a national sample of older adults. *The Journal of Gerontology: Social Sciences, 50*(2), S101–S109.

This article presents national estimates of self-care practices, assistance from others, and functional status from the longitudinal National Survey of Self-Care and Aging. The study is based on a national probability sample of 3,485 noninstitutionalized older adults from Medicare beneficiary files, stratified by gender and age groups (65–74, 75–84, and 85+) and geographically clustered in urban and rural areas. Using baseline in-person interviews conducted in 1990–1991, the authors examine older adults' self-care practices for coping with functional status limitations. A composite score of functional status reflects the presence and severity of disability in three dimensions: basic, mobility, and instrumental activities of daily living. Three types of self-care coping strategies were use of special equipment, changes in behavior, and environmental modifications. Results showed that likelihood of engaging in self-care coping strategies increased as severity of disability increased, except among the most severely disabled. In general, those receiving assistance from others were more likely to engage in self-care activities, suggesting that receiving assistance supplemented, rather than supplanted, self-care coping strategies. (See also in this section Kincade et al., 1996; Rabiner et al., 1997.)

Keywords: aged, behavior change, chronic self-management, conceptual, demographics, environment, functional status, predictor, prevalence, psychosocial factors.

Omenn, G. S. (Ed.). (1992). Health promotion and disease prevention [Special issue]. *Clinics in Geriatric Medicine, 8*(1).

This comprehensive issue highlights research and recommendations pertaining to effective health promotion and disease prevention strategies specifically for older adults. Although older adults were excluded or underrepresented in studies during the 1960s and 1970s, adequate evidence now exists to support beneficial effects of preventive strategies and to propose

clinical recommendations for this population. Articles review findings on preventing frailty (see above, Buchner & Wagner, 1992) and cognitive decline, beneficial effects of exercise (see above, Elward & Larson, 1992), cancer screening, smoking consequences and cessation, screening and treating cholesterol and high blood pressure, prophylactic aspirin for preventing stroke, moderate alcohol consumption, overcoming polypharmacy, preventing depression, interventions for hearing and visual impairments, vaccinations, preventive oral medicine, and preventive care counseling.
Keywords: aged, behavior change, chronic self-management, HPDP, medical self-care, policy, predictors, psychosocial factors, review.

Potts, M. K., Hurwicz, M. L., Goldstein, M. S., & Berkanovic, E. (1992). Social support, health-promotive beliefs, and preventive health behaviors among the elderly. *Journal of Applied Gerontology, 11*(4), 425–440.
Previous research shows that social support is important to the physical and mental health of older adults, and that it may facilitate practice of health behaviors. This study determines the extent that high social support levels and health beliefs are related to preventive health behaviors, when controlling demographics, health status, and perceived frailty. Data were collected in a panel study through telephone interviews with 936 elderly enrollees at a health maintenance organization. Health behavior beliefs were the strongest predictor of preventive behavior. Nevertheless, high social support levels also consistently predicted preventive behaviors, such as reducing red meat consumption, taking vitamins, and exercising regularly. This relationship held when controlling health beliefs. Health beliefs were more strongly associated with preventive behaviors among subjects who lived alone, suggesting that subjects may be more likely to behave based on their beliefs when no other person can directly influence their behavior. Among other variables, only gender consistently predicted preventive behaviors: Women were more likely to practice prevention. While both beliefs and social support predicted preventive behavior, these variables explained only a modest amount of variance (from 4% to 15%).
Keywords: aged, behavior change, HPDP, psychosocial factors.

Prohaska, T. R., Keller, M. L., Leventhal, E. A., & Leventhal, H. (1987). Impact of symptoms in aging attribution on emotions and coping. *Health Psychology, 6*(6), 495–514.
Findings characterize the process of selecting self-care coping activities and medical care in response to symptoms by means of "common sense

models of illness" (p. 495). Symptom responses are analyzed in terms of the interactions among symptom characteristics, age, and tendency to attribute symptoms to aging (see also in this section Cameron et al., 1993; Leventhal et al., 1992). In experimental studies, individuals ranked the likelihood of employing particular coping responses to four scenarios involving varying symptom characteristics (severity, duration, and symptom label), and indicated whether or not they attributed the specific symptoms to aging. Generally, symptom characteristics and interpretations were major determinants of self-care and medical care coping strategies. Severe symptoms elicited the highest incidence of self-care, medical treatment, and emotional distress. Severity had greater impact than duration of symptoms, but longer enduring symptoms also increased the seeking of medical care. Attributing symptoms to aging was greater for older adults, was related to reduced emotional distress, and resulted in significant delays in seeking treatment. The investigators conclude that coping processes depend on the characteristics of symptoms, not just on specific illness.

Keywords: aged, behavior change, conceptual, medical self-care, predictors, utilization.

Rabiner, D. J., Konrad, T. R., DeFriese, G. H., Kincade, J. E., Bernard, S. L., Woomert, A., Arcury, T. A., & Ory, M. G. (1997). Rural urban differentials in functional status and self-care practice: Findings from a national sample of community-dwelling older adults. *Journal of Rural Health, 13*(1): 14–28.

This paper compares the functional status and self-care practices of older adults residing in nonmetropolitan and metropolitan communities based on a national probability survey of the noninstitutionalized older adult population (see, above, Norburn et al., 1995). Weighted bivariate and multivariate logistic regression analyses determine the relationship between geographic residence and the ability to perform basic, mobility, and instrumental activities of daily living without assistance from others. Analyses also assess effects of functional limitations on self-care practices. Bivariate logistic analyses point to modest, often insignificant, metropolitan versus non-metropolitan differences in the ability of older adults to perform functional tasks. Once other factors likely to account for some of these differences were taken into account, larger positive effects of nonmetropolitan residence generally were observed. Older adults from nonmetropolitan areas generally are more likely to report being able to perform functional activities, but also were more likely to report performing self-care activities both in the presence and absence of disability. Among their explanations, the authors suggest that nonmetropolitan older adults may normalize the process of aging in different ways.

Keywords: aged, functional status, policy, predictor, rural, self-care (general).

Rakowski, W., Julius, M., Hickey, T., & Halter, J. B. (1987). Correlates of preventive health behavior in late life. *Research on Aging, 9,* 331–335.

In-person interviews and daily diaries from community-based older adults aged 64 to 96 years focused on a broader range of preventive and health-related practices than previous studies. Factor analyses and correlations confirmed the appropriateness of grouping the 37 behaviors into four types of health practices: information seeking, regular health routines, medical and self-examination, and risk avoidance. Evidence did not support a general factor of health behavior. Only modest associations were found. Generally, each of the four health practice types was characterized by a separate set of predictor variables. Being a woman and having a supportive family environment most consistently predicted positive health practices.

Keywords: aged, behavior change, HPDP, policy, psychosocial factors.

Rakowski, W., Julius, M., Hickey, T., Verbrugge, L. M., & Halter, J. B. (1988). Daily symptoms and behavioral responses: Results of a health diary with older adults. *Medical Care, 26,* 278–295.

This study explores self-care and other health care behaviors by which older adults respond to daily symptoms. It also contributes to understanding methods data collection in older populations, specifically, the use of daily diaries of symptoms and responses. Analyses identify useful predictors covering sociodemographic, economic, psychological, social, health, and health care utilization factors. The overwhelming symptom responses were "no action" and "self-treatment." Compared to men, women were more likely to respond actively and with self-treatment. Symptom responses and preventive health behaviors may be independent health behaviors, since they were not strongly associated with each other. Nevertheless, information seeking may be generally important. Overall, the study identified no dominant predictors for health behaviors. Thus, each dependent measure may represent different dimensions of symptom-related behavior, and no single theory may adequately explain all health behaviors.

Keywords: aged, behavior change, conceptual, medical self-care, methods, psychosocial factors, utilization.

Rakowski, W., & Schmidt, R. M. (Eds.). (1994). Preventive healthcare and health promotion for older adults [Special issue]. *Generations, 28*(1).

This special issue presents a generic view that treats older adults, their families, and health professionals as consumers of the diverse research data and literature on preventive health care and health promotion for older adults. The first articles discuss the historical context and measurement of prevention and health promotion. The second section covers guidelines and recommendations for health promotion and disease prevention for older adults. The third section reviews current issues in implementing preventive and health-promoting care, including the contexts of value judgments for objectives, risk assessment measures, and impact on costs of care. Individual articles cover changing perceptions about the meaning of prevention for older people, societal and individual preventive health care services, health promotion for ethnic minorities, locus of responsibility for prevention, current state and future trends of health status and risk assessment, (mis)interpretation of health status and risk assessments, cost-effectiveness of prevention programs, older people as consumers of health promotion recommendations, information management, and an international example of health promotion in Budapest.

Keywords: aged, conceptual, costs, HPDP, interventions, minorities, policy, review.

Segall, A. (1987). Age Differences in lay conceptions of health and self-care responses to illness. *Canadian Journal on Aging, 6*(1), 47–63.

Hypothesizing that elderly adults are more likely than others to have "popular" health beliefs and to practice self-care, this study examines the nature and extent of self-care in a random sample of Winnipeg residents. The study found complex relationships between age and lay health beliefs and self-care responses to illness. By itself, age did not explain much variance in any of the health belief or self-care practice dependent variables. Lay self-care beliefs and self-care practices existed throughout the population; they were not more pronounced among older adults. Evidence was found for a supplemental relationship between self-care and professional care. Rather than being mutually exclusive, self- and professional care coexisted. Medical skepticism did not decrease use of medical care, but was among the best predictors of all lay belief and self-care variables.

Keywords: aged, behavior change, HPDP, informal vs. formal care, medical self-care, prevalence, psychosocial factors.

Shephard, R. J. (1990). The scientific basis of exercise prescribing for the very old. *Journal of the American Geriatric Society, 38*(1), 62–70.
Emphasizing the heterogeneity of physical ability among older adults, the author reviews the contributions to independent living that active functional ability can make. He presents ways that exercise can benefit frail, older adults, even beginning at 75 years or older, and summarizes comprehensive research evidence supporting each benefit. Exercise by frail older adults can improve their health by lowering cardiovascular risk, reducing body fat and rate of osteoporosis, and by improving functional capacity, nutritional uptake, and sleep patterns. Furthermore, it can increase social contacts, improve cerebral function, and reduce anxiety and depression. The author offers specific ways medical practitioners can identify and encourage healthy exercise interventions appropriate for older persons. Key issues are ways to achieve safety, encourage compliance, and determine requirements for an effective but safe intervention. Finally, the author summarizes the psychological and physiological responses that can be expected for older adults. For example, older adults may progress relatively slowly from a sedentary to trained state. Although moderate exercise is likely to enhance deteriorating immune function, heavy exercise can depress immune function. In conclusion, exercise can protect against some diseases, and can improve quality of life by improving physical function.
Keywords: aged, behavior change, frail/oldest-old, review.

Stoller, E. P., & Forster, L. E. (1992). Patterns of illness behavior among rural elderly: Preliminary results of a health diary study. *The Journal of Rural Health, 8*(1), 13–26.
Exploring patterns of illness behavior and lay care, the authors interviewed older adults from a probability sample in rural upstate New York. Multiple indicators of health status included 26 diagnosed conditions from the Duke-University of North Carolina (UNC) Health Profile and 36 symptoms from the Older Americans Resources and Services Program (OARS) protocol. Each participant completed 3-week structured health diaries. Respondents experienced an average of 4.3 out of 26 health diary symptoms. The most common in descending order were muscle or joint pain, fatigue, and runny nose. Generally, nonmedical and medical explanations were combined. Almost 89% reported a nonmedical cause, with weather mentioned most often, while 75% cited a medical cause, usually associated with a previously diagnosed chronic condition. Most discussed symptoms

with others; family and friends, not health professionals, were the most likely consultants. The primary symptom response was to do nothing. The most common intervention actions were using over-the-counter (OTC) medications, limiting activity, and using previously prescribed medications. Rural-urban differences generally disappeared after controlling demographic and socioeconomic background (covariates of residence). Persisting residential differences were: urban residents were more likely to explain symptoms by previous chronic conditions, use nonmedical explanations, report more symptoms that were very troublesome, use OTC medications for indigestion and nervousness, and to pray about nervousness. Rural subjects were less likely to take no action, and more likely to use exclusively medical explanations and ignore nervousness. (See also the three following reviews.)

Keywords: aged, behavior change, chronic self-management, medical self-care, rural, utilization.

Stoller, E., Forster, L. E., Pollow, R., & Tisdale, W. A. (1993). Lay evaluation of symptoms by older people: An assessment of potential risk. *Health Education Quarterly, 20,* 505–522.

One major research issue is the appropriateness of lay decisions about when it is safe to self-treat symptoms. Stoller and colleagues explore appropriateness and safety of assessments of the potential risk of symptoms among rural older adults. Interviews and diaries provided prevalence, lay interpretations of risk, and consultation decisions about 26 common symptoms. These evaluations and decisions were compared with conservative clinical assessments of potential risk of the symptoms. About 73% of the older adults experienced at least one potentially risky symptom, such as fatigue, headache, sleep difficulties, nervousness, depression, or shortness of breath. About one in eight older adults were judged to be medically at risk because they experienced potentially risky symptoms but had not consulted a medical professional in the past 6 months. At-risk persons were most likely to be women, widowed, and at the young end of the sample. They were likely to assess their health more positively than those not at medical risk. The most common sources of health information for elders who contacted physicians were their physician, media, and discussion with family members, while those without physician contact relied most heavily on the media.

Keywords: aged, interventions, medical self-care, prevalence, rural, utilization.

Stoller, E. P., Forster, L. E., & Portugal, P. (1993). Self-care responses to symptoms by older people: A health diary study of illness behavior. *Medical Care, 31*(1), 24–42.

Lay care is becoming increasingly important to illness behavior research, which previously emphasized formal service utilization. This study, too, explores self-treatment of symptoms by older adults. Analyses describe patterns of self-medication and self-treatments (other than medication) for 26 symptoms. Nonmedication self-treatments included prayer, dietary home remedies, other home remedies such as a warm bath, behavior changes such as quitting smoking, and leisure activity. Analyses also examine symptom interpretation (e.g., seriousness) and symptom experience as potential predictors of self-care responses. Most older adults self-treated most of their symptoms. A minority took no action, although no action was common for some symptoms. The most frequently reported treatments were prescriptions and over-the-counter medicines. Nevertheless, treatment patterns varied greatly for subjects and symptoms. According to multivariate analyses, both symptom interpretation and symptom experience were important in making treatment decisions. Decisions to self-treat rather than not act tended to be made based on presence of pain and discomfort, interference with daily activities, and belief the symptom might be serious. Familiarity with the symptom and attributed cause were less important in these decisions.

Keywords: aged, behavior change, chronic self-management, HPDP, medical self-care, psychosocial factors.

Stoller, E. P., & Pollow, R. (1994). Factors affecting the frequency of health enhancing behaviors by the elderly. *Public Health Reports, 109,* 377–389.

The authors considered primary, secondary, and tertiary prevention models in their examination of the frequency of personal preventive health behaviors of older adults who completed in-depth interviews. (See preceding Stoller et al. reviews.) Almost all subjects regularly practiced at least one of nine health-enhancing behaviors; dietary practices were reported most often. The mean was 4.6 regularly practiced behaviors. Multivariate analyses were consistent with previous studies in showing few consistent predictors of health behaviors. Women were more likely than men to practice most of the health behaviors. Analyses indicated that illness and disability may have an important impact on the frequency of preventive health practices. This article presents illustrative analyses for relationships of hypertension diagnosis with relevant preventive health management strategies. Analyses support the work of others who suggest that different conceptual models may be needed to explain health behaviors of those with disease and/or disability and those without. Because chronic disease and disability more often characterize older adult than young populations, the need to develop separate models for the different levels of prevention becomes particularly important. The authors encourage use of qualitative methodologies.

Keywords: aged, behavior change, chronic self-management, conceptual, functional status, HPDP, informal vs. formal care, methods, psychosocial factors, prevalence.

Strawbridge, W. J., Cohen, R. D., Shema, S. J., & Kaplan, G. A. (1996). Successful aging: Predictors and associated activities. *American Journal of Epidemiology, 144*(2), 135–141.

Six-year predictors of successful aging were analyzed for 356 Alameda County study men and women aged 65–95 years measured prospectively in 1984 and followed to 1990. Successful aging was defined as needing no assistance and having no difficulty on any of 13 activity/mobility measures plus little or no difficulty on 5 physical performance measures. After adjusting for baseline successful aging, sex, and age, the authors found that 1984 predictors of 1990 successful aging included income, years of education, ethnicity, diabetes, chronic obstructive pulmonary disease, arthritis, and hearing problems. Adjusting for all variables, the authors found that behavioral and psychosocial predictors included the absence of depression, presence of close personal contacts, and walking for exercise. Cross-sectional comparisons at follow-up revealed significantly higher community involvement, physical activity, and mental health for those aging successfully.

Keywords: aged, functional status, psychosocial factors, health status.

Struyk, R. J., & Katsura, H. M. (1988). *Aging at home: How the elderly adjust their housing without moving.* New York: Haworth.

Some conceptualizations of self-care incorporate housing and environmental modifications that help older adults maintain community residence. This book takes a comprehensive look at "in-place" housing adjustments and a multitude of predictors. The study was part of the longitudinal Community Development Strategies Evaluation of urban households, and focuses on the 177 households headed by an older adult. It examines repairs, housing unit modification to accommodate disabled persons, alternative room use, and boarders on the premises. Large proportions of households repaired their homes; for example, 69% of elderly-headed and 80% of other-headed households made at least one repair in both years. Other types of housing adjustments were rarely made, although unexpectedly high proportions of households modified their homes (10% of elderly-headed and 5% of non–elderly headed) in the prior 2 years. At least one room change was made over the past 2 years by 5% of elderly-headed and 6% of non–elderly headed households. Multivariate analyses indicated that activity limitations consistently predicted use of rooms; changes were likely when there was a disabled member. Activity limitations and using special equipment also were significant determinants of modifications in dwelling units. Outside support and services attenuated some effects; economic status showed limited or no effects. The authors caution that interventions must be tailored to wide ranges of specific needs and complement the ongoing assistance.

Keywords: aged, behavior change, costs, environment, functional status, HPDP, psychosocial factors.

Teno, J. M., Lynn, J., Phillips, R. S., Murphy, D., Youngner, S. J., Bellamy, P., Connors, Jr., A. F., Desbiens, N. A., Fulkerson, W., & Knaus, W. A. (1994). Do formal advance directives affect resuscitation decisions and the use of resources for seriously ill patients? *The Journal of Clinical Ethics, 5*(1), 23–30.

One new area of self-care research addresses how patients' preferences shape medical decision making through advance directives concerning incompetence. This article reports findings on the effect of advance directives by seriously ill adult patients in five hospitals. Interviews identified 618 subjects (20.2%) with written directives including living wills, durable power of attorney, or both. Results showed that advance directives, including actual do-not-resuscitate (DNR) orders, and decisions to forgo resuscitation at time of death, had no clinically important effects on decision making about resuscitating patients. Furthermore, analyses of patients who died during their first hospital stay after enrollment showed no significant effects of advance directives on use of resources, as indicated by hospital bill, intensity of therapy, or length of stay. Even among subjects most likely to show effects (i.e., patients with a living will or who preferred to forgo resuscitation), no significant effect of advance directives was found. The authors conclude that advance directives did not seem to be relevant to the outcomes of decision making.

Keywords: aged, chronic self-management, conceptual, costs, policy, quality of life, self-care (general), utilization.

Wykle, M. L., & Haug, M. R. (1993). Multicultural and social-class aspects of self-care. *Generations, 17*(3), 25–28.

The authors discuss older adults and their self-care practices, defined as self-treatment for symptoms. They use a health belief model to analyze cultural differences between the United States and Japan and social class differences in the United States. In the cross-cultural study, a greater proportion of the Japanese adults used only self-care for both mild and more serious symptoms than did the American counterparts, despite greater proportions of physician error and greater presence of chronic illness reported by Americans. Cultural factors may explain these differences, such as Eastern medical methods that more closely parallel self-care patterns. Among 28 self-care practices to treat symptoms of arthritis, the authors found few ethnic differences, although variation did occur by cultural groups. For example, Hispanics were more likely to use herbal teas and home remedies, while Eastern Europeans were more likely to use dry heat, copper bracelets, and change in routines. Much ethnic variation seems to be related to education or social class measures, although larger studies are needed. More research is needed to disentangle relationships among ethnic, cultural, and social class variables.

Keywords: aged, behavior change, chronic self-management, conceptual, HPDP, international, medical self-care, minorities, psychosocial factors.

SECTION III. DESIGN, IMPLEMENTATION AND EVALUATION OF SELF-CARE PROGRAMS FOR OLDER ADULTS

Buchner, D., Beresford, S., Larson, E., LaCroix, A., & Wagner, E. (1992). Effects of physical activity on health status in older adults. II. Intervention studies. *Annual Review of Public Health, 13*, 469–488.

The authors review experimental evidence from intervention studies about effects of exercise on health status and physical and cognitive functioning of older adults. They focus on effects of exercise on disabilities (i.e., restricted ability to perform an activity). The role of exercise on impairments (i.e., psychological or physiological losses in structure or function) is already well known for heart disease, hypertension, diabetes, pulmonary disease, obesity and depression. This review finds clear evidence that exercise promotes health or physical function of both healthy and chronically ill older adults when improved physical function is measured as increased aerobic capacity, muscle strength, and endurance. Evidence to support beneficial effects of exercise on functional status is not conclusive. Nevertheless, some studies suggest possible improvements in gait and balance. Arthritis patients may gain improved long-term functional status, including increased mobility and decreased pain. According to some nonrandomized trials, exercise may increase bone mineral density and thus decrease risk of fractures. Intervention studies are inadequate to determine whether or not exercise improves cognitive functioning.

Keywords: aged, functional status, HPDP, interventions, review.

Carter, W. B., Elward, K., Malmgren, J., Martin, M. L., & Larson, E. (1991). Participation of older adults in health programs and research: A critical review of the literature. *The Gerontologist, 31,* 584–592.

Identifying methodologies appropriate for use with older adults is important for conducting research and implementing effective programs. This article provides an extensive review on participation of older adults in surveys, clinical trials, health promotion interventions, and health programs. All aim to maintain or improve functional status among chronically ill older adults. Appropriate and feasible recruitment strategies are discussed. Tables summarize participation rates by age of participants, study characteristics, and participation variables. Despite scant literature, it appears that older adults through 74 years of age can be included in surveys, clinical trials, and health promotion programs just as feasibly as other age groups. Their participation rates, compliance with study protocols, and response quality are comparable or only slightly lower than those of younger adults. Somewhat longer recruitment periods may be necessary since older adults sometimes are reluctant and may be more difficult to locate. For oldest-old adults, adequate participation, compliance, and quality responses seem to become more problematic, but their participation still is feasible.

Keywords: aged, functional status, HPDP, interventions, methods, review.

Clark, N. M., Janz, N. K., Becker, M. H., Schork, M. A., Wheeler, J., Liang, J., Dodge, J. A., Keteyian, S., Rhoads, K. L., & Santinga, J. T. (1992). Impact of self-management education on the functional health status of older adults with heart disease. *The Gerontologist, 32,* 438–443.

Few rigorous studies have evaluated self-management interventions for chronic disease among older adults. This article evaluates effects of a self-management education program on functional status of older adults with

heart disease. The "Take PRIDE" intervention, based on social cognitive theory, bolsters self-efficacy and teaches participants to use self-regulation principles to identify and resolve problems of managing heart disease. It provided videotapes, a workbook, instruction from a health educator, meetings with other older adults, and strategies to improve patient-physician communication and family support. At the 12-month follow-up, no differences were found between the program and control groups on the overall Sickness Impact Profile score or the physical function dimension, but program participants showed significantly greater psychological functioning. Within the psychological dimension, the program group had lower emotional behavior scores (e.g., less hopelessness) and greater alertness than the control group. Better psychological functioning was evident for both male and female program participants compared with their respective control counterparts, but the difference was significant only for women. In terms of disease impact on overall psychological functioning, there were no differences between males and female program participants. Gender differences were apparent for items within all dimensions. The authors conclude that the self-regulation program did help participants identify and change heart disease management problems, and reduced negative factors. They suggest that education seems likely to affect women differently than men and may improve psychological functioning of older women.
Keywords: aged, behavior change, chronic self-management, functional status, informal vs. formal care, interventions, predictor, psychosocial factors.

FallCreek, S., Muchow, J., & Mockenhaupt, R. E. (1994). Health promotion with rural elders. In R. T. Coward, C. N. Bull, G. Kukulka, & J. M. Galliher (Eds.), *Health services for rural elders* (pp. 182–202). New York: Springer Publishing.

Very few studies have examined health promotion in rural aging populations. This chapter summarizes the state of knowledge. The limited evidence based on a few health status indicators suggests that rural older adults may be at greater risk for disease and disability than their nonrural counterparts, but it is not known whether the need patterns for health promotion differ for older adults in rural versus nonrural areas. The authors discuss access barriers to health promotion services that characterize rural areas, older adults and rural elder populations. Barriers include myths about aging and rural elders, program costs and funding issues amidst scarce resources and high poverty rates, shortages of health professionals in rural areas, lesser availability of programs and particular attitudes and beliefs. The authors summarize research and demonstration programs conducted with rural older adults: Growing Younger and Growing Wiser of Healthwise, Dartmouth's Self-Care for Senior Citizens project, Wallingford Wellness Project, programs by the USDA Cooperative Extension Service, and several regional and statewide initiatives. Using volunteers seems to be an important way to extend limited resources, and innovative strategies such as mailed interventions appear to be effective, cost-containing methods. The authors note the importance of addressing the diversity within the rural aging population.

Keywords: aged, demographics, health status, HPDP, interventions, minorities, policy, psychosocial factors, review, rural.

Fries, J. F. (1994). *Emerging data on the effectiveness of self care among older adults in western industrial societies.* Stanford University School of Medicine, Department of Medicine. Available from: Dr. J. F. Fries, 1000 Welch Road, Suite 203, Palo Alto, CA 94304-1808.

The author argues that increasing data support the effectiveness of self-management approaches for older adults, and suggests that national dissemination of such programs is needed. To support this argument and illustrate the state of the art, he provides brief overviews of six recent studies of self-management interventions for seniors conducted by the Stanford University School of Medicine. These include a large observational study and randomized controlled trials of a mail-delivered health promotion program, a longitudinal study of aerobic exercise, and randomized controlled trials of self-management programs for Parkinson's disease and arthritis.

Keywords: aged, chronic self-management, HPDP, interventions, medical self-care, self-care (general), review.

Fries, J. F., Bloch, D. A., Harrington, H., Richardson, N., & Beck, R. (1993). Two-year results of a randomized controlled trial of a health promotion program in a retiree population: The Bank of America study. *The American Journal of Medicine, 94,* 455–462.

This randomized control trial evaluated the effectiveness of the Senior Healthtrac health promotion program for Bank of America retirees. The program aimed to improve health habits and self-sufficiency, and increase appropriate health care use. This individualized mailed program cost about $30 per person per year. Program materials included two books on healthy

habits and algorithms for appropriate symptom response, health habit questionnaires, personal health risk reports, personal letters recommending ways to correct risks, and newsletters. When compared with controls, overall health risk scores improved substantially for the intervention group at 1 year (12%) and at 2 years (23%). Participants made favorable changes in their health habits, for example, in seat belt use, salt and fat intake. Participants also made favorable health changes in systolic blood pressure and body weight. Most changes were statistically significant. At 12 months, the study found significant cost reduction differences by both self-report (more than 20%) and by claims experience (10%). The intervention group averaged a $164 medical cost reduction compared with the control group average increase of $15. The authors conclude that the program effectively changed health behaviors by reducing health risks, and lowered medical costs.
Keywords: aged, behavior change, costs, HPDP, interventions, utilization.

Fries, J. F., Fries, S. T., Parcell, C. L., & Harrington, H. (1992). Health risk changes with a low cost individualized health promotion program: Effects at up to 30 months. *American Journal of Health Promotion, 6,* 364–371.

Findings are reported from a prospective, longitudinal, observational study of 103,937 consecutive participants in a low-cost, mailed health promotion program for young and older adults. It is one of few studies of large-scale interventions analyzing medium-term benefits (30 months) with different age and socioeconomic groups. The design uses baseline data from new participants to approximate concurrent comparison groups. Interventions were the Healthtrac and Senior Healthtrac programs. These included mailed health risk assessments, individualized reports, self-management and health promotion materials and newsletters. The intervention cost an average of $30 per participant. The program showed strong positive effects overall. At 12-month and 18-month follow-ups, both younger adults (mean of 41 years) and older adults (mean of 68 years) had improved in all target health habits except pounds over ideal weight. Improved habits included smoking, dietary fat and cholesterol intakes, alcohol, exercise, and stress management. Health risk changes were consistently progressive over time and were consistent over all age and socioeconomic subgroups. This program illustrates the potential of low-cost, mailed interventions for large populations, seniors, and lower socioeconomic groups.
Keywords: aged, costs, HPDP, interventions, utilization.

Fries, J. F., Harrington, H., Edwards, R., Kent, L. A., & Richardson, N. (1994). Randomized controlled trial of cost reductions from a health education program: The California Public Employees' Retirement System (PERS) study. *American Journal of Health Promotion, 8*(3), 216–223.

The authors evaluate cost reduction trends by the active and passive Healthtrac and Senior Healthtrac health promotion programs. The design was a 12-month randomized controlled trial of claims data for employees and retirees of California's Public Employees' Retirement System. Secondary analyses examined changes in self-reported health habits and estimated costs. Active interventions included mailed health risk assessments, individualized reports, and self-management books. Passive subjects received only printed educational materials. Results indicated the intervention was associated with (a) reduced health risk scores at 12 months, (b) reduction in self-reported medical care use (doctor visits per year, hospital days per year, and sick days per year) from baseline, and (c) decreased rate of claims growth compared to controls. The authors suggest that when designed appropriately, health promotion programs can reduce both health risks and the medical care claims cost trend. Among features that facilitate cost reductions are self-management books with algorithms for appropriate response, enhancing self-efficacy, and improving health risks. Programs must be evaluated individually for effects on risks and costs.

Keywords: aged, costs, HPDP, interventions, medical self-care, policy, psychosocial factors, utilization.

Goeppinger, J., Arthur, M. W., Baglioni, Jr., A. J., Brunk, S. E., & Brunner, C. M. (1989). A reexamination of the effectiveness of self-care education for persons with arthritis. *Arthritis and Rheumatism, 32*, 706–715.

For these authors, self-care complements professional care for chronic conditions. Their study differs from other research by comparing effectiveness of two types of arthritis self-care education interventions, a home study model with videotapes and a small group model taught by trained lay leaders. Both models covered the same content, based on the Stanford Arthritis Self-Management Program. Results indicated that arthritis self-care interventions work. Both models increased arthritis knowledge and self-care behavior, reduced perceived helplessness, and improved pain management. Controlling education, disease diagnosis and duration, social support, and program choice did not change these relationships, suggesting broad applicability of self-care interventions. The home study model more effectively maintained reduced helplessness over time, while the small group model was associated more strongly with short-term improvements in pain and depression. Voluntary selection seemed no more effective than random assignment to program type. Improvements in self-care behavior and reduced feelings of helplessness partially explained improved pain outcomes.

Keywords: aged, chronic self-management, informal vs. formal care, interventions, psychosocial factors.

Hornbrook, M. C., Stevens, V. J., & Wingfield, D. J. (1993). Senior's program for injury control and education. *Journal of the American Geriatric Society, 41,* 309–314.

The focus of this Frailty and Injuries: Cooperative Studies of Intervention Techniques (FICSIT) study (see below, Ory et al., 1993) is on effects of a multifaceted intervention involving endurance building (walking), developing balance and lower limb strength, improving home safety, and mental imagery to prevent injuries such as falls among high risk adults 65 years or older. The subjects in this randomized trial are 1,323 older HMO enrollees living in the community. The article describes study design, setting, intervention, recruitment, measurements, and data collection. Analyses will assess effectiveness of the intervention in terms of health status, physical functioning, and health care use and cost outcomes.

Keywords: aged, costs, interventions, health status, HPDP, utilization.

Kemper, D. W., Lorig, K., & Mettler, M. (1993). The effectiveness of medical self-care interventions: A focus on self-initiated responses to symptoms. *Patient Education and Counseling, 21,* 29–39.

This article provides an excellent overview of self-care behaviors and educational interventions from ancient history through the 1960s' consumer health movement. It focuses on medical self-care or symptom responses by lay persons, thus excluding traditional patient education programs. It reviews findings from the few studies about effects of medical self-care behavior and interventions on health and use of professional health care services, including evaluations of impact and effectiveness of the interventions. It includes interventions directed at elderly populations, Medicare households, or retirees. Findings are congruent, indicating wide use of self-care. In fact, self-care seems to be universal, as it is not explained by demographic, attitudinal, or behavioral factors. Furthermore, self-care actions often are beneficial and seldom are harmful or inappropriate. Fifteen program evaluations that aimed to help participants choose appropriate self-

care responses to symptoms or to use the formal medical care system appropriately in response to symptoms are reviewed. All studies used self-care handbooks; some addressed a broad range of health problems, while others addressed specific symptoms. All found that self-care education was effective in reducing use of physicians or medical services, although some samples were small and results were not always statistically significant.
Keywords: aged, conceptual, history, interventions, medical self-care, prevalence, review.

Lorig, K., & Gonzalez, V. (1992). The integration of theory with practice: A 12-year case study. *Health Education Quarterly, 19*, 355–368.
    This case study describes the process of integrating health education theory and practice in the development and evaluation of the widely disseminated Arthritis Self-Management Program (ASMP) or Arthritis Self-Help Course (ASH). It provides insights into the realities of health education research. It describes the interaction and linkages between theory and practice, showing how theoretical exploration and program applications contribute to each others' development. It illustrates how a specific theory of behavior change mechanisms, self-efficacy theory, was used to develop the patient education program. Descriptions of the program and discussions of the findings about the program's effectiveness and mechanisms of behavior change can be found in Clark, Janz, Becker, Schork, Wheeler, Liang, Dodge, Keteyian, Rhoades, and Santiga, 1992; Goeppinger, Arthur, Baglioni, Brunk, and Brunner (in this section) 1989; Kemper, Lorig, and Mettler, 1993, this section; Lorig and Holman, 1993 (this section); and Lorig, Mazonson, and Holman, 1993 (see below).
Keywords: aged, chronic self-management, conceptual, history, interventions, psychosocial factors, review.

Lorig, K., & Holman, H. (1993). Arthritis self-management studies: A twelve-year review. *Health Education Quarterly, 20*(1), 17–28.
Arthritis, one of the most common chronic diseases, is the major cause of disability among older adults. This article describes the Arthritis Self-Management Program (ASMP), reviewing the 12-year history of the program and its evaluation. The program incorporates Bandura's social learning theory which employs self-efficacy as a mechanism of behavior change. Three versions of the ASMP incorporate efficacy. The investigators developed valid, reliable scales of self-efficacy specific to arthritis (for manag-

ing pain and other symptoms, and for function). Using randomized trials, the study has established the effectiveness of the intervention in terms of improving health care behaviors, self-efficacy, and health status. The changes in self-efficacy were more highly associated with changes in health status than with behaviors, and behavior change was not highly associated with health status changes. Formal reinforcement from newsletters and an Arthritis Reinforcement Program (ARP) did not appear to improve long-term outcomes of the ASMP, but the ASMP did have lasting effects for as long as 4 years without reinforcement. The study also demonstrated that the ASMP was cost-effective, and showed potentially important cost savings for use of health services. The program has been widely disseminated in the United States, Canada and Australia, and, by 1991, had 120,000 participants.

Keywords: aged, behavior change, chronic self-management, conceptual, costs, health status, interventions, policy, psychosocial factors.

Lorig, K. R., Mazonson, P. D., & Holman, H. R. (1993). Evidence suggesting that health education for self-management in patients with chronic arthritis has sustained health benefits while reducing health care costs. *Arthritis Rheumatism, 36*, 439–446.

This article describes the Arthritis Self-Management Program (ASMP) and study methodology used by Lorig and Holman and their colleagues, summarizing evidence about health benefits and cost effectiveness 4 years after program participation. Participants' psychological attributes, especially levels and growth of perceived self-efficacy (confidence) to cope with pain and other consequences of chronic arthritis, correlated strongly with ASMP outcomes. Among participants, pain and visits to physicians declined, respectively, by a mean of 20% and 40%; but physical disability increased by 9%. Similar changes did not appear for comparison groups. Not participating in ASMP to improve self-efficacy, the comparison group arthritis patients experienced increased pain, disability, and use of physician services. Estimated savings after 4 years based on reduced physician visits were $648 per rheumatoid arthritis patient and $189 per osteoarthritis patient. The investigators conclude that when compared with conventional therapy, health education for chronic arthritis may have sustained and significant health benefits and can reduce costs.

Keywords: aged, chronic self-management, costs, functional status, health status, interventions, predictors, utilization.

Mayer, J. A., Jermanovich, A., Wright, B., Elder, J. P., Drew, J. A., & Williams, S. J. (1994). Changes in health behaviors of older adults: The San Diego Medicare Preventive Health Project. *Preventive Medicine, 23,* 127–133.

This article describes follow-up findings from a controlled clinical trial, the San Diego Medicare Prevention Health Project being conducted to evaluate the cost-effectiveness of health promotion benefits for Medicare beneficiaries in a health maintenance organization. The intervention is based on Bandura's social learning theory and Kanfer's model of self-control and self-change. It consists of goal setting and counseling based on Health Risk Appraisal assessments, and eight health promotion sessions from two self-care manuals for older adults published by Healthwise, Inc. The intervention was broad, but emphasized exercise and nutrition. When compared to controls, intervention subjects had significantly greater improvement in aerobic exercise, exercise for flexibility and strength, appropriate fat intake and caffeine intake. No differences in change were seen for blood pressure, body mass indices (BMI), sodium intake, nutrition pattern, meal regularity, or home and motor vehicle safety. The control group showed greater increase in fiber consumption. The program had high participation and satisfaction by subjects, and can be successfully implemented on a large scale. The intervention demonstrated significant increases in physical activity among older adults.

Keywords: aged, behavior change, costs, HPDP, interventions, functional status, psychosocial factors.

Montgomery, E. B., Lieberman, A., Gurkirpal, S., Fries, J. F, & the PROPATH Advisory Board. (1994). Patient education and health promotion can be effective in Parkinson's disease: A randomized controlled trial. *American Journal of Medicine, 97*(5): 429–435. Also available from: Dr. J. F. Fries, 1000 Welch Road, Suite 203, Palo Alto, CA 94304-1808 (as *Report for the PROPATH advisory board,* January 28, 1994).

This report evaluates the effectiveness of a mailed health promotion program for Parkinson's disease (PROPATH) through a randomized controlled trial. Objectives were to provide information, to improve physical function by increasing exercise levels and/or perceived self-efficacy (health confidence) and decreasing side effects, and to facilitate medical treatment and compliance. The intervention group received disease assessment questionnaires with individualized computer reports and recommendations for patients and physicians. The controls received questionnaires only. Generally, the intervention group improved or stabilized, while the control group worsened. For example, summary scores of rate of progression increased sharply for the control group, but progression rates remained primarily stable for the intervention. Outcomes favoring the intervention were present for quality of life assessments, self-efficacy measures, stress scores for spouses, and spousal assessments of positive changes. Medication doses increased for controls but remained about constant for the intervention group. Medical care use was lower for the intervention; these decreases were significant for doctor visits and overall costs. The authors suggest that improvements (or stabilization) in symptom progression occurred through improved exercise and/or improved self-efficacy. They conclude that a "low-cost patient education program provides a useful adjunct to medical therapy of Parkinson's disease, may reduce costs, and can improve intermediate term outcomes" (p. 429).

Keywords: aged, behavior change, chronic self-management, costs, functional status, HPDP, interventions, predictor, psychosocial factors, utilization.

National Institute on Aging and Pfizer Pharmaceuticals. *Help yourself to good health.* Bethesda, MD: National Institutes of Health, National Institute on Aging. [No date]

This book illustrates self-care educational literature for use by older adults seeking to take an active role in prevention and maintaining health and independence. It compiles 94 information summaries on chronic and acute conditions, health, and safety issues. Printed in large readable type, the fact sheets describe the health concern, symptoms and detection, self-treatment and medical care, tips on prevention and behavior change, and resources. Topics include accidents and falls, arthritis, cancer, crime, dietary supplements, flu, health quackery, osteoporosis, prostate problems, safe use of medicines, sexuality, smoking cessation, and urinary incontinence.

Keywords: aged, chronic self-management, HPDP, interventions, medical self-care, review.

Ory, M. G. (1988). Considerations in the development of age-sensitive indicators for assessing health promotion. Measuring health-related behaviors and health: Towards new health promotion indicators. *Health Promotion: An International Journal, 3*(2), 139–150.

Most health promotion research has focused on young and middle-aged populations and, when conducted on older populations, ignores age-related differences. Biases or inappropriateness can occur by blindly applying methodological strategies developed with younger populations to older populations. This article reviews crucial methodological issues in research on older populations, and calls for developing age-sensitive data collection methodologies and indicators for assessing health, health promotion, and health lifestyle variables. Given new evidence of benefits of health promotion activity for older adults, accompanied by growing interest in developing and assessing health promotion programs to delay onset and reduce impact of illness and disability in older populations, these issues have become even more important. Among 10 issues raised here are the need to consider age in developing measures, determining the stability through old age of health behavior risks on health outcomes, the heterogeneity of older populations, and avoiding potentially faulty interpretations of findings that may be explained by cohort or other age-related differences. The author points to implications for developing effective health promotion programs targeted to the diversity of needs of older populations.

Keywords: aged, HPDP, interventions, methods.

Ory, M. G., Schechtman, K. B., Miller, J. P., Hadley, E. C., Fiatarone, M. A., Province, M. A., Arfken, C. L., Morgan, D., Weiss, S., Kaplan, M., & the FICSIT Group. (1993). Frailty and injuries in later life: The FICSIT trials. *Journal of the American Geriatric Society, 41,* 283–296.

Major threats to functional status of older adults include physical frailty and injuries from falls. In 1990, the National Institute on Aging and the National Center for Nursing Research launched a set of coordinated clinical trials called "Frailty and Injuries: Cooperative Studies of Intervention Techniques" (FICSIT). The eight FICSIT trials examine relationships among biomedical, behavioral, and environmental variables in frailty and injuries among the elderly. This report summarizes the background and organization of FICSIT, preliminary research, and characteristics of the FICSIT database, including measures and analytic strategies. Most of the interventions include some form of exercise for community resident elders. For example, one study focuses on effects of walking, lower limb strength, and mental imagery to prevent falls in high risk older adults (see above, Hornbrook, Stevens, & Wingfield, 1993). Another examines effects of reducing risk factors such as vision impairment, limb weakness, and medication use on frail adults (Tinetti, Baker, Garrett, Gottschalk, Koch, & Horwitz). Wolf, Kutner, Green, and McNeely compare effects of Tai Chi with conventional Western balance training.

Keywords: aged, functional status, HPDP, interventions.

Rakowski, W. (1992). Disease prevention and health promotion with older
adults. In M. G. Ory, R. P. Abeles, & P. D. Lipman (Eds.), *Aging, health
and behavior* (pp. 239–275). Newbury Park, CA: Sage.

This chapter considers complex issues facing research and community-
based interventions for both well and ill or disabled elderly populations,
and presents illustrative programs. Conceptual distinctions that health
behavior research must recognize to demonstrate change or health benefits
are unpatterned behavior occurring at single points versus habits maintained
over time, and unintended health-related actions versus intentionally preventive actions. Few studies used "true" random experimental/control
designs. Health promotion/disease prevention interventions and research
may focus on disease-specific or functional objectives, high risk of disease
onset versus community-wide eligibility to reduce population-based risk,
and existing disease status versus preclinical risk-factor status. Interventions also vary in terms of targets, phase of behavior change, and philo-
sophical underpinnings. Mediating factors affecting program success include unknown ceilings of health status necessary to make behavioral
changes, and the possibility that different models apply to certain segments
of the population. Rakowski also reviews measurement and design issues,
including how to select multiple indicators of behavior change and self-
selection bias. While some programs address general HPDP and self-care
skills, perhaps the predominant trend is toward more disease- and illness-
related programs. Most programs follow didactic models, and have more
women as participants. While short-term follow-ups are common, efforts
have moved toward long-term evaluations.
Keywords: aged, behavior change, chronic self-management, conceptual,
HPDP, interventions, methods.

Rimer, B. K., Orleans, C. T., Fleisher, L., Cristinzio, S., Resch, N.,
Telepchak, J., & Keintz, M. K. (1994). Does tailoring matter? The
impact of a tailored guide on ratings and short-term smoking-related
outcomes for older smokers. *Health Education Research, 9*(1), 69–84.

Much evidence shows protective effects of smoking cessation for older
adults, yet a common belief says it is "too late" for older adults to quit. This
article reports findings from a randomized control trial to evaluate effectiveness of the first behavioral smoking cessation materials and model
specifically targeted to older smokers. Based on focus groups and a national
random survey of older adults, the authors created a self-help guide, *Clear
Horizons,* with telephone counseling tailored for older adults. At 3 months,

compared with a generic guide, older smokers gave higher ratings to the tailored guides and were more likely to read them. Quit rates at 3 months were significantly higher for smokers who received the combination of the tailored guide and counseling. Those using the tailored guides reported significantly more quitting strategies than control subjects. Subjects believed that the tailored guide was more helpful, easy to use, written for people like them, and that it contained new ideas. When compared to the control condition at 12 months, quit rates were higher for both of the tailored guide interventions, although the tailored guide interventions did not differ statistically. The authors speculate this may reflect a fading of the effect of the telephone counseling protocol over time.

Keywords: aged, behavior change, HPDP, informal vs. formal care, interventions, psychosocial factors.

Simmons, J. J. (Ed.). (1989). Staying healthy after 50: Experiences in creating and disseminating a health promotion program. *Health Education Quarterly, 16*(4).

This special issue features five articles describing the development, evaluation, and dissemination of the Staying Healthy After Fifty (SHAF) course which derived from the Health Promotion for Older Americans Program (HPOA). Articles describe SHAF's evaluation and revision as a national program, discuss interorganizational collaboration and dissemination of the HPOA program, discuss training for delivering SHAF, evaluation and impact of the course, and describe the Hawaii Asian-American response to SHAF.

Keywords: aged, HPDP, interventions, medical self-care, review.

Simmons, J. J., Nelson, E. C., Roberts, E., Salisbury, Z. T., Kane-Williams, E., & Benson, L. (1989). A health promotion program: Staying healthy after fifty. *Health Education Quarterly, 16*(4), 461–472.

The authors describe Staying Healthy After Fifty (SHAF), a comprehensive health promotion program for older adults, and evaluate its national dissemination. Based on the Self-Care for Senior Citizens program developed at Dartmouth, the authors summarize collaborative organizational efforts to develop, evaluate, and revise the program for national dissemination as SHAF. (See below, Salisbury, Kane-Williams, Kauffman, & Quaintance, Simmons, 1989.) The aim is to help older adults gain confidence and take responsibility for their health, develop skills, change attitudes, and modify health behaviors. Education and behavioral theory are discussed. Content covers health concerns and emergency situations, lifestyle, and consumer planning. Topics include basic skills, treating common health problems, exercise, and designing a self-change plan. Recommended educational methods encourage active participation, role playing, and skill practice. Materials include an instructor's manual, personal health planner notebook, and a reference book covering 60 medical problems appropriate for self-care. Courses are taught by instructors trained by the AARP and Red Cross, which administer the program. Findings from a quasi-experimental study design demonstrated success. For example, participants scored significantly higher than comparison groups on perceived ability to perform health skills such as taking blood pressure, understanding food labels, and reducing stress levels.

Keywords: aged, HPDP, interventions, medical self-care, psychosocial factors, review.

Simmons, J. J., Salisbury, Z. T., Kane-Williams, E., Kauffman, C. K., & Quaintance, B. (1989). Interorganizational collaboration and dissemination of health promotion for older Americans. *Health Education Quarterly, 16,* 529–550.

This article describes how Health Promotion for Older Adults (HPOA) was adapted and disseminated through collaboration of the Dartmouth Institute for Better Health with national organizations—the American Association of Retired Persons and the American Red Cross. Components of HPOA include the Staying Healthy After Fifty (SHAF) course, adaptation for minorities, national dissemination, and obtaining continuing financial support. The article presents a conceptual framework for building the collaborative relationship. The implementation process involved forming a multiorganizational system; developing decision making mechanisms; collaborating on program adaptation and delivery; gaining support for SHAF at national, regional and local levels; implementing SHAF in the community; and determining the cost at local levels. Outcomes and experiences are discussed in terms of the diffusion of innovations in organizations. Important factors contributing to development and dissemination of such a program include selecting an optimal setting, creating necessary preconditions for change, demonstrating program effectiveness, and dispersing innovative programs through example.

Keywords: aged, conceptual, costs, HPDP, interventions, medical self-care, minorities, policy, review.

Vickery, D. M., Golaszewski, T. J., Wright, E. C., & Kalmer, H. (1988). The effect of self-care interventions on the use of medical service within a Medicare population. *Medical Care, 26,* 580–588.

This is one of the first studies of older adults to examine potential effects on medical care of prevention and self-care programs emphasizing decision making. The prospective, randomized, control trial hypothesized that the low-cost, self-care education intervention would reduce use and cost of medical care services of the Medicare population of an HMO. Program materials emphasized personal decision making and included self-care reference books featuring clinical algorithms, lifestyle brochures, self-help groups, and newsletters and education packages designed for subjects over 60 years. A telephone information service was used only 4 times. Results demonstrate the effectiveness of the preventive, self-care program in reducing ambulatory care use among older adults. When compared with the control group, total medical care visits significantly decreased 15% for the experimental group. A significant decrease in number of follow-up visits from pre- to postentry was observed for the experimental but not control group. The decrease in medical visits saved $35.65 per household, yielding a benefit-cost ratio of $2.19 saved for every program dollar spent. The authors found no evidence of impaired health quality.

Keywords: aged, costs, HPDP, interventions, medical self-care, predictor, utilization.

KEYWORDS

This list shows keywords in boldface accompanied by a brief description of content area for each keyword. Keywords appear after each abstract to provide further detail about the content of the documents.

Aged (usually 65 years and older)
Behavior change (includes mechanisms and dynamics of behavior change, reinforcement, or maintenance; compliance to medical regimes and physician perspectives; program adherence)
Costs
Demographics (includes epidemiology of aging population)
Frail/oldest-old
Functional status (includes daily activities of living, disability rates)

Health status (includes morbidity)
International
Interventions (includes programs)
Methods (includes measurement)
Minorities
Policy
Psychosocial factors (includes beliefs, attitudes, cognitive status, self-effi-
   cacy, social support, correlates and predictors of self-care)
Quality of life
Review
Rural
Self-Care:
   Conceptual (includes definition, theory and models)
   History (includes self-care movement)
   Informal vs. formal care (systems of care, social support networks)
   as Predictor (of health-related outcomes such as health, morbidity, mor-
      tality, functional status, quality of life, institutionalization, use of ser-
      vices, costs)
   Prevalence (or extent of self-care)
Self-care (general) (general or unspecified definition of self-care)
Self-Care, Types:
   Alternative healing
   Chronic self-management for disease or disability (includes self-man-
      agement of arthritis, diabetes, heart disease, disabilities)
   Environment (refers to physical environment, including self-care tech-
      nology and equipment)
   HPDP (health promotion/disease prevention includes health habits,
      lifestyle behaviors, preventive behaviors, general health behaviors, risk
      avoidance)
   Medical self-care (includes acute illness, self-medication, symptom
      response)
Social support (see informal vs. formal care, psychosocial factors)
Utilization (includes use of health, medical, and social services)

Index

Personalized interventions, future of, 93–94

Physical activity, and health status, 241

Physician(s)
 responsibilities of, in designing self-care, 136–137
 skepticism about, *xx–xxi*

Piggybacking of self-care research on other research, 195–196

Policy agenda, in self-care, 18–20

Policy on healthcare. *See* Public health policy

Population health research, as precursor of self-care research, 181

Practical implications of self-care research, 52–54

Practitioner, responsibilities of, in designing self-care, 136–137

Precontemplation stage of behavior change, 65

Prediction of main effect, vs. understanding cause, 134–135

Preparation stage of behavior change, 65

Preventive health behavior, 234

Preventive health care, 235

Process evaluation, 90–92
 vs. outcome evaluation, 109–111

Psychosocial factors in behavior change, 65

Public health policy
 implications of self-care research for, 52–54
 importance of self-care to, 197–198

Quality of life
 and aging, 203
 and assistive technology use, 162–163
 and self-care, 206–207

Reasoned action, theory of, 121–122

Recruitment for self-care programs, need for further research in, 67–73, 80

Relevance of threat, and motivation for self-care, 131–132

Research on self-care. *See also* Comparison group(s) for self-care research; Intervention(s), research on;

Methodology(ies) in self-care research; Outcome evaluation; Process evaluation
 in Europe, 188–189
 future directions for, 18–20, 54–55, 193–197
 in assistive technologies, 164–165
 in minority cultures, 177
 history of, 180–182
 policy and practical implications of, 52–54
 progress of, 62–63
 role of social sciences in, 155–165
 utility of, 201

Responsibility
 imputation of, in disease, 27, 54
 individual, for health maintenance, 183–185

Risk
 modeling perception of, 121–124
 psychosocial factors for, and age, 7–9

Role compromise, desire of elderly to minimize, 29–30, 32. *See also* Containment of symptoms

Rural elderly
 and health promotion, 243–244
 illness behavior among, 236–237
 strategies of self-care for, vs. urban elderly, 233–234

Sampling issues, in research on self-care, 50–51, 108

San Diego Medicare Prevention Health Project, 250

Scandinavia, health care attitudes in, 183

Seasonal change, and symptom interpretation, 26

Self-care, *xiv–xv,* 9–10, 11–12, 34. *See also* Folk medicine traditions
 categories of, *xviii–xix,* 11
 context of. *See* Context of self-care behavior, cultural
 cultural differences in. *See* Context of self-care behavior, cultural; Culture
 effectiveness of, 38–41, 212, 244, 247–248